THE CLASSICS OF WESTERN SPIRITUALITY

Bernard McGinn—Professor of Historical Theology and History of Christianity, University of Chicago Divinity School, Chicago, Ill.

John Meyendorff—Professor of Church History, Fordham University, Bronx, N.Y., and Professor of Patristics and Church History, St. Vladimir's Seminary, Tuckahoe, N.Y.

Seyyed Hossein Nasr—Professor of Islamics, Department of Religion, Temple University, Philadelphia, Pa., and Visiting Professor, Harvard University, Cambridge, Mass.

Heiko A. Oberman—Director, Institute fuer Spaetmittelalter und Reformation, Universitaet Tuebingen, West Germany.

Alfonso Ortiz—Professor of Anthropology, University of New Mexico, Albuquerque, N. Mex.; Fellow, The Center for Advanced Study, Stanford, Calif.,

Raimundo Panikkar—Professor, Department of Religious Studies, University of California at Santa Barbara, Calif.

Jaroslav Pelikan—Sterling Professor of History and Religious Studies, Yale University, New Haven, Conn.

Fazlar Rahman—Professor of Islamic Thought, Department of Near Eastern Languages and Civilization, University of Chicago, Chicago, Ill.

Annemarie B. Schimmel—Professor of Hindu Muslim Culture, Harvard University, Cambridge, Mass.

Sandra M. Schneiders—Assistant Professor of New Testament Studies and Spirituality, Jesuit School of Theology, Berkeley, Calif.

Huston Smith—Thomas J. Watson Professor of Religion, Adjunct Professor of Philosophy, Syracuse University, Syracuse, N.Y.

John R. Sommerfeldt—Professor of History, University of Dallas, Irving, Texas.

David Steindl-Rast—Monk of Mount Savior Monastery, Pine City, N.Y.

William C. Sturtevant—General Editor, Handbook of North American Indians, Smithsonian Institution, Washington, D.C.

David Tracy—Professor of Theology, University of Chicago Divinity School, Chicago, Ill.

Victor Turner—William B. Kenan Professor in Anthropology, The Center for Advanced Study, University of Virginia, Charlottesville, Va.

Kallistos Ware—Fellow of Pembroke College, Oxford; Spalding Lecturer in Eastern Orthodox Studies, Oxford University, England.

John Climacus

THE LADDER OF DIVINE ASCENT

TRANSLATION
BY
COLM LUIBHEID and
NORMAN RUSSELL

NOTES ON TRANSLATION
BY
NORMAN RUSSELL

INTRODUCTION
BY
KALLISTOS WARE

PREFACE
BY
COLM LUIBHEID

PAULIST PRESS
NEW YORK • RAMSEY • TORONTO

Cover Art
A graduate of The Pennsylvania Academy of the Fine Arts in Philadelphia, cover artist ANDRIJ MADAY has won numerous awards for his graphic designs and prints. He has exhibited his paintings and woodcuts in approximately eighty shows in the United States and has permanent collections at universities in Italy, Canada, and the United States. Mr. Maday's art, based on simple rectangular and circular designs, is inspired by ancient Ukrainian icons and conveys Mr. Maday's own deep mystical experience and rich Ukrainian Eastern Orthodox heritage.

Library of Congress
Catalog Card Number: 82-60540

ISBN: 0-8091-2330-4 (paper)
0-8091-0312-5 (cloth)

Published by Paulist Press
545 Island Road, Ramsey, N.J. 07446

Printed and bound in the
United States of America

Contents

Translators of This Volume

COLM LUIBHEID was born in Dublin in 1936 and received his B.A. and M.A. from University College, Dublin. He was awarded a Ph.D. in Classics from Princeton University. Since 1961 he has been a member of the teaching staff at University College, Galway. His scholarly interests focus on the early Church in the eastern half of the Mediterranean between the third and fifth centuries. In addition to publishing two books on Eusebius, he is preparing a volume on John Cassian for this series. Dr. Luibheid lives with his wife and four children in the village of Abbeyknockmoy, near Galway.

REV. NORMAN VICTOR RUSSELL was born in Belfast in 1945 and was educated at King's College, University of London. Subsequently he took his theology degrees at Oxford. In 1971 he was ordained Deacon in the Church of England. After being received into the Catholic Church a year later he was ordained a priest of the Congregation of the Oratory. Father Russell is an editor of *Sobornost* and has contributed to the English editions of the *Philokalia* and *The Lives of the Desert Fathers.*

Author of the Introduction

BISHOP KALLISTOS WARE was born in Bath in 1934 and was educated at the Westminster School, London, and Magdalen College, Oxford where he studied Classics, Philosophy and Theology. Received into the Orthodox Church in 1958, he was ordained a priest in 1966, the same year he took monastic vows at the Monastery of St John the Theologian in Patmos. In 1982 he was consecrated titular Bishop of Diokleia and appointed assistant bishop in the Orthodox Archdiocese of Thyateira and Great Britain. Since 1966 he has been been Spalding Lecturer in Eastern Orthodox Studies at Oxford, and in 1970 he became a Fellow at Pembroke College. He is the co-editor of *Sobornost* and the author of many books, including *The Orthodox Church.*

FOREWORD

If there are numerous and well-founded doubts concerning the few spare details of the biography of John Climacus, or John Scholasticus, there is little risk of over-estimating the influence of the treatise which emerged from the pen of this notably elusive figure whose life touched the end of the sixth and the beginning of the seventh centuries. *The Ladder of Divine Ascent* is undeniably a classic of early Christian spirituality. It offers advice, counsel and guidance to those capable of embarking on that difficult road whose summit is encounter with God, and it embodies the fruit both of long personal experience and of the intensely dynamic insights of earlier generations of men caught up in the first great surge of monasticism.

The present translation is based on the text printed by Migne—*Patrologia Graeca* 88. Apart from the details to be gathered in the standard handbooks of patrology, a most useful and wide-ranging bibliography has been supplied by Guerric Couilleau at the end of his article, *Jean Climaque* in *Dictionnaire de Spiritualité*, Fasc. lii-liii (Paris) 1972. This is to be strongly recommended to anyone wishing to explore the various issues raised by the impact of *The Ladder of Divine Ascent*.

ABBREVIATIONS

DHGE:	*Dictionnaire d'histoire et de géographie ecclésiastiques* (Paris)
DS:	*Dictionnaire de spiritualité* (Paris)
DTC:	*Dictionnaire de théologie catholique* (Paris)
ET:	English translation
HTM:	St. John Climacus, *The Ladder of Divine Ascent,* translated by Archimandrite Lazarus (Moore) (revised edition by the Holy Transfiguration Monastery: Boston, Massachusetts 1978).
PG:	J.-P. Migne, *Patrologia Graeca* (Paris)
PL:	J.-P. Migne, *Patrologia Latina* (Paris)
Phil.:	St. Nikodimos of the Holy Mountain and St. Makarios of Corinth, *The Philokalia,* translated by G.E.H. Palmer, P. Sherrard and K. Ware, vol. 1 (London & Boston 1979).
Rader:	Matthew Rader, editor of the text printed in Migne.

References to St. John Climacus, *The Ladder,* are given as follows: first the number of the step; then the column number from *PG* 88; finally the page number of the present translation. Thus "4 (677C), p. 45" signifies: Step 4, *PG* 88, col. 677C, p. 45 below.

To the Shepherd (Ad Pastorem) is cited as *Past.*, followed by the chapter number and the column number in *PG* 88, and then the page number of the HTM translation.

Old Testament references are to the Septuagint.

PREFACE

To Western eyes, the monk increasingly is a figure of yesterday, and the commonest images of him are of the kind to make easy the patronizing smile, the confidently dismissive gesture, or that special tolerance extended to the dotty and the eccentric. Around Friar Tuck, with his cheerful obesity, and Brother Francis, harming no one as he talks to birds and animals, vaguer ghosts manage to cluster, gaunt, cowled, faintly sinister, eyes averted or else looking heavenward, a skull clutched in a wasted hand, with gloom arising and laughter dead. Somewhere in the background there are bells and hymns, and psalms chanted long after midnight; and, as if to confirm that these are only the leftovers of a past surely and mercifully gone, there is the dumb presence of all those European monasteries visited for ten scheduled minutes during a guided tour, or else sought out on warmer evenings by courting couples.

But for the Christian, that is, for someone who believes that there is a God, that God has manifested Himself in historical surroundings in the person of Christ, and that insights and obligations are thereby held up to everybody, the monk cannot easily be shrugged off. Certainly in the aftermath of the immense changes that have occurred in the outlook of Christians since the end of World War II, the future of the religious order or community as such may well be problematic, but this in no way alters the deeper challenge presented by the monk. For here is someone who, so it would appear, has deliberately withdrawn from the usual patterns of living.

In this matter, of course, one has to tread with great care, since the meaning of such a withdrawal is not absolute, but is conditioned by and must be understood in terms of the norms and customs of the era in which it occurs. And even if historical evidence can help to isolate what seem to be the characteristic features of a widely shared outlook at a given time, this still leaves mostly untouched the precise set of reasons impelling a particular person to choose a type of living that involves some form of renunciation, some decision to opt out of the way of the world.

But again, the difficulties begin to multiply. A linguistic usage, so long employed by Christians that it has the look of being quite simply "natural," surrounds the individual monk with a wall of venerable words, a wall more solid and enduring than any that may set the boundaries of the area where he actually lives. For the talk is of "withdrawal" from "the world," of "renunciation," of a "monastic life" in contrast with the way other people happen to live, of being "apart from," "away from" the rest of mankind, of pursuing a "dedicated" and "consecrated" path. And this language, with its emphasis on the differences between the monk and all others, very quickly begins to generate something more than a mere set of descriptions. It begins to imply a value system, a yardstick of achievement and worth until at last, and not surprisingly, there grows the irresistible urge to speak of a "higher," "fuller," and "more perfect" way of life.

Words of this sort, words lined and laced with implications of particular values, are the co-relations of belief, of commitment, and of action. Language of this kind, endlessly repeated by ecclesiastical writers and preachers, has long been characteristic of Christian practice and has been received largely without demur. But the power of words is not a constant; and the impact of a terminology that claims, among other things, that the clerical, and specifically the monastic, way is a "higher" calling grows greater or lesser in proportion to the number and availability of competing terminologies. And when, as in the last quarter of the twentieth century, there is in fact a proliferation of serious and compelling value systems, then the force of an exclusively Christian rhetoric is inevitably weakened, even for Christians. The mere assertion of a value is no longer matched, as it used to be in other days, by a willingly affirmative response, and the timely quotation from Leo XIII or from Thomas Aquinas cannot now be relied on to still doubts or to answer questions.

There is in all of this a situation unique in Christian experience, for it has long been a popular notion that Christianity is a religion of the book; and it has certainly been the case that the Bible, the commentary, and the exegetical tract have supplied the material and the language in which the sermon, the homily, and the theological analysis have been firmly grounded. The pastoral letter, the authorized hymn, and the training manual for future clerics have extended the range and the reach of a discourse whose themes and elaborations have reverberated ceaselessly in the consciousness of believers. Year after year, scripted prayers have been read aloud to a congregation that is either silent or else invited to repeat them, and stock themes of petition or praise, with all that this implies by way of what is acceptable or not, have directed the minds of worshipers to a landscape of concern, a domain of reality that for long had the appearance of being unique. Until, that is, the coming of other rhetorics and other certainties. So that now there are, in a sense, too many books, too many claims to attention in a world geared for the instant transmission of every idea, event, and apocalypse. And the Christian, bombarded from every quarter by the exigencies of the day, is less and less able to operate exclusively within the frontiers established for his forebears by a language rooted in biblical detail.

Given those circumstances, it is reasonable to wonder how a Christian may now cope with the vast literature to which he is heir. It is also reasonable to anticipate that he will approach it with something less than automatic deference. And amid all the competing voices, his capacity to deploy a commitment and a sustained interest may well diminish as he strives to assemble for himself and for his friends criteria of evaluation that make some kind of accepted sense. How, for instance, is he to approach a work like *The Ladder of Divine Ascent* by John Climacus? By what means can he integrate it within his own heritage and his immediate environment? How can this text, over fourteen hundred years old, have any bearing on the problems of a Christian in the last quarter of the twentieth century? Such questions arise in relation to any classic book. But for the moment they must be directed to this treatise, which had a very considerable influence during a lengthy era in the history of the Church. And, in any case, if something useful can be said of *The Ladder of Divine Ascent*, it may contribute a little to the resolution of the problem presented today by the figure of the monk.

The setting at least can be readily established. The *Ladder* is a product of that great surge of monasticism which appeared first in Egypt during the third century, spread rapidly through all of Eastern Christendom, and eventually reached the West by way of the mediating zeal of figures such as John Cassian. The general history of this most influential development in the life of the early Church is well known, even if details and certain interpretations continue to preoccupy scholars, and there is no need to attempt here a sketch of what has been so well described by others. But in justice to the author of the *Ladder* it would be important to make a few preliminary comments in order to lessen the possibility of serious misunderstanding.

First, it should be observed that no discussion of early monasticism is complete without its due quota of lugubrious tales. The appalled scholar and the generous opponent of zealotry can choose from and grade a seemingly endless supply of horror stories, and someone familiar with the relevant literature finds himself on the lookout for the better-known figures: the monk who constructed for himself a cell too tiny to permit him ever to stand up or to lie down, the stylites who perched for decades on top of their sunscorched pillars, the Egyptian whose boast was that he was closer to being a corpse than anyone else. These are not the figments of some Gothic imagination, and frequently one may construct from various sources solid biographical details. Take, for instance, the case of Barsauma, a fifth-century monk from Syria, a region notable for the numbers who displayed a positive genius in the extravagant penances they managed to devise for themselves. Barsauma first had himself chained to a rock-face, and only when it was pointed out to him that he would be unlikely to survive long enough to practice the penance he had in view did he change his plans. Instead he took to wearing an iron tunic, vowed never to sit or to recline, hung himself in an upright position whenever he had to sleep, and attracted in this way fascinated and uncritical disciples who, at his bidding, wrecked and looted synagogues in the name of the God they all worshiped.

Barsauma was not unique, and the *Ladder* too has its own contribution to make to this image of extremism:

> . . . there were men in hardship and bowed down to the end of their lives, going about each day in sadness, their bodies' wounds stinking of rottenness and yet unnoticed by them. They forgot to eat their bread; their drink was mixed with tears. They ate dust and ashes instead of bread; their bones stuck to their flesh and they were dried up like grass. . . . You could see the tongues on some of them dry and hanging

> from their mouths in the manner of dogs. Some punished themselves in the blazing sun, others tortured themselves in the cold, while others, again, drank only as much water as would keep them from dying of thirst. . . . With knees like wood, as a result of all the prostrations, with eyes dimmed and sunken, with hair gone and cheeks wasted and scalded by many hot tears, with faces pale and worn, they were no different from corpses. Their breasts were livid from all the beatings, which had even made them spit blood. There was no rest for them in beds, no clean and laundered clothing. They were bedraggled, dirty, and verminous. (Step 5)

Such tales earn a disproportionate measure of attention among many of those dealing with the phenomenon of early monasticism. The stories are too vivid, too imperious for the imagination to be able to remain unengaged, and the decent witness or the gentle historian, accustomed to worthy ideals and the advantages of hygiene, recoils in distaste from what he takes to be the repulsive excesses of guilt-ridden and maddened wretches. Indeed, so intense is the inclination to dwell on the spectacular or the repulsive aspects of the first Christian monks that the attempt to describe their hopes and practices regularly degenerates into caricature or well-bred irony. And this is surely regrettable since even the available evidence points unambiguously to the fact that very many of the first monks were wholly admirable men, gentle, wise, and loving, capable of great heroism and moved by an abiding trust in God. Figures remarkable by any standard emerged from their monastic surroundings to leave an enduring mark on the character and quality of their times; and in the fourth and fifth centuries some of the most effective men, some of the men most able to provide leadership and inspiration to countless thousands, were actually dedicated ascetics. In other words, the emphasis on the sensational features of early monastic life is apt to provide a lopsided and seriously misleading historical picture.

But whether the focus of attention be on the saint, on the fanatic, or indeed on the common and ordinary human, no one would deny that hardship and strict regimentation marked the lives of the early monks. And this too calls for brief comment, since a complex network of incentives—religious, psychological, social, and anthropological—is in play whenever the issue of discipline is seriously invoked. There seems to be an attraction in the spectacle of discipline, irrespective of the values that may happen to underlie it in a given context. A strangely recurrent terminology shows up among Christians, Marxists, Manichees, army officers, revolutionaries, right-wing extremists, and racists, and it consecrates the inherent worth of restraint, self-sacrifice, manliness, solidarity with one's comrades, the "cause," the need to struggle, and the requirement to fight against sin, corruption, and weakness. Translated into practice, this vocabulary can be brought to exemplify what is manifestly right—or righteous. Such proclaimed values draw continued admiration, regardless of the brotherhood that may happen to have betrayed them; and precisely because they have long held so great an appeal for so many, it is foolish to try (as some do) to confine within a comfortable generalization the reasons why men in their thousands join a particular movement. A student of motives is not much helped by the statement that, for instance, the national humiliation stemming from the Versailles treaty was the cause of the growing membership of the Nazi party, or the economic and social dislocation of the third century was responsible for the rise of monasticism.

However, there is one feature of the unrelaxed severity and discipline of early monastic life that certainly ought to be adverted to and that offers a clue to the reasons why some men resolve to join a religious community; namely, the undeniable correlation between hardship and an intense marshaling of inner, and frequently unsuspected, resources. Words cannot really encompass what happens here. But the fact seems well established. In the evidence of the Gulag Archipelago, in the testimony of men like Solzhenitsyn, Tertz, Panin, and Shifrin, in the records of the tidal wave of misery let loose by German Nazism, there is a persistent and humbling proof of the capacity of individuals, trapped amid the worst conditions of deprivation, to unlock an inner dynamism, which often is manifested as a commanding faith in God and which must never be confused with the understandable motive of escapism. It has happened too often in twentieth-century experience to be trivialized or explained away; and somewhere within it lies a common bond with the ordeals, voluntarily undertaken, and the achievements of the first monks of the Church. Sharp differences of time and circumstance do not alter the shared character of the early saint and that prisoner of our day who has climbed beyond gross suffering and oppression to arrive at a level of richness beyond all common imagining. And because this is so, the decision of a man to take on himself the discipline of a hard religious life may not, after all, be so odd and unintelligible.

That many of the first monks had glimpsed a connection between the experience of hardship and an enhanced spirituality is evident in the writings of the early Church. And in the neighborhood of that perceived connection were other sources of the resolve to enter on a monastic life. There was, for instance, the belief that, given the right conditions and preparation, a man may even in this life work his passage upward into the actual presence of God; and there, if God so chooses, he can receive a direct and intimate knowledge of the Divine Being. Such knowledge is not the automatic or the guaranteed conclusion of a process. It is not like the logical outcome of a faultlessly constructed argument. There is no assurance that a man will come to it at the end of a long journey. But to many it was a prize and a prospect so glittering that all else looked puny by comparison; and, besides, there were tales told of some who, so it seemed, had actually been granted that supreme gift of a rendezvous.

Something of what was meant is found in a section of the *Confessions* of Augustine:

> Imagine a man in whom the tumult of the flesh goes silent, in whom the images of earth, of water, of air and of the skies cease to resound. His soul turns quiet and, self-reflecting no longer, it transcends itself. Dreams and visions end. So too does all speech and every gesture, everything in fact which comes to be only to pass away. All these things cry out: "We did not make ourselves. It is the Eternal One who made us." And after they have said this, think of them falling silent, turning to listen to the One Who created them. And imagine Him speaking. Himself, and not through the medium of all those things. Speaking Himself. So that we could hear His word, not in the language of the flesh, not through the speech of an angel, not by way of a rattling cloud or a mysterious parable. But Himself. The One Whom we love in everything. Imagine we could hear Him without them. Reaching out with speeding thought we come to Him, to the Eternal Wisdom which outlasts everything. And imagine if sight of Him were kept available, while all lesser sights were

> taken away. Think of this encounter, seizing, absorbing, drawing the witness into the depths of joy. Eternal life would be of a kind with this moment of understanding. (*Confessions* ix, 10, 25)

Augustine is talking of a one-to-one encounter with God. That anyone should dream of such an encounter in this life may seem bold and surprising to a believer from the twentieth century, surrounded as he is by countless men of goodwill unable to accept that there is a God at all. But the dream was clearly there, and there was much to keep it alive. To writers of the fourth, fifth, and sixth centuries, the cultural and intellectual resources of the age supported them and cooperated with them as they confidently formulated convictions of the kind laid out by Augustine. They had, too, a thriving, dynamic sense of the reality of God. And from this they turned to the life and, especially, the resurrection of Christ as an unambiguous proof of the existence of a sure road, a high road, into the actual living presence of the Creator. Journey's end might not perhaps be reached until the afterlife, but to these men, with their great capacity to love, their hunger for salvation, and their bitter awareness of the fact of sin, the way was already marked out, and only the obstacles had to be overcome.

But whatever the combination of motives that might operate for individuals entering on the path of monasticism, there was one factor that set the tone of all else; namely, the distinction, profoundly felt, between soul and body, a distinction regularly understood in terms of a conflict, endless and without respite, between two irreconcilable antagonists yoked together for a lifetime. The body was the foe—gross, corrupt, and greedy, reaching out for its own crass satisfactions or else generating subtle, even civilized, needs against which the soul had always to struggle. This notion of a deadly antagonism at the very center of a man's own being was a theme older than Christianity, but in the literature of early monasticism it became a focal point of agonized reflection. For to be alive at all is to be in the world, ensuring one's survival, entering into relationships with others, gazing on the beauty rising before the eye, encountering at every turn the achievements of art and intellect, feeling the stirrings of delight, and discovering the outward reach of desire, of passion, and of the urge to possess. And all this in the arena where the body feels most at home. Even the hours awake and the sleep of the night are but aspects of the body in command; and, seemingly, no hour or place can offer the soul an instant of unthreatened peace and recreation.

And so it is that John Climacus, facing the spectacle of unending war between soul and body, finds himself compelled to write as follows:

> By what rule or manner can I bind this body of mine? By what precedent can I judge him? Before I can bind him he is let loose, before I can condemn him I am reconciled to him, before I can punish him I bow down to him and feel sorry for him. How can I hate him when my nature disposes me to love him? How can I break away from him when I am bound to him forever? How can I escape from him when he is going to rise with me? How can I make him incorrupt when he has received a corruptible nature? How can I argue with him when all the arguments of nature are on his side? . . . If I strike him down I have nothing left by which to acquire virtues. I embrace him. And I turn away from him. What is this mystery in me? What is the principle this mixture of body and soul? (Step 15)

More typical, perhaps, was the following reflection by Basil of Caesarea, himself the single most influential figure in the monasticism of the eastern half of the Roman Empire:

> There is only one way out of this, namely, total separation from all the world. But withdrawal from the world does not mean physical removal from it. Rather, it is the withdrawal by the soul of any sympathy for the body. One becomes stateless and homeless. One gives up possessions, friends, ownership of property, livelihood, business connections, social life and scholarship. The heart is made ready to receive the imprint of sacred teaching, and this making ready involves the unlearning of knowledge deriving from evil habits. To write on wax, one has first to erase the letters previously written there, and to bring sacred teaching to the soul one must begin by wiping out preoccupations rooted in ordinary habits. (Basil, *Letter 2*)

John Climacus, Basil, and many other leading figures were proclaiming in effect that the only safe gaze was heavenward, that the only unblemished gesture was the signal of prayer or of compunction, that the only secure involvement with others was the unstinted offer of charity. Temperament and available insights would determine the extent and the degree to which, for individuals, all this would be translated into hatred of the body and hence of the world. But whatever the disparate motives at work, a man seized by a love of God and a man lacerating himself in a frenzy of penance had at least in common the abiding sense of a war within them, of the soul facing the body in an unending and possibly mortal combat. No other factor was more decisive in shaping the morality and the disciplinary practices of the first monks, and its influence can still be seen at work, for instance, in many of the pronouncements on the subject of marriage or in the nervous efforts of some ecclesiastical celibates to cope with the fact that half, if not more, of the members of the human race are women.

But a vastly more troublesome problem arises in the context of this deeply felt antagonism between soul and body, and it is a problem that will today strike someone reading *The Ladder of Divine Ascent*. It is also an issue that can be touched on here in only the briefest fashion. There is now in the consciousness of the West a terminology and a set of value judgments centered on the person. From the era of the Renaissance and Reformation up to the present time, there has been a steady progress in the insistence on the reality and the inherent worth of the individual. Some philosophers, of course, would argue that man the word-spinner has in this merely demonstrated once again his capacity to sublimate reality and has only succeeded in hiding from himself that he is no more—and no less—than a very complex organism. But this is not a widely shared view. Instead, there is much talk of human rights, of one man's being as good as another, of the right of the poor to share in the goods of the world, of one-man-one-vote. What all this has done to belief in God is a theme of major import. However, on a more restricted plane, a difficulty for anyone today reading *The Ladder of Divine Ascent* or similar texts is that in these a somewhat different view of the person is at work. If modern Christianity has invested heavily in the notion of the value of the individual person, it has been at the cost of a seeming incompatibility with much that was felt and believed in the early Church.

Still, whether incompatible or not with the modern sense of the self and of identity, *The Ladder of Divine Ascent* remains what it has long been, a text that had a profound influence, lasting many centuries, in the monastic centers of the Greek-speaking world. As such it deserves at least a hearing, if only to ensure that the awareness of the Christian past is not impoverished. And in any case it has in its own fashion a contribution to make to the problem of what the monk could possibly signify in the life of today. For the *Ladder* was, of course, addressed specifically to monks.

Hardly anything is known of the author, and the most reliable information about him can be summarized in the statement that he lived in the second half of the sixth century, survived into the seventh, passed forty years of solitude at a place called Tholas; that he became abbot of the great monastery of Mount Sinai and that he composed there the present text. The *Ladder* was written for a particular group, the abbot and community of a monastic settlement at Raithu on the Gulf of Suez. It was put together for a restricted audience and to satisfy an urgent request for a detailed analysis of the special problems, needs, and requirements of monastic life. John Climacus was not immediately concerned to reach out to the general mass of believers; and if, eventually, the *Ladder* became a classic, spreading its effects through all of Eastern Christendom, the principal reason lay in its continuing impact on those who had committed themselves to a disciplined observance of an ascetic way as far removed as possible from daily concerns.

Not much is actually said of the reasons for joining a monastery. Men become monks "either for the sake of the coming kingdom, or because of the number of their sins, or on account of their love of God" (Step 1). But once inside the walls, the monk, according to John, has to live under the scrutiny of a God Who is undoubtedly loving, merciful, and omnipotent, but Who is also just, stern, and conscious of protocol. Like the emperor, in fact:

> Those of us wishing to stand before our King and God and to speak to Him should not rush into this without some preparation, lest it should happen that—seeing us from afar without arms and without the dress appropriate to those who appear before the King—He should command His servants and His slaves to lay hold of us, and to drive us out of His sight, to tear up our petitions and to throw them in our faces. (Step 28)

The emperor, in the world known to John, presided over a society rigidly stratified, with the common man living at the base of a triangle whose apex was remote, distant, and fearsome. Most of those who came into the imperial presence would do so with nervous apprehension, with a sense of risking some terrible displeasure. But at least for the majority of his subjects the emperor lived far away in a distant capital, whereas God is ever present, ever on the watch, noting and recording, ever directing toward the individual His knowing stare. And in case the analogy here is not properly understood, John offers some others:

> If you ever found yourself having to appear before a human judge, you may use that as an example of how to conduct yourself in prayer. Perhaps you have never stood before a judge nor witnessed a cross-examination. In that case, take your cue from the way patients appeal to surgeons prior to an operation or a cautery. (Step 28)

"With no anaesthetic," the modern scholiast might add.

Before the face of this King, the monk puts on a lifetime performance, one, moreover, that at every turn is imperiled by virtually unlimited hazards. Had John lived in the twentieth century, he might have spoken of the monk as journeying through a minefield; but, as it is, the image of the strait way suffices, and that a moment might ever come when it would be otherwise, when a man might briefly relax, is nowhere hinted at in the course of the long, often melancholy, analysis of the spiritual life. For not only is the monk caught up in an endless fight against a host of obstacles, but he has also to live in perpetual insecurity, with perhaps never an intimation of whether his struggle has been a success or whether it has produced compensation sufficient for the weight and gravity of his sins:

> Let no one who grieves for his sins expect reassurance at the hour of death. There can be no reassurance about the unknown. (Step 5)

And he has to beware even this insecurity, since "to despair is . . . to inflict death on oneself" (ibid.).

Yet the whole point of *The Ladder of Divine Ascent* is that a great amount of wisdom and insight is available to enable the monk to cope with the perils of his situation. There is knowledge to be handed on to him, and practical steps that, if taken, must show him how to transform his life, how to transcend his condition, provided he has within himself the necessary faith and zeal. The form of John's text—with its thirty sections or steps—is suggested by the biblical image of the ladder of Jacob, and such an image, rooted in the certainties of scripture, must be taken to imply that despite the myriad difficulties rising up before him, the way of the monk is not in fact impassable. But it has its own special character and its own particular objectives, and these must be understood from the beginning and accepted for what they are. The monk, after all,

> finds himself in an earthly and defiled body, but pushes himself into the rank and status of the incorporeal. . . . Withdrawal from the world is a willing hatred of all that is materially prized, a denial of nature for the sake of what is above nature. (Step 1)

In other words, the monk, unlike the majority of believers, is so overwhelmed by his sense of the reality of God and of the afterlife that he turns away, by a deliberate choice, from the concerns of the here and now, renounces as far as possible the alliance of soul and body, and lives to the extent that he can the life of the spirit. Of all tasks this is surely the most formidable; and yet, John is saying, at the top of the ladder, on the thirtieth step of striving, there awaits a promise for the man whose heart longs to be there: love clarified, God made present.

To get there, however, the monk has first to enter the arena of renunciation. It is easily said, and the inexperienced onlooker will have his own way of constructing the image of the bolt on the cloister gate, of the cell entered for a lifetime. Or the talk can be of what a man has decided to forego—a varied diet, physical comfort, sexual experience, possessions, the security and self-respect provided by the love and esteem of one's time, of neighbors, of society. And these are indeed among all that the monk has decided to renounce. But wherever a man is, however far he has retreated from what the world may have to offer, he remains a man, endowed, among other attributes, with a capacity to remember and to imagine, and in the drabbest byway of the rockiest desert he would be less than human if he did not think sometimes of the road not taken—which would mean that he had not yet achieved renunciation.

And suppose that he manages at least to reduce to a minimum his taste—real, remembered, dreamed—for the first-line comforts of the world. He has still to run a gauntlet of entanglements, all centered on his genuine humanity, all deriving from the fact that as a person, an amalgam of body and soul, he has an inherent tendency to impinge voluntarily on his surroundings. He has the urge to speak, to act, to form judgments about whatever he hears and sees, and, on this account, John maintains, catastrophe looms over him, since the assertion of his own opinion, of his own proposal for how things should be done, of his own criteria of evaluation, may well amount to an illegitimate and unwarranted promotion of the self at the expense of that goal of "denying nature for the sake of what is above."

As if this were not more than enough to cope with, there is a further problem with which the monk must somehow deal, namely, the unending assault of demons, of evil spirits hovering and lurking everywhere, restless and vicious, ever on the watch for an opportunity to turn a believer, but especially a monk, away from the path of right conduct. In this matter John is at one with his numerous predecessors and, like them, he refers constantly to the war on two fronts, against the self and against the hosts of marauding devils.

> We have countless hidden enemies—evil enemies, harsh, deceitful, wicked enemies with fire in their hands, wishing to set the Lord's temple alight with the flame that is in it. These enemies are powerful, unsleeping, incorporeal and unseen. (Step 1)

And they cooperate, these enemies, this self and these circling demons, to lift their persuasive words toward the monk, calling him and enticing him to whatever corner of the world where he is most likely to weaken.

In these conditions he must therefore decide if his vocation is more likely to be realized in solitude than in a religious community, as an anchorite rather than a cenobite. The two options lie before him, and he has numerous exemplars to help him make up his mind. As an anchorite, living totally alone or with fellow anchorites nearby, he can choose for himself the ascetical regime that appears most suitable to his needs. While he may seek guidance from many quarters and may feel bound to follow in detail the advice of someone else, the decision as to how he should conduct himself remains within his own person and under his own control. The cenobite, on the other hand, while renouncing the world as the anchorite does, also abdicates his capacity to decide his future for himself. To him, the "I," with its power of decision, is the enemy, always insidious, ever exploited by demons, endlessly a prey to deceit from within and from outside; and because of this, the solitary life appears too hazardous, too filled with risk. So he joins a community, a resolve in which he will be encouraged by John, who is convinced of the fact that only a special few are able to live in solitude and that in community life the monk will find at least one major instrument for his own progress, namely, the strategy of obedience.

It is no accident that one of the longest and most impressive sections in *The Ladder of Divine Ascent* is given over to obedience, which is variously described, but which involves above all the decision "to put aside the capacity to make one's own judgment." With care and foresight the monk, knowing his own special failings and proclivities, chooses a director or superior and then submits completely to him in everything great or small, reserving to himself not even the tiniest domain of personal initiative.

> I have seen men there who lived in total obedience for all of fifty years, and when I begged them to tell me what consolation they had won from so great a labor, some answered that having arrived thereby at the lowest depths of abasement they could repel every onslaught, while others declared that they had attained complete freedom from the senses and had obtained serenity amid every calumny and insult. (Step 4)

To emphasize this aspect of the matter, John puts forward several anecdotes of which the following is typical:

> The superior . . . said to (Isidore): "Brother, this is what I want you to do. You are to stand at the gate of the monastery, and before everyone passing in or out, you are to bend the knee and say: 'Pray for me, Father, because I am an epileptic.' " And Isidore obeyed (and) spent seven years at the gate. . . . I asked this great Isidore how he had occupied his mind while he was at the gate. . . . "At first I judged that I had been sold into slavery for my sins," he said. "So I did penance with bitterness, great effort and blood. After a year

> my heart was no longer full of grief, and I began to think of a reward for my obedience from God Himself. Another year passed and in the depths of my heart I began to see how unworthy I was to live in a monastery, to encounter the fathers, to share in the Divine Mysteries. I lost the courage to look anyone in the face, but lowering my eyes and lowering my thoughts even further, I asked with true sincerity for the prayers of those going in and out." (Step 4)

From this, and from the many other incidents and comments set down by John, it becomes clear that the requirement of obedience implies very much more than what the term would suggest today. It is not a question of agreeing to accept the rules of a club that one has voluntarily joined. Nor is the obedience invoked here the phenomenon one associates with a soldier, who, in following highly dangerous and even very stupid orders, can still preserve an independence of view concerning them. The submission of the monk goes much farther and includes the surrender of even the capacity to hold a private and unspoken attitude of critical reserve or judgment regarding the commands meted out to him. And this is not to be confused with blind obedience. For the obedience is indeed purposeful, because the monk in his awareness within himself of particular failings, actual or potential, has chosen a superior who will correct these; and his total unquestioning submission will then be the avenue by which to transcend weakness and to advance toward increasingly important spiritual goals:

> The surest sign of our faith is when we obey our superiors without hesitation, even when we see the opposite happening to what we had hoped. (Step 4)

> Let what we call quicksilver be a paradigm of perfect obedience. Roll it with any substance you wish and it will nevertheless run to the lowest place and mix with nothing defiled. (Ibid.)

> When a monk living in solitude has realized what his weak point is, and when he changes place and sells himself to obedience, then, blind that he was once, he recovers sight and can see Christ without difficulty. (Ibid.)

> He who strives for dispassion and for God considers lost any day on which he was not criticized. Like trees swayed by the wind and driving their roots deeper into the ground, those who live in obedience become strong and unshakable souls. (Ibid.)

All this because the self, reduced through obedience not only to a humble recognition of its own insignificance, but also to an actualization of that insignificance, will then lie open to receive the grace of becoming someone pleasing in the sight of God, pleasing as a showplace of the virtues.

These virtues, and the vices that shadow them, form the subject matter of the greater part of *The Ladder of Divine Ascent*. They are submitted to penetrating analysis, classification, and subdivision. They are treated in a sequence more or less logical and in a manner occasionally reminiscent of a soul owner's manual. Yet this too can be misleading, as indeed the image of the ladder itself is somewhat misleading. For it would be wrong to think in terms of a solid progression up from one firm level to that above it. A more appropriate metaphor would be the text of a play or the notations of a musical composition whose internal patterns and consistencies may well be described and established, but which really come to true being only in a living enactment. In *The Ladder of Divine Ascent* the monk can study the virtues as an actor studies his lines, but the exercise is only of secondary interest if it is not followed by the actual performance, a performance that, in the case of the monk, will be in an ambience of prayer, in a continuous "dialog and union of man and God" (Step 28).

Here, perhaps, is the crucial point. For John Climacus is concerned not so much with the outward trappings of monasticism as with its vital content. To him the monk is a believer who has undertaken to enter prayerfully into unceasing communion with God, and this in the form of a commitment not only to turn from the self and world but to bring into being in the context of his own person as many of the virtues as possible. He does not act in conformity with virtues of one kind or another. Somehow, from within the boundaries of his own presence, he emerges to *be* humility, to be gentleness, to be sin abhorred, to be faith and hope and, above all else, to be love. Such a vocation turns him into a marked man, not just in the sort of milieu known to John Climacus, but at any time, even where the name of God is something to be shrugged off or rejected. He offers an example of love and courage, something to be followed by others in their own way and as their own insights and circumstances dictate, because

> the monastic life is a light for all men. Hence monks should spare no effort to become a shining example in all things, and they should give no scandal in anything they say or do. For if the light becomes dark, then all the deeper will be the darkness of those living in the world. (Step 26)

Such, in outline, is the perspective in which *The Ladder of Divine Ascent* was written, and the work was quickly recognized as important. Influential texts, of course, have a life and season of their own. They supply the dominant themes of an era, acquire eventually the status of the honorably mentioned and the unread, emerge once again to promote undreamed-of perceptions, and then slip, perhaps forever, out of sight and out of reckoning. But in a time of rapid change, such as today, even the capacity to ponder or to remember can be so blunted that not only will an individual work sink from view, but the very realm it opened up, the vein it disclosed, will also disappear, leaving men with an impoverished vision and a diminished grasp of the available images and ideals from which to construct for themselves a worthwhile sense of meaning and purpose. To lose the awareness of the choices on offer, to be locked without respite into a single, all-pervasive bias, is a disaster. This much at least is clear amid the unfinished history of the twentieth century, with its countless grim examples of unsheathed bigotry, rampant prejudice, and dreadful unreason. But in the meantime, there is still the influential text, like some shining life, presenting as does *The Ladder of Divine Ascent* one of the many opportunities to confront a view of being and of man. And if the fruit of such a confrontation is a researched "No," or a reasoned acquiescence, then indeed the sum of human enrichment can confidently be held to have been augmented.

INTRODUCTION

I. THE AUTHOR AND HIS BACKGROUND

Sinai and Tabor

With the exception of the Bible and the service books, there is no work in Eastern Christendom that has been studied, copied and translated more often than *The Ladder of Divine Ascent* by St. John Climacus. Every Lent in Orthodox monasteries it is appointed to be read aloud in church or in the refectory, so that some monks will have listened to it as much as fifty or sixty times in the course of their life. Outside the monasteries it has also been the favorite reading of countless lay people in Greece, Bulgaria, Serbia, Russia, and throughout the Orthodox world. The popularity of *The Ladder* in the East equals that of *The Imitation of Christ* in the West, although the two books are altogether different in character.

The author of *The Ladder* lived in the desert of Sinai, at the foot of Jebel Musa, Moses' Mount, that rises rocky and precipitous to a height of nearly 7,500 feet. The surroundings would often have called to his mind the scene in Exodus: the lightning and thunder, the mountain shrouded in thick cloud, and Moses climbing up alone into the darkness to speak with God face to face (Exod. 20:18–21). But St. John Climacus was also reminded constantly of another mountaintop, belonging to the New Covenant—Tabor, "the high mountain apart" (Matt. 17:1), where our Lord was transfigured before the three disciples. For, when he prayed in the church built for the monks of Sinai by the Emperor Justinian in 556–7, each time he looked up John would have seen in the apse at the east end the great mosaic that still survives to this day, depicting Christ's Transfiguration.[1]

Visually and spiritually, then, John's imagination was dominated by these two mountains, Sinai and Tabor, and both alike are reflected in the book that he wrote. In its severity, its refusal of compromise, and its demand for total dedication, *The Ladder* calls to mind the arid desert, and the rocks and darkness of Sinai. But those prepared to look deeper will discover that the book speaks not only of penitence but of joy, not only of self-denial but of man's entry into divine glory. Together with the gloom of Sinai there is also the fire of the Burning Bush and the light of Tabor.

The Three Monastic Paths

Little is known, beyond the bare outlines, about the life of St. John Climacus.[2] In Greek he is called *Ioannis tis Klimakos,* "John of the Ladder," after the book that he wrote. In Latin this came to be rendered *Joannes Climacus,* and so in English his title has become "Climacus." In Greek he is also named "John the Scholastic" (*scholastikos*); while the term used here could mean a lawyer, it is often more broadly applied to someone well educated or widely read, and this seems to be the sense in John's case.

John's dates have been much debated. According to the view most commonly accepted, he was born in or shortly before 579, and he died around 649;[3] but some scholars put his birth as early as 525 and his death around 600,[4] while others place his death as late as 670–

1. The mosaic dates probably from 565–6, nine years after the building of the church. See V. Beneševič, "Sur la date de la mosaïque de la Transfiguration au Mont Sinaï", *Byzantion* i (1924), pp. 145–72.

2. The main source is the *Life* by Daniel of Raithu: Greek text in *PG* 88, 596–608; ET, HTM, pp. xxxiv–xxxviii. Daniel writes as if he were John's contemporary but he is not very well informed. For further details about John's life, see the *Narratives* attributed to Anastasius of Sinai, §§ 5–7, 32, 34, 39: ed. F. Nau, *Oriens Christianus* ii (1902), pp. 58–89; cf. *PG* 88, 608–9, and HTM, pp. xxxix–xl. There is some doubt how much of this material in Anastasius in fact refers to Climacus.

3. F. Nau, "Note sur la date de la mort de S. Jean Climaque", *Byzantinische Zeitschrift* xi (1902), pp. 35–37.

4. S. N. Sakkos, *Peri Anastasion Sinaïton* (Thessalonica 1964), p. 180. An early date is also preferred by Beneševič, *art. cit., Byzantion* i (1924), pp. 168–9: in his view Climacus was born before 532 and died before 596.

80.[5] While certainty is not possible, it seems reasonable to regard John as an author of the seventh rather than the sixth century, as a contemporary, that is to say, of St. Maximus the Confessor (*c.* 580–662). It is not known where he was born. His delight in metaphors drawn from the sea has led some to conclude that his early years were spent near the coast,[6] but this is no more than a speculation.

John was sixteen when he came to Sinai.[7] Here he would have found a monastic center already well established, containing in close proximity all the three forms of the monastic life that he describes in Step 1 of *The Ladder*.[8] First, inside the fortress walls built at the orders of Justinian, and occupying the buildings around the church with its mosaic of the Transfiguration, there was a fully organized *cenobium*, a monastic brotherhood pursuing the common life under the direction of an abbot (*higoumenos*). Second, scattered through the surrounding desert there were hermits dedicated to the solitary life. And in the third place there were monks following the middle way, intermediate between the cenobitic and the anachoretic forms, whereby small groups lived as close-knit families, each under the immediate guidance of a spiritual father. For this third way, "the life of stillness shared with one or two others," as he terms it, John himself expresses a preference: it avoids the dangers of excessive isolation, while being at the same time less "structured" and more personal than life in a large-scale monastery, and providing more opportunities for silence.

In the course of his life St. John Climacus had experience of all these three forms. Initially, so it seems, he adopted the middle way, taking as his spiritual father a certain Abba Martyrius. After three years, when John was nineteen or twenty, Martyrius took him to the

---

5. H.-G. Beck, *Kirche und Theologische Literatur im Byzantinischen Reich* (Munich 1959), p. 451.

6. S. Rabois-Bousquet, "Saint Jean Climaque: sa vie et son oeuvre", *Echos d'Orient* xxii (1923), pp. 442–3.

7. Daniel of Raithu, *Life* (597A). But L. Petit, *DTC* viii (1924), cols. 690–3, doubts whether Climacus entered the monastic life so young, and prefers to identify him with a certain John the Rhetorician, a married man in Alexandria, who is mentioned by Sophronius, *Miracles of St. Cyrus and St. John*, §§ 61, 70 (*PG* 87, 3640A, 3673A); in Petit's view, Climacus is also the John mentioned in Moschus, *The Spiritual Meadow*, § 102 (*PG* 87, 2960D). But this theory that Climacus only became a monk at a mature age, after marriage and a secular career, remains hypothetical and has not been widely accepted.

8. 1 (641D), p. 79.

chapel at the top of Moses' Mount and there, following the custom of the time, he tonsured John as a monk. Coming down from the summit, the two met Anastasius, the abbot of the central monastery, who had not seen John before. "Where does this boy come from," asked Anastasius, "and who professed him?" Martyrius replied that he had done so. "How strange!" Anastasius exclaimed. "Who would have thought that you had professed the abbot of Mount Sinai!" Martyrius and John Climacus continued on their way, and paid a visit to the celebrated solitary John the Sabbaite, who washed John Climacus' feet and kissed his hand, but took no notice of Martyrius. John the Sabbaite's disciple was scandalized by this, but after the two visitors had left the old man assured him: "Believe me, I don't know who that boy is; but I received the abbot of Sinai and washed his feet."[9] Forty years later these prophecies were fulfilled.

Martyrius, so it seems, died soon after John's profession.[10] John now retired into solitude, settling as a hermit at Tholas, some five miles from the fortress housing the main monastery. Yet he was not altogether isolated, for there were certainly other monks in the immediate vicinity. According to John's biographer Daniel of Raithu, during his years of retreat at Tholas he received the gift of tears and the grace of continual prayer. He reduced sleep to a minimum but displayed a prudent moderation in his fasting, for it was his custom to eat everything allowed by the monastic rule, but in extremely small quantities. In time he became known and respected as a spiritual guide, and he began to receive frequent visits from his fellow monks—so frequent, indeed, that some criticized him for being a gossip and a chatterbox. Thereupon John kept total silence for a year, only agreeing to speak once more with his visitors when entreated to do so by the very monks who had been his critics.[11]

At some point during his time in Tholas John made a journey to Egypt, staying at a large monastery on the outskirts of Alexandria. What he witnessed in this community of several hundred monks made a lasting impression on him, as can be gauged from the lengthy description that he gives in Steps 4 and 5 of *The Ladder*. Since his own

9. Anastasius, *Narratives*, §§ 34 and 6.

10. Daniel of Raithu's language (597B) is ambiguous: it may mean that Martyrius died, not when John was nineteen years of age, but when John had been nineteen years in the monastic life (i.e. when he was about thirty-five).

11. Daniel, *Life* (600A–601A, 604D–605A).

early years as a monk had been spent in the third way, in a small hermitage and not in a large *cenobium,* it is easy to understand the impact which life at the Alexandrian house must have had upon him. He was struck in particular by the abbot's power of insight, and by the combination of sternness and affection which he showed in his treatment of the monks. John was also impressed by the "Prison," a mile from the main monastery, in which erring monks were confined; here he stayed for a month.[12] His vivid account of the physical austerities and the mental anguish undergone by the monks in this "Prison" is likely to prove, for most Western readers, by far the least attractive section of *The Ladder;* at times, so one modern critic has complained, it sounds like "a badly run psychiatric institution." But John was impressed by other things as well during his visit to the Alexandrian monastery—by the unity prevailing among the brethren, by the warmth and sensitivity of their mutual love, and by their unceasing inward prayer.[13]

After forty years of hermit life at Tholas, against his will John was elected abbot of the central monastery at Sinai. On the day of his installation as abbot, a party of six hundred pilgrims chanced to arrive at the monastery. While they were all being given a meal, John saw "a man with short hair, dressed like a Jew in a white tunic, going round with an air of authority and giving orders to the cooks, cellarers, stewards and other servants." Once the meal had finished, the man was nowhere to be found. "It was our lord Moses," said John. "He has done nothing strange in serving here in the place that is his own."[14] To the monks the sign was significant; for they were soon to feel that, in the person of their new abbot John, they had indeed found another Moses.[15]

How long John continued in office is unknown. It was during this last period of his life, while abbot, that he composed *The Ladder of Divine Ascent,* at the request of another John, the superior of a nearby monastery at Raithu.[16] "Tell us in our ignorance," asked John of Raithu, "what like Moses of old you have seen in divine vision upon the mountain; write it down in a book and send it to us as if it were

12. 5 (776B), p. 128.
13. 4 (685ABC), pp. 95–96.
14. Anastasius, *Narratives,* § 7.
15. Daniel, *Life* (605B).
16. Probably to be identified with Tor, on the Gulf of Suez near the southern tip of the Sinai peninsula.

the tables of the Law, written by God." In his reply John Climacus protests that the task is beyond his strength: "I am still among the learners." But, he says, constrained by the virtue of obedience, he has complied with the request, composing "in my stammering way" what is no more than "an outline sketch."[17]

Shortly before his death John, longing to enjoy once more the stillness in which he had lived as a solitary, resigned his position as abbot, appointing his brother George to replace him.[17a]

There is nothing to indicate that St. John Climacus was ever ordained a priest. His appointment as abbot is not in itself proof that he was in holy orders.

II. THE LADDER: PURPOSE AND STRUCTURE

John's Audience

The Ladder was written, then, by one who, after living for most of his monastic life as a hermit, had in old age been entrusted with the pastoral care of a large community; it is the work of a solitary writing for cenobites. The audience that John has in view is monastic. He begins his book, however, with a clear affirmation of God's loving care for the entirety of humankind. Salvation is offered to all alike:

> God is the life of all free beings. He is the salvation of believers or unbelievers, of the just or the unjust . . . of monks or those living in the world, of the educated or the illiterate, of the healthy or the sick, of the young or the very old. He is like the outpouring of light, the glimpse of the sun, or the changes of the weather, which are the same for everyone without exception. "For God is no respecter of persons" (Rom. 2:11).[18]

To the married Christian John insists that matrimony is not an obstacle to salvation:

---

17. For John of Raithu's letter and John Climacus' reply, see *PG* 88, 624–8; ET, HTM, pp. xli–xliv.

17a. Anastasius, *Narratives*, §32, mentioning John the Sabbaite, but probably referring to John Climacus (cf. *PG* 88, 609A).

18. 1 (633A), p. 74.

> Do whatever good you may. Speak evil of no one. Rob no one. Tell no lie. Despise no one. . . . Show compassion to the needy. . . . Be satisfied with what your own wives can provide you. If you do all this, you will not be far from the kingdom of heaven.[19]

Later in the work, he points out that purity is by no means the monopoly of those who have never married, and he cites as proof the example of the apostle Peter, "who had a mother-in-law and who nevertheless received the keys of the kingdom."[20]

But, having insisted in this manner upon the universality of God's saving love, John makes it clear that he himself is writing specifically for monks. This needs to be remembered by the modern reader. Yet does it therefore follow that *The Ladder* is of no interest to those in the "world"? Surely not. It has in fact been read with the utmost profit by many thousands of married Christians; and, whatever the author's original intention, there is nothing surprising in that. Monasticism, as St. Basil the Great observes, is nothing else than "life according to the Gospel."[21] Whether monastic or married, all the baptized are responding to the same Gospel call; the outward conditions of their response may vary, but the path is essentially one.

The Need for Personal Experience

St. John Climacus, like St. Symeon the New Theologian and St. Gregory Palamas at a later date,[22] lays heavy emphasis upon the need for personal experience. Christianity, as he sees it, is much more than the exterior acceptance of doctrines and rules. No one can be a true Christian at second hand; there must be a personal encounter, in which each knows, sees, tastes and touches for himself.

This applies first of all to anyone who teaches others:

> The true teacher is one who has received directly from heaven the tablet of spiritual knowledge, inscribed by God's own finger, that is, by the active working of illumination. Such a

19. 1 (640D), p. 78.
20. 15 (896A), p. 181.
21. *Letter* 207, 2 (*PG* 32, 761B).
22. Cf. K. Ware, "Tradition and Personal Experience in Later Byzantine Theology", *Eastern Churches Review* iii (1970), pp. 131–41.

> man has no need of other books. It is not right for teachers to give instruction by copying out what other people say.[23]

And just as the true teacher is the man of personal experience, who has seen for himself, so likewise the teacher's aim in giving instruction is to bring his disciples to the point of crisis and confrontation, where they too will see for themselves. John, as we shall see, attaches profound importance to the role of the spiritual father, affirming that none should embark upon the inward journey without a guide. The spiritual father, however, is not in his view a substitute figure but an initiator. His function is not to experience things on our behalf, thereby dispensing us from the need to experience them personally, but the precise opposite. He is the very one who says to us: Open your own eyes, look and see for yourselves. To see, so John insists, it is not sufficient to listen to directions from other people; you need to use your own natural power of sight. "In the same way, you cannot discover from the teaching of others the beauty of prayer."[24] He takes as an example the taste of honey:

> Do you imagine that plain words can . . . describe the love of God . . . and assurance of the heart? Do you imagine that talk of such matters will mean anything to someone who has never experienced them? If you think so, then you will be like a man who with words and examples tries to convey the sweetness of honey to people who have never tasted it. He talks uselessly.[25]

This firm belief in the necessity for personal experience has determined the character which John gives to his book. Convinced as he is of the need for encounter and participation, for direct tasting and touching, John's aim in *The Ladder* is not to inculcate abstract teaching or to impose a formal code of ascetic rules, but to evoke in his readers an experience similar to his own. As the late Fr. Georges Florovsky put it, "*The Ladder* is an invitation to pilgrimage." It is an existential work, and only those who read it existentially will appreciate its true value.

---

23. *Past.* 1 (1165C), p. 231.
24. 28 (1140C), p. 281.
25. 25 (988AB), p. 218.

Faithful to this existential stance, in *The Ladder* John usually refrains from giving detailed directions about what foods to eat, how much and when, about hours of sleep and the daily program of manual labor. We search in vain through the pages of *The Ladder* for that kind of guidance. When discussing prayer, he likewise gives no description of the liturgical offices, no advice about preparation for Holy Communion and its frequency, no specific instructions about methods of private prayer, about formulae, bodily posture, breathing exercises and the like. These omissions are surely deliberate. His interest is in the inward rather than the outward. What matters for him is not physical asceticism but humility and purity of heart:

> In Scripture are the words, "I humbled myself, and the Lord hastened to rescue me" (Ps. 114:6); and these words are there instead of "I have fasted," "I have kept vigil," "I lay down on the bare earth."[26]

What he offers is not techniques and formulae but a way of life, not regulations but a path of initiation.

Because his aim is to impart a living, personal experience, John is often intentionally enigmatic. Like our Lord with His parables, like the Zen masters with their *koans* or the Sufis with their "scatter" technique, John avoids spelling out his conclusions too plainly, for he wants the reader to work out the answer for himself. When the point of his examples is left unclear, or he seems to jump in arbitrary fashion from one idea to another, normally this is due, not to carelessness or incompetence, but to deliberate purpose. He takes a conscious pleasure in cryptic phrases:

> If all are not saved who have been baptized, I will pass in silence over what follows.

> In the entire universe there is a unique place that saw the sun just once.

> Let us summon the Holy Trinity to help us as we marshal three against three.

26. 25 (992D), p. 221.

> Why is it that there were not as many lights among the holy fathers at Tabennisi as at Scetis? Cope with that question if you can. I cannot say why. Or rather, I do not wish to.[27]

In posing such riddles, John's aim is pastoral: to elicit a response, to provoke the reader into a leap of faith, to bring him to the moment of personal encounter.

Style and Structure: The Thirty Steps

With this objective in view, St. John Climacus has adopted a distinctive literary style in *The Ladder*. At first sight the Greek may seem abrupt and rough, but the book is in fact composed with subtlety and conscious art, in a rhythmic prose often not far removed from poetry. The abruptness is intended. The author loves short, sharp sentences, pithy definitions, paradoxical aphorisms, for his purpose is to wake the reader up. He excels in quaint illustrations, marked by a monastic sense of humor that has amused his audience over the centuries:

> . . . like someone trying at the same time to swim and to clap his hands. . . .
>
> . . . like someone who pelts [a] dog with bread. . . .
>
> Do not imitate those who in burying the dead first lament them—and then go off and get drunk.
>
> A man who has heard himself sentenced to death will not worry about the way theaters are run.
>
> The thought of the hesychast keeps hold of his spiritual mouse.[28]

We are left with the impression that, behind the unusual style and picturesque images, here is an author with a strongly marked personality: exacting, with a sharp eye for the weaknesses of his fellow monks, yet also full of humor and unexpected compassion, realistic—but with the realism that springs from living prayer.

John's basic image, around which the entire book is structured, is

27. 1 (636C), p. 76; 25 (993A), p. 221; 26 (1021A), p. 234; 27 (1105C), p. 265.
28. 6 (796A), p. 133; 7 (804D–805A, 813D), pp. 138, 143–4; 27 (1097C), p. 262.

of a ladder stretching from earth to heaven like that which Jacob saw (Gen. 28:12). Earlier writers, such as St. Gregory of Nazianzus[29] and St. John Chrysostom[30] in the fourth century, and Theodoret of Cyrrhus[31] in the fifth, had already spoken of the spiritual life as a ladder, up which by God's grace we mount step by step. But in St. John Climacus the analogy is far more developed. His ladder has thirty rungs or steps, one for each year in the hidden life of Christ before His baptism.[32] John's ingenious use of the ladder-image at once catches the reader's attention, giving to his book as a whole a distinctive flavor and unity. Indeed, his symbolic ladder soon became part of the spiritual imagination of the Christian East, and is frequently represented in panel ikons, refectory frescoes and illuminated manuscripts.[33] John is usually shown standing to one side, near the foot, holding a scroll and pointing to the ladder. The monks are struggling laboriously upward, while at the top Christ reaches out His arms to welcome those who have completed the ascent. On the right of the ladder angels encourage the monks as they climb, on the left demons try to trip them up and pull them off, and at the bottom the dragon of the abyss waits with open jaws.

As a supplement to the thirty steps of *The Ladder*, John also wrote a short treatise entitled *To the Shepherd*, describing the task of the abbot or spiritual father. Sometimes reckoned as the thirty-first step, this is likewise addressed to John of Raithu.[34]

While *The Ladder of Divine Ascent* is not in the strict sense a systematic treatise—John modestly calls himself a "second-rate architect"[35]—it is evident that he has arranged his rungs with care, according to a precise scheme. John embraces in his scope the whole extent of the spiritual life, starting with the initial "turning" or con-

---

29. *Oration* 43, 71 (*PG* 36, 529D).

30. *Homilies on John* 83, 5 (*PG* 59, 454).

31. *History of the Monks in Syria* 27 (*PG* 82, 1484C). The image of a "soul ladder" is widespread in the ancient world: see A. B. Cook, *Zeus. A Study in Ancient Religion*, vol. ii (Cambridge 1925), pp. 114–40; E. Bertaud and A. Rayez, 'Echelle spirituelle', *DS* iv (1958), cols. 62–86.

32. *Brief Summary* (1161A), p. 291.

33. See J. R. Martin, *The Illustration of the Heavenly Ladder of John Climacus* (Princeton 1954); M. Heppell, introduction to St. John Climacus, *The Ladder of Divine Ascent*, ET Archimandrite Lazarus (London 1959), pp. 29–31.

34. Greek text, *PG* 88, 1165–1208; ET, HTM, pp. 231–50; not included in the present volume.

35. 27 (1105B), p. 265.

version, continuing with a detailed analysis of the virtues and vices, and ending with the mystical union. The work falls into three main sections, of unequal extent. In the first three steps John describes the break with the "world," the renunciation both outward and inward that forms the presupposition of any spiritual ascent. Then, in a far longer section (Steps 4–26), he discusses the "active life" or "practice of the virtues" (*praxis, praktiki*), along with the corresponding passions that must be uprooted. Finally, the last four steps are devoted to the "contemplative life" (*theoria*), to stillness, prayer and union with God.

As this summary implies, John accepts in general terms the distinction drawn by Evagrius of Pontus (*c.* 345–99) between the active and the contemplative life. But, as Dr. Christos Yannaras rightly observes,[36] John does not follow the Evagrian scheme with any great exactness. In contrast to Evagrius, he holds that the supreme end of the spiritual way is not contemplation or *gnosis* but love. Much in the earlier steps of *The Ladder* relates to the contemplative as well as to the active life, while the final step on love is concerned with both the active and the contemplative life at once; in the context of divine love there can be no sharp differentiation between the two.

The basic pattern of the thirty steps of *The Ladder* can be presented thus:[37]

I. *The Break with the World*

1. Renunciation
2. Detachment
3. Exile

II. The Practice of the Virtues ("*Active Life*")

(i) *Fundamental Virtues*

4. Obedience
5. Penitence
6. Remembrance of Death
7. Sorrow

36. *I metaphysiki tou somatos* (Athens 1971), pp. 58–62.

37. This scheme is taken, with some modifications, from G. Couilleau, *DS* viii (1972), col. 373. I am in general much indebted to this article.

(ii) *The Struggle Against the Passions*

(a) Passions That Are Predominantly Non-physical

8. Anger
9. Malice
10. Slander
11. Talkativeness
12. Falsehood
13. Despondency

(b) Physical and Material Passions

14. Gluttony
15. Lust

16–17. Avarice

(c) Non-Physical Passions (cont.)

18–20. Insensitivity

21. Fear
22. Vainglory
23. Pride (also Blasphemy)

(iii) *Higher Virtues of the "Active Life"*

24. Simplicity
25. Humility
26. Discernment

III. *Union with God (Transition to the "Contemplative Life")*

27. Stillness
28. Prayer
29. Dispassion
30. Love

While the book as a whole has in this way a clearly defined structure, many of the individual steps have also an internal structure of their own. Thus most of the chapters on the vices are arranged on the following pattern:

Brief introductory statement, indicating the source of the vice and its place in the sequence of *The Ladder;*

Short definitions;

More detailed analysis: causes, symptoms, effects, remedies (with illustrative anecdotes);

Final summary.

Glancing through the outline given above, a reader may gain the impression that John's approach is for the most part negative. For, out of thirty chapters, sixteen are concerned with the vices to be overcome, and only fourteen with the virtues to be acquired; and several of these fourteen chapters seem also to be mainly negative, concerned as they are with such themes as "penitence," "sorrow," "dispassion." But this initial impression is misleading. First, the chapters on the vices are usually shorter than those on the virtues; so the fourteen steps on the virtues, added together, are considerably more than twice as long as the sixteen steps on the vices. Second, the chapters on the vices speak also of the corresponding virtues: Step 8, for instance, deals with meekness as well as anger, Step 11 with silence as well as talkativeness, Step 15 with purity as well as lust, Steps 18–20 with vigilance as well as insensitivity. Third and most fundamentally, as we shall see shortly, penitence, sorrow and dispassion are far from being predominantly negative.

Within this general scheme that we have indicated, there are skillfully balanced correspondences and contrasts:

I (1–3) balances III (27–30).

II i (4–7) balances II iii (24–26).

II ii b (14–17), on passions of a material type, is flanked by two balancing sections, each of six steps—II ii a (8–13) and II ii c (18–23)—on passions of a less physical character.

Closer examination reveals more detailed structures of "type" and "antitype." A theme is adumbrated in the earlier part of the work, and then taken up again at a higher level in the second part:

Step 2 (detachment)	:	Step 29 (dispassion)
Step 4 (obedience)	:	Step 26 (discernment)[38]
Step 5 (penitence)	:	Step 25 (humility)
Step 13 (despondency)	:	Step 18 (insensitivity)

Underlying these various parallels and oppositions there is, in *The Ladder* as a whole, a basic progression from human effort to divine gift, from *kopos* to *charisma*. Certainly, God's grace is absolutely indispensable for the attainment of any virtue, however humble. Yet,

38. The connection is made clear in the definition of obedience as "with all deliberateness, to put aside the capacity to make one's own judgment"; or, more literally, as "an abandonment of discernment in a wealth of discernment": 4 (680A), p. 92.

while both the divine and the human elements are present throughout the ascent of the ladder, on the earlier rungs we are chiefly conscious of our own toil and struggle, while on the higher rungs we are more and more aware of the freely granted grace of God. What begins as painful warfare ends as spontaneous joy:

> At the beginning of our religious life, we cultivate the virtues, and we do so with toil and difficulty. Progressing a little, we then lose our sense of grief or retain very little of it. But when our mortal intelligence turns to zeal and is mastered by it, then we work with full joy, determination, desire, and a holy flame.[39]

Two further things are apparent in the structure of *The Ladder*. First, by far the larger part of the work is concerned with the practice of the virtues and the struggle against the vices; by comparison, the section on the contemplative life (Steps 27–30) is relatively brief—to many, no doubt, disappointingly so. But John has good reasons for concentrating in this way on the active life. He does not want his readers willfully and prematurely to seek after visions and ecstasies, instead of learning penitence and humility. *The Ladder* displays in this regard a marked sobriety. John is highly cautious about dreams;[40] and it is significant that much the longest chapters in the book are those on obedience (Step 4) and on discernment or discretion (*diakrisis;* Step 26).

John is constantly warning us not to attempt too much too soon; we cannot "climb the entire ladder in a single stride."[41] When, in the monastery at Alexandria, John tried to start a discussion about stillness or inner silence (*hesychia*), he was kindly but firmly rebuked by his hosts:

> Father John [they said], we are corporeal beings and we lead a corporeal life. Knowing this, we choose to wage war according to the measure of our weakness.[42]

39. 1 (637C), p. 77.
40. 3 (669B–672B), pp. 89–90.
41. 14 (865B), p. 166; cf. 25 (997D), p. 225.
42. 4 (700B), p. 103.

John took the point. In *The Ladder* he insists that *hesychia*—meaning both the solitary life and the more advanced forms of inner prayer—is only for "very few,"[43] only for those who have been prepared through long years of training in the practice of the virtues. No one should embark on "theology," in the sense of the contemplative life, without first struggling against the passions: "It is risky to swim in one's clothes. A slave of passion should not dabble in theology."[44] That is why John speaks at length about the warfare against sin, but offers no more than a few veiled hints about the final transfiguration of the human person, in soul and body, by the uncreated light. His reticence is deliberate. He does not want us to reach out for the iced cakes before we have eaten the bread and butter.

Secondly, John did not mean the image of the ladder, which dominates the book, to be interpreted too literally. While placed in ordered sequence, the different steps are not to be regarded as strictly consecutive stages, the one terminating before the next commences. For, even though by God's grace we gradually progress to the higher steps, we still continue to live and develop simultaneously on the lower levels as well. This is true in particular of the fifth step, penitence, and of the seventh step, sorrow or mourning (*penthos*). These are things that in this present life we never outgrow; they continue unceasing up to the gates of death. As John insists:

> When we die, we will not be criticized for having failed to work miracles. We will not be accused of having failed to be theologians or contemplatives. But we will certainly have some explanation to offer to God for not having mourned unceasingly.[45]

In our beginning is our end. In one sense, the supreme aim of the spiritual path is indeed "theology," the contemplation or vision of God. But in another and perhaps more vital sense, our end-point is our starting-point: penitence.

---

43. 4 (725C), p. 119.
44. 27 (1097C), p. 262.
45. 7 (816D), p. 145.

III. THE SPIRITUAL TEACHING OF ST. JOHN CLIMACUS

Imitation of Christ, Spirituality and Dogma, Grace and Free Will

Without attempting a full analysis, let us consider a few master themes in the spiritual teaching of *The Ladder*.

In the first step, at the very beginning of the work, St. John Climacus briefly indicates the essence of the spiritual life:

> A Christian is an *imitator of Christ* in thought, word and deed, as far as this is humanly possible, and he believes rightly and blamelessly in the Holy Trinity.[46]

In the final step he returns to the same idea:

> Love, by its nature, is a *resemblance to God*, insofar as this is humanly possible.[47]

Such is the aim throughout the ascent of the ladder: to follow Christ, to become "like God," to imitate and resemble Him in His divine love.

The Christian, however, does not only imitate; he also "believes rightly." For St. John Climacus spirituality and dogma are essentially connected; there can be no true life of prayer without a right faith in God. "It is characteristic of *The Ladder*," writes the Serbian D. Bogdanović, "that in it dogmatic themes are constantly overflowing into the ethical realm. Dogma forms here . . . the theoretical basis of ethics."[48] As Archimandrite Sophrony observes, throughout *The Ladder* John raises the discussion "from the purely ascetic to the mystical and theological level."[49]

From this it follows that *The Ladder*, in common with any authentically Christian work of spirituality, is theocentric rather than an-

46. 1 (633B), p. 74. Compare the last letter of the spiritual alphabet, 26 (1017C), p. 232: "With God's help an imitator of the Lord."

47. 30 (1156B), p. 286.

48. *Jean Climaque dans la littérature byzantine et la littérature serbe ancienne* (Belgrade 1968), p. 218.

49. "De la nécessité des trois renoncements chez St. Cassien le Romain et St. Jean Climaque", *Studia Patristica* v (*Texte und Untersuchungen* 80: Berlin 1962), p. 395.

thropocentric; its purpose is not to analyze psychological states, considered in themselves, but to see the human person always in its relationship with God. To quote Bogdanović once more, "For Climacus the virtues are not so much qualities of man as qualities of God; they are divine attributes."[50] Man becomes virtuous by participating in the virtues or energies of God.

John usually takes for granted this link between spirituality and dogma without alluding to it explicitly, but such occasional references as he makes to dogmatic questions are sufficient to indicate the closeness of the connection. He explains, for example, the relation between obedience and stillness (*hesychia*) by comparing the doctrine of the Trinity with that of Christ,[51] and goes on to illustrate the interdependence between prayer and the remembrance of death by invoking the definition of Chalcedon (451):

> Some claim that prayer is better than the remembrance of death. But for my part, my praise goes out to the two natures in one person.[52]

In other words, prayer and the remembrance of death are both equally necessary: the two form a unity similar to that between Christ's humanity and His divinity.

The most significant among the Christological references in *The Ladder* is the brief allusion to Gethsemane in Step 6:

> Christ is frightened of dying but not terrified, thereby clearly revealing the properties of His two natures.[53]

John is thinking here of the Monothelete controversy which was raging in his day, and in which his contemporary St. Maximus the Confessor was deeply involved. Although John was less directly concerned with the dispute, from his words here it is evident that he took the same view as Maximus. The Monotheletes held that our

50. *Op. cit.*, p. 218.
51. 27 (1117A), p. 273.
52. 28 (1137A), p. 279.
53. 6 (793C), p. 132. On this passage, see D.J. Chitty, *The Desert a City* (Oxford 1966), p. 174.

Lord, while possessing two natures, was endowed with only a single will. Against this Maximus argued that human nature without a human will is an unreal abstraction. If Christ is truly man, then He has two wills as well as two natures; and it is precisely at His agony in the garden that we see the presence of these two wills most plainly manifested—in tension, yet in ultimate reconciliation. John's standpoint in Step 6 is similar. The passage quoted is to be understood as a gloss on Hebrews 4:15, ". . . tempted in everything just as we are, only without sin." Christ's fear of death indicates that He has a genuinely human nature, and so a genuinely human will, for He could not experience such fear in His divine nature or His divine will. At the same time John makes a further point by distinguishing *fear* of death from *terror* of death. It is, he says, natural for man, living under the conditions of the fall, to fear death; terror of death, on the other hand, comes from a sense of unrepented sins. Now Christ is not Himself a sinful man, but at His Incarnation He accepts to live out His earthly life under the conditions of the fall. He therefore accepts the fear of death natural to fallen man; but, being Himself sinless, He does not experience the sinful terror of death.

In all this John, like Maximus, is not just splitting hairs. The doctrinal point, technical though it may be, is vital for spirituality. Imitation of Christ, in a full and genuine sense, is only possible because God has become completely man, taking upon Himself the entirety of our human nature—including a human will—and so experiencing *from within* all our moral conflicts, our fears and temptations, "only without sin." Because we see in Christ a human will exactly like ours, yet freely obedient to the will of God, we know that such free obedience is also possible for us. Here it becomes evident, in a very clear and direct manner, how a correct spirituality depends upon correct doctrinal teaching.

Faith in the two natures and two wills of the incarnate Savior implies that the spiritual way, understood as an "imitation of Christ," involves the convergence or "synergy" (*synergeia*) of two factors, unequal in value but both equally necessary: divine grace and human freedom. "Without Me you can do nothing" (John 15:5): what God does is incomparably the more important. Yet our part is also essential, for God does not save us against our will. This is exactly the position of St. John Climacus. At first sight it might appear that in *The Ladder* he overstresses the human aspect, putting too great an emphasis on man's effort and saying too little about God's initiative. But in fact he is in no doubt whatsoever about the necessity for divine grace:

> Anyone trained in chastity should give himself no credit for any achievements. . . . When nature is overcome it should be admitted that this is due to Him Who is above nature. . . . The man who decides to struggle against his flesh and to overcome it by his own efforts is fighting in vain. . . . Admit your incapacity. . . . What have you got that you did not receive as a gift either from God or as a result of the help and prayers of others?. . . It is sheer lunacy to imagine that one has deserved the gifts of God.[54]

John is certainly no Pelagian!

"Joyful Sorrow": The Ladder as Dialectical Theology

". . . always bearing about in our body the dying of the Lord Jesus, that the life of Jesus may also be made manifest in our body" (2 Cor. 4:10): the imitation of Christ signifies sharing at one and the same time both in His death and in His resurrection. But does not St. John Climacus lay too much stress upon the burdens of cross-bearing, and too little upon the joyfulness of the risen life? Does not *The Ladder* serve to repel rather than to encourage?

It is certainly true that *The Ladder* offers no encouragement to those who look for compromise. John asks from us, in Christ's name, a complete, unsparing dedication. Nothing is ever enough. Yet he is not cruel or inhuman. He criticizes Evagrius' directives on fasting precisely for their lack of humanity: Evagrius fails to allow for human weakness, John says; we need to grow accustomed gently to the rigors of fasting, advancing little by little.[55] Although his strictures on the failings of his brother monks come close at times to caricature, John is scarcely ever censorious: "his attitude," as Dr. Muriel Heppell remarks, "is that of the Publican rather than the Pharisee."[56] He freely admits his own defects, confessing that he cannot say much, for in-

54. 15 (881A, 884BC, 900B), pp. 172, 173, 184; 23 (968B), pp. 208–9.
55. 14 (865AB), p. 166.
56. Introduction to *The Ladder of Divine Ascent*, ET Archimandrite Lazarus, p. 17.

stance, about insensitivity because he is himself "very sorely tried by this vice."[57]

The key to a true appreciation of *The Ladder* is to recognize throughout its pages a dialectical approach. Those who see in the work nothing except harsh demands for self-denial and ascetic struggle have discerned only one side of the dialectic. But, alongside the negations, again and again there is a positive note of reassurance and hope.

Fundamental to John's dialectical attitude is his sense of the reality of the fall. Throughout *The Ladder* an all-important distinction of levels has to be made: *Is John speaking about the fallen or the unfallen state?* Concerning the fall and the resulting distortion of human nature, John is indeed highly negative, although never sweepingly condemnatory in the manner of Augustine or Calvin; he nowhere suggests that the fall has led to a total corruption. But when he speaks about the condition prior to the fall—about humankind's true and natural state, which in Christ we can now regain—he is not only affirmative but optimistic. John is no Manichaean. Human nature in its entirety, body as well as soul, is God's creation, and is therefore good: "God neither caused nor created evil."[58] Sin is extrinsic to our true personhood: "No one wants to sin against God."[59] There are many natural virtues, but no natural vices:

> Evil or passion is not something naturally implanted in things. God is not the creator of passions. On the other hand, there are many natural virtues that have come to us from Him

—and these include the highest virtues of all, faith, hope and love.[60]

Such, then, is the basic dualism underlying John's ascetic theology: not a dualism between God and matter, for God is the creator of matter; not a dualism between soul and body, for *The Ladder* views the human person as an integral unity; but a dualism between the unfal-

57. 18 (933B), p. 192.
58. 26 (1068C), p. 251.
59. 10 (845D), p. 156.
60. 26 (1028A), p. 238.

len and the fallen, between the natural and the contranatural, between immortality and corruption, between life and death.

True to this dialectical approach, throughout *The Ladder* John balances negations with affirmations. The monk is "a soul pained by the constant remembrance of death," yet the motives for his renunciation are positive: not just sorrow for sins and fear of punishment, but love of God and longing for the future Kingdom.[61] The monastery is "a tomb before the tomb," but it is also "heaven on earth."[62] Exile involves a painful sacrifice—the loss of parents, friends, familiar surroundings—but its overriding motive is creative, to make us free for God: "Exile is a separation from everything, in order that one may hold on totally to God."[63] Obedience is "a total renunciation of our own life . . . death freely accepted," but it is also a "resurrection."[64] We are to hold the hour of death in constant remembrance, regarding each day as our last;[65] at the same time we should await death "as though it were life."[66]

Everywhere John negates in order to affirm. This is true in particular of the chapter which to most contemporary readers appears the harshest and most distasteful of all: Step 5 on repentance, with its grim portrayal of the "Prison" at the Alexandrian monastery. Perhaps John meant us to be shocked by it: "One may suppose," says Fr. Derwas Chitty, "that the writer intended those who were not ready for his work to be put off by this chapter."[67] Yet, even so, the image of repentance that emerges is ultimately positive. If repentance is "hell,"[68] it is also and more fundamentally "resurrection."[69] It is not just death but life—the renewal of our baptismal regeneration.[70] It is not despair but hope:

61. 1 (633C), p. 74.
62. 4 (716B, 713B), pp. 113, 111.
63. 3 (664C), p. 85.
64. 4 (680A), pp. 91–92.
65. 6 (797C), p. 135.
66. 4 (705B), p. 106.
67. *The Desert a City*, p. 174.
68. 5 (769B), p. 124.
69. 5 (781A), p. 131.
70. 5 (764B), p. 121.

> Repentance is the daughter of hope and the refusal to despair. (The penitent stands guilty—but undisgraced.) Repentance is reconciliation with the Lord.[71]

To repent is not only to fear God's wrath but to respond to His love: the grief that accompanies penitence is "the grief that comes from loving God."[72]

John's dialectical approach is similarly evident in Step 7, on sorrow and weeping. This chapter on the gift of tears has proved to be one of the most influential in the whole of *The Ladder*.[73] God, so John points out forcefully—and here his basic optimism is plainly in evidence—created us for laughter, not for tears:

> God does not demand or desire that someone should mourn out of sorrow of heart, but rather that out of love for Him he should rejoice with the laughter of the soul. Take away sin and then the sorrowful tears that flow from bodily eyes will be superfluous. Why look for a bandage when you are not cut? Adam did not weep before the fall, and there will be no tears after the resurrection when sin will be abolished, when pain, sorrow and lamentation will have taken flight.[74]

Tears, then, reflect man's fallen state and express his mourning for sin. Yet there is more to them than that. Tears can be "sweet" as well as "bitter."[75] Tears that begin by being "painful" become in course of time "painless"; tears of fear develop into tears of love.[76]

---

71. *Ibid.*

72. 5 (776D), p. 128.

73. The basic modern study on the gift of tears is still I. Hausherr, *Penthos. La doctrine de la componction dans l'Orient chrétien (Orientalia Christiana Analecta* 132: Rome 1944), especially pp. 137–73. See also M. Lot-Borodine, "Le mystère du 'don des larmes' dans l'Orient chrétien", *La vie spirituelle* (supplement for September 1936), reprinted in O. Clément and others, *La douloureuse joie (Spiritualité orientale* 14: Bellefontaine 1974), pp. 131–95; L. Gillet, "The Gift of Tears", *Sobornost* n.s. 12 (1937), pp. 5–10; G.A. Maloney, *The Mystic of Fire and Light: St Symeon the New Theologian* (Denville, N.J. 1975), pp. 129–37; K. Ware, "The Orthodox Experience of Repentance", *Sobornost* ii (1980), pp. 26–28.

74. 7 (809C), p. 141.

75. 5 (776A), p. 127.

76. 7 (813B), p. 143.

True to his fundamental dialectic, John insists that for the penitent Christian sorrow is constantly interwoven with joy. Tears, like the experience of repentance, spring from a sense not only of our sinfulness but of God's mercy; there is gladness in them as well as grief. John sums up the point in the composite word *charmolypi*, apparently of his own invention, signifying "joyful sorrow."[77] The repentant person is like a child who cries, yet smiles in the middle of his tears.[78] Spiritual mourning leads to spiritual laughter; it is a wedding garment, not a funeral robe:

> The man wearing blessed, God-given mourning like a wedding garment gets to know the spiritual laughter of the soul.[79]

Joy goes with sorrow like honey in a comb:

> As I ponder the true nature of compunction, I find myself amazed by the way in which inward joy and gladness mingle with what we call mourning and grief, like honey in a comb.

Such compunction, he immediately adds, is a divine charism, not just the fruit of human striving:

> There must be a lesson here, and it surely is that compunction is properly a gift from God[80]

—a gift, he notes, not conferred upon all, but only upon such as God chooses in His own wisdom.[81]

There are, however, many different kinds of tears, and it is important to discriminate between them. The basic distinction is between tears that are simply the consequence of our own efforts, and those that come as a gift from God[82]—in other words, between "ordi-

77. 7 (804B), p. 137.
78. 7 (813B), p. 143.
79. 7 (809A), p. 140.
80. 7 (812A), p. 141.
81. 7 (808A), p. 139.
82. 7 (805D), p. 139.

nary and natural tears" and tears that are "spiritual."[83] As John observes, this is a distinction not always easy to apply in practice:

> This problem of tears, especially where it concerns beginners, is a very obscure matter and hard to analyze since tears can come about in various ways. Tears come from nature, from God, from suffering good and bad, from vainglory, from licentiousness, from love, from the remembrance of death. . . .[84]

Here John indicates at least three levels; these may be designated—although John himself does not actually use this terminology—as contranatural, natural, and supranatural. First, tears may come "from vainglory, from licentiousness." Tears of this kind, tears of frustration, anger, jealousy or self-pity, are contranatural, an expression of our fallen self, and as such they are sinful and injurious. Second, our tears may be natural, the result of spontaneous human feelings; in that case they may be neutral, neither good nor bad, or they may have an effect for good, as with the healing and purifying tears that we shed for the departed. It is not always easy to distinguish between the second level and the third, between natural tears that are pure and beneficial, and the spiritual or supranatural tears that are, in a direct and special sense, "from God." Nature presupposes grace, and grace builds upon nature; so it is possible for natural tears to develop, gradually and almost unnoticed, into spiritual tears, without the point of transition being clearly evident to the one who weeps. John believes, nevertheless, that a distinction needs to be made, and that it is only to the supranatural or spiritual tears that the title "*gift* of tears" can properly be applied.

When John speaks of "spiritual" tears, it should not be imagined that he means tears that are merely inward and metaphorical. Tears, in his view, even when spiritual, are still manifested visibly and physically; by the "gift of tears" he means something specific and concrete. Spiritual tears are not merely an event within the soul, but form part of the spiritualization of the body and its physical senses.

---

83. 7 (808C), p. 140.
84. 7 (808B), pp. 139–40.

When genuinely spiritual, tears are a renewal of baptism, and even stand on a level higher than baptism itself:

> The tears that come after baptism are greater than baptism itself, though it may seem rash to say so. Baptism washes off those evils that were previously within us, whereas the sins committed after baptism are washed away by tears. The baptism received by us as children we have all defiled, but we cleanse it anew with our tears. If God in His love for the human race had not given us tears, those being saved would be few indeed and hard to find.[85]

Here the positive character of spiritual tears is manifest. Baptism is renunciation of sin, but it is also in a positive sense rebirth, resurrection, entry into new life. The same is true of the "joyful sorrow" of supranatural tears: negatively it involves mourning for our sins, but positively it expresses joy at our reconciliation. The prodigal son wept as he sat in exile among the swine, shedding tears of sorrow for his sins. But no doubt he also wept on his return home, when the Father embraced him, clothed him in the festal robe, and put a ring on his hand; and this time the tears were sweet rather than bitter, expressing joy at the love with which he had been welcomed back. The gift of tears includes both these moments on our inward pilgrimage.

St. Isaac the Syrian, John's younger contemporary—but there is no reason to believe that they knew each other—develops this same point in his own characteristic way. Tears, he says, mark the point of transition, the frontier between the present age and the age to come. The newborn child weeps on first coming into the world; in the same way the Christian weeps as he is reborn into the age to come:

> The fruits of the inner man begin only with the shedding of tears. When you reach the place of tears, then know that your spirit has come out from the prison of this world and has set its foot upon the path that leads towards the new age. Your spirit begins at this moment to breathe the wonderful air which is there, and it starts to shed tears. The moment for the birth of the spiritual child is now at hand, and the

85. 7 (804B), p. 137.

> travail of childbirth becomes intense. Grace, the common mother of us all, makes haste to give birth mystically to the soul, God's image, bringing it forth into the light of the age to come. And when the time for the birth has arrived, the intellect begins to sense something of the things of that other world—as a faint perfume, or as the breath of life which a newborn child receives into its bodily frame. But we are not accustomed to such an experience and, finding it hard to endure, our body is suddenly overcome by a weeping mingled with joy.[86]

Here we catch precisely the same note as we have heard already in *The Ladder;* as John puts it, "joy and gladness mingle with what we call mourning and grief."

The cardinal importance of tears is manifest, but are they *essential*? Did St. John Climacus consider that only those who have passed through this particular experience of weeping can be regarded as truly repentant and genuinely reborn into the "new age"? St. Symeon the New Theologian (949–1022), who is much influenced by John's theology of tears, certainly came close to adopting such a view. But John himself is more cautious. We should allow, he urges, for differences in temperament: some shed tears with the utmost difficulty, "like great drops of blood," while others do so "with no trouble at all"; God looks, not at the outward intensity of weeping, but at the inward struggles of our heart. Those who have been granted the gift of tears should on no account imagine themselves superior to those who lack it. "Some are not granted the gift of mourning," but the desolation that they feel at their lack of tears may take the place of the gift itself.[87]

It seems that John's attitude is more qualified than Symeon's. While Symeon thinks in terms of the *way* of tears, John thinks rather of the *gift* of tears. For Symeon tears are the King's highway, the royal road that all are to follow. For John tears are a charism conferred only upon some, whereas on others God bestows some different gift that takes its place.

---

86. *Mystic Treatises by Isaac of Nineveh*, ET A. J. Wensinck (Amsterdam 1923), p. 85 (adapted).

87. 7 (805C, 809D), pp. 138–9, 141. Cf. 26 (1088D), p. 259.

"My Helper and My Enemy": The Ambivalence of the Body—Eros, the Passions, Apatheia

The dialectical stance displayed by St. John Climacus in his treatment of repentance and tears is to be seen equally in his attitude to the human body. The body is both adversary and friend: adversary inasmuch as it has been marred by the fall, friend inasmuch as it remains God's creation and is called to share in the resurrection glory. To appreciate John's attitude aright, and to avoid unjustly accusing him of an anti-Christian body-soul dualism, it is important to determine on what level he is speaking in each particular passage: whether of the body in its true and natural state, as formed by the Creator, or of the body as we know it now, in its contranatural or fallen condition.

It is not difficult to find negative statements about the body in *The Ladder*:

> Those gifted with the heart's depth of mourning regard their lives as detestable, painful, and wearying, as a cause of tears and suffering, and they turn away from their body as from an enemy.
>
> Treat your body always as an enemy, for the flesh is an ungrateful and treacherous friend. The more you look after it, the more it hurts you.
>
> The man who pets a lion may tame it but the man who coddles the body makes it ravenous.
>
> Some wise men have said that renunciation is hostility to the body.
>
> A monster is this gross and savage body.[88]

But, as the context makes clear in these passages, it is the body in its *fallen* state that John has here in view. Elsewhere he treats the body not as irreclaimably hostile but as ambivalent. By virtue of the

88. 7 (808B), p. 139; 9 (841C), p. 153; 14 (864D), p. 165; 15 (881D), p. 173; 26 (1016D), p. 232.

fall it is hindrance and enemy; but by virtue of its creation by God it is partner and friend:

> By what rule or manner shall I bind this body of mine?... How can I hate him when my nature disposes me to love him? How can I break away from him when I am bound to him forever? How can I escape from him when he is going to rise with me? How can I make him incorrupt when he has received a corruptible nature? ... He is my helper and my enemy, my assistant and my opponent, a protector and a traitor.... I embrace him. And I turn away from him. What is this mystery in me? What is the principle of this mixture of body and soul? How can I be my own friend and my own enemy?[89]

In this passage, significantly John implies that there is a continuing link between soul and body: "I am bound to him forever ... he is going to rise with me." For the Christian the body is not a tomb or prison, not a piece of clothing to be worn for a time and then cast aside, but an integral part of the true self. Scripture teaches us to believe not just in the immortality of the soul but in the resurrection of the body. Even though, as a result of the fall, body and soul are separated at death, this severance is no more than temporary, and we look beyond it. The body's vocation, therefore, is to be sanctified and transfigured along with the soul: it is to be rendered spiritual, without thereby losing any of its God-given materiality. "Your body," we are told, "is a temple of the Holy Spirit ... glorify God with your body" (1 Cor. 6:19–20); Christ "will transfigure the body of our humiliation, so as to conform it to His own glorious body" (Phil. 3:21).

St. John Climacus shares the standpoint of St. Paul. Alongside the passages in *The Ladder* which treat the body as an enemy, there are others that speak positively about its participation in the spiritual life, its resurrection and its final glory. The gift of tears, already discussed, is part of the process of bodily transfiguration: it represents the spiritualization of the senses. Nor is it only in Step 7 that this theme of bodily glory is in evidence. At the very outset of *The Ladder* John affirms that the monk's aim is "a body made holy";[90] we seek "to

89. 15 (901C–904A), pp. 185–6.
90. 1 (633C), p. 74.

ascend to heaven with the body."[91] The same point recurs later in the work: "Everyone should struggle to raise his clay, so to speak, to a place on the throne of God. . . . I do not think anyone should be classed as a saint until he has made holy his body, if indeed that is possible."[92] And what he here regards as a doubtful eventuality, elsewhere he affirms as a realized fact:

> A man flooded with the love of God reveals in his body, as if in a mirror, the splendor of his soul. . . . Men who have attained this angelic state often forget to eat, and I really think they do not even miss their food. . . . Indeed I suspect that the bodies of these incorruptible men are immune to sickness, for their bodies have been sanctified and rendered incorruptible.[93]

In certain instances, so John believes, bodily resurrection has actually been anticipated; one example is Hesychius the Horebite, whose tomb was found to be empty.[94] Hesychius' experience is a striking case of the "inaugurated eschatology" assumed in *The Ladder;* the blessings of the age to come, in John's view, are not merely a future hope, but are also in some measure a present reality in the lives of the saints. Already in this life the righteous enjoy the first-fruits of the last things, having "risen to immortality before the general resurrection,"[95] and in this anticipation of the End the body also has its part.

John believes, then, in a *total* sanctification of soul and body together. Even the passions, although a consequence of the fall and therefore no true part of human nature, are merely the distortion of the natural impulses implanted in the body (or the soul) by God. While repudiating the passions, we should not reject the natural, God-given impulses that underlie them, but should restore to good use that which has become misdirected as a result of the fall. In the

---

91. 1 (636B), p. 75.

92. 26 (1064A), p. 248; 15 (889C), p. 178.

93. 30 (1157B), p. 288. Cf. the story of the monk Menas at Alexandria, whose body flowed with myrrh after his death: 4 (697C), p. 102.

94. 6 (797A), p. 134.

95. 15 (893A), p. 179; cf. 15 (904C), p. 186; 28 (1129B), p. 274.

warfare against the passions, our watchword should be "transfigure," not "suppress"; "educate," not "eradicate":

> We have taken natural attributes of our own and turned them into passions. For instance, the seed that we have for the sake of procreating children is abused by us for the sake of fornication. Nature has provided us with anger as something to be turned against the serpent, but we have used it against our neighbor. . . . We have a natural desire for food, but not surely for profligacy.[96]

Gluttony, so John tells us here, is a vice, but eating as such is by no means sinful; there is nothing wrong about enjoying our food. The practice of fasting implies no condemnation upon the action of eating, but serves to make that action sacramental and eucharistic. Even anger can be turned to good use. As for the sexual impulse, this too is a divine gift, and has its role to play in the life of the spirit. John is not afraid to take the term for physical love, *eros*—which has in Greek many of the same associations as the English word "erotic"—and to apply it to our love for God. The erotic impulse is not to be suppressed but redirected:

> I have watched impure souls mad for physical love (*eros*) but turning what they know of such love into a reason for penance and transferring that same capacity for love (*eros*) to the Lord.
>
> A chaste man is someone who has driven out bodily love (*eros*) by means of divine love (*eros*), who has used heavenly fire to quench the fires of the flesh.[97]

Although John says that "bodily love"—meaning in this context *fallen*, impure *eros*—is to be "driven out," yet its place is to be taken, not by a state of frigid detachment, but by a "divine erotic impulse." Fire is quenched by fire, not by water! Even when speaking of physical

96. 26 (1068C), p. 251.
97. 5 (777A), p. 129; 15 (880D), p. 171.

and divine love as "opposites," John still regards the earthly as a true image of the heavenly:

> Physical love can be a paradigm of the longing for God. . . .
>
> Lucky the man who loves and longs for God as a smitten lover does for his beloved. . . .
>
> Someone truly in love keeps before his mind's eye the face of the beloved and embraces it there tenderly. Even during sleep the longing continues unappeased, and he murmurs to his beloved. That is how it is for the body. And that is how it is for the spirit.[98]

The importance of these passages has been rightly emphasized by Dr. Yannaras.[99]

Physical *eros*, then, is not to be considered sinful, but can and should be used as a way of glorifying God. Sin is evil, but not the body and its natural impulses. The sinfulness of passion resides, not in materiality—for as God's creation the material body is good, and in any case not all passions are physical—but in the misdirection of the human will. Sin is not material but spiritual in its origin; for the devil fell before man did so, and the devil has no body.

These conclusions about *eros*, the body and the passions are confirmed by an analysis of the term "dispassion" (*apatheia*), as used by John in Step 29 and elsewhere in *The Ladder*. Dispassion is not negative but positive: St. Diadochus of Photice (mid fifth century) even speaks of "the fire of dispassion."[100] It is a denial of the passions, regarded as the contranatural expression of fallen sinfulness; but it is a reaffirmation of the pure and natural impulses of our soul and body. It connotes not repression but reorientation, not inhibition but freedom; having overcome the passions, we are free to be our true selves, free to love others, free to love God. Dispassion, then, is no mere mortification of the passions but their replacement by a new and better energy. Using once more the language of "inaugurated eschatology,"

98. 26 (1024B), p. 236; 30 (1156CD), p. 287.

99. *I metaphysiki tou somatos*, pp. 149–66; "Eros divin et éros humain selon S. Jean Climaque", *Contacts* xxi (1969), pp. 190–204.

100. *Century* 17: ET *Phil.*, p. 258.

John defines dispassion, not as a form of death, but as "resurrection of the soul prior to that of the body."[101]

John underlines the dynamic, affirmative character of dispassion by associating it closely with love, to such an extent that he virtually identifies the two:

> Love, dispassion and adoption are distinguished by name, and name only. . . .
>
> To have dispassion is to have the fullness of love, by which I mean the complete indwelling of God.[102]

Dispassion, then, is not indifference or impassivity but burning love, not emptiness but the fullness of divine indwelling. Whereas in Stoic ethics it tends to be a state of individualistic and self-centered detachment, as used in *The Ladder* it implies a personal relationship. To be "dispassioned" is to relate to God, to have His energy active within us: "A man is truly dispassionate . . . when he keeps his soul continually in the presence of the Lord."[103]

One thing that dispassion certainly does *not* mean for John is immunity from temptation, impeccability, a condition in which we are no longer capable of sinning. John is entirely clear that no such state is possible "this side of the grave,"[104] and he quotes with approval the words of the archdeacon Macedonius:

> It is said of angels that they do not, or, as some would have it, that they cannot fall. But men fall, yet they can quickly rise again, as often as this may happen to them.[105]

John agrees with Isaac the Syrian: "Dispassion consists, not in no longer feeling the passions, but in not accepting them."[106]

As inward resurrection, as a personal relationship with God in love, dispassion signifies the return to man's unfallen state in para-

101. 29 (1148C), p. 282.

102. 30 (1156B), p. 287; 26 (1092C), p. 260.

103. 29 (1148B), p. 282. On the "relational" character of *apatheia*, see Yannaras, *I metaphysiki tou somatos*, p. 178.

104. 14 (865A), p. 166.

105. 4 (696D), pp. 101–2.

106. *Mystic Treatises*, ET Wensinck, p. 345 (adapted).

dise, the recovery of the "undying beauty" which he possessed "before this clay."[107] In paradise man was not a disembodied soul, but a unity of soul and body, a psychosomatic whole; and so dispassion, as the return to paradise, involves not the repudiation of the body and its impulses but their reintegration with the soul and their deliverance from "corruption."[108]

The Monk and the World: Brotherhood, Obedience, the Spiritual Father

The Ladder has been blamed, not only for what its critics see as undue severity and pessimism, but also for its apparent individualism. It has been pointed out that in none of the thirty steps does St. John Climacus say anything at all about the Church. He never speaks of the episcopate, and his few allusions to the clergy are on the whole uncomplimentary.[109] He writes for the most part as if the monastic community existed entirely on its own, without forming part of any wider ecclesial structure; the all-embracing unity of Christ's Body seems to be ignored. Scarcely any reference is made to the heavenly Church: the Mother of God is not once mentioned, and although John does speak regularly about the angels, there is very little about the communion of saints. The liturgy, the sacraments, the Church festivals are only touched on once or twice in passing.

Silence, however, does not necessarily imply contempt. Pope Gregory the Great in his huge masterpiece the *Moralia* says almost nothing about the Eucharist, although the work was written at the very heart of ecclesiastical life in Rome; Bernard of Clairvaux, in a sermon delivered at Mass on Maundy Thursday, makes no more than a single brief allusion to Holy Communion.[110] Failure to mention such things need not mean that they are being dismissed as peripheral; perhaps they are everywhere presupposed, like the air we breathe and the light that enables us to see.

John in any case is writing specifically for monks, and so it is not surprising if he has little to say about Church life outside the monastery. As a matter of fact, he does sometimes speak of the monk's service to society. The monk helps others, so he believes, not so much

107. 29 (1149D), p. 284.
108. 29 (1148B), p. 282.
109. See, for example, 4 (701C), p. 104; 14 (865A), p. 166.
110. C. Butler, *Ways of Christian Life* (London 1932), pp. 51–52.

visibly as invisibly—not through exterior works but through inward prayer, and by acting as a presence, a sign, an example:

> Angels are a light for monks and the monastic life is a light for all men. Hence monks should spare no effort to become a shining example in all things, and they should give no scandal in anything they say or do.[111]

When dealing with his primary theme, life inside the monastery, John is certainly no individualist. On the contrary, he insists very strongly upon the communal character of the monastic life. No one, he stresses, should embark on the solitary life unless he has first undergone the experience of living with others, either in a fully organized monastery or in some smaller spiritual "family" pursuing the third way. Throughout Step 4, in particular, John underscores the necessity for adequate preparation before withdrawing into solitude, and the dangers of pride to which the hermit is exposed.[112]

The two aspects of community life to which John attaches particular importance are *brotherly love* and *obedience*. Love forms the topmost rung on the spiritual ladder—love for God, but also love for neighbor, since the two are inseparable: "He who loves the Lord has first loved his brother, for the latter is proof of the former."[113] Love for neighbor signifies first of all love for my *immediate* neighbor, and so in the monk's case it means love for his fellow monks dwelling with him in the same community. The true monk shares to the full in the joys and sorrows of each brother—"he weeps for the sins of that brother and is delighted by his progress"[114]—although this love does not need always to be expressed outwardly in words.[115] As we have noted, what most impressed John at the monastery that he visited in Egypt was precisely the quality of loving compassion shown by the monks toward one another:

> An unbreakable bond of love joined these men together. . . . Above all, they strove never to injure a brother's conscience.

111. 26 (1020D), p. 234.
112. 4 (708A, 709C, 712A), pp. 107, 109, 110, etc.
113. 30 (1157C), p. 288.
114. 4 (705A), p. 106.
115. 6 (797C), p. 135.

> And if ever someone showed hatred of another, the shepherd banished him like a convict to the isolation monastery. Once when a brother spoke ill of a neighbor, the holy man, on hearing him, had him expelled immediately. "I'm not having a visible devil here along with the invisible one," he said.[116]

Whenever a quarrel arose, those in authority at the Alexandrian house worked at once to secure a reconciliation. The brethren themselves, obedient to St. Paul's injunction, "Bear one another's burdens" (Gal. 6:2), in mutual love gladly took responsibility for each other's faults.[117] It was these features above all that made the monastery at Alexandria a model in John's eyes.

Along with brotherly love, the second fundamental virtue of the monk in community is obedience. By this John does not mean primarily obedience to a written monastic rule; in fact, he nowhere makes any reference to such a rule. He is thinking in more personal terms—of obedience to Christ, and of obedience to the spiritual father as the earthly ikon of Christ the Good Shepherd. For a monk in a fully organized monastery, the spiritual father will normally be the abbot; for a monk following the third way, he will be the *geron* or *abba*, the "old man" who heads the small monastic "family."

John is emphatic about the importance of the spiritual father. The ascent of the ladder is not to be undertaken in isolation, but under the immediate direction of a guide. Here John takes up a theme central to monasticism from its earliest days.[118] In the words of the father of Egyptian monasticism, St. Antony:

> I know of monks who fell after much toil and lapsed into madness, because they trusted in their own work and forgot the commandment that says, "Ask your father and he will tell you" (Deut. 32:7). So far as possible, for every step that a monk takes, for every drop of water that he drinks in his cell,

116. 4 (685A), p. 95; cf. 4 (701A), p. 104.

117. 4 (685D), p. 96.

118. On spiritual fatherhood, see I. Hausherr, *Direction spirituelle en orient autrefois* (*Orientalia Christiana Analecta* 144: Rome 1955); K. Ware, "The Spiritual Father in Orthodox Christianity", *Cross Currents* xxiv (1974), pp. 296–313.

> he should entrust the decision to the old men, to avoid making some mistake in what he does.[119]

Such also is John's conviction. At the start of *The Ladder* he speaks of the monk's need for "some Moses" to guide him to the Promised Land:

> Those of us who wish to get away from Egypt, to escape from Pharaoh, need some Moses to be our intermediary with God, to stand between action and contemplation, and stretch out his arms to God, that those led by him may cross the sea of sin and put to flight the Amalek of the passions.[120]

He returns to the point in the summary at the end of Step 26:

> A ship with a good navigator comes safely to port, God willing. A soul with a good shepherd climbs easily heavenward, even if it has earlier done much wrong.
>
> A man, no matter how prudent, may easily go astray on a road if he has no guide. The man who takes the road of monastic life under his own direction may easily be lost, even if he has all the wisdom of the world.[121]

The disciple receives guidance from his spiritual father chiefly in two ways: first, by modeling himself on the personal example which the spiritual father sets in daily life;[122] second, through the "disclosure of thoughts," through opening his heart to the spiritual father in what John terms "confession" (*exomologisis*), a word that can also mean "thanksgiving." This is not exactly the same as the sacrament of confession, understood as part of the official structure of ecclesiastical penance; for while it may sometimes overlap with sacramental confession, it is broader in scope:

---

119. *The Sayings of the Desert Fathers,* Alphabetical collection, Antony 37–38 (*PG* 65, 88B): ET Sister Benedicta Ward (London 1975), p. 7.

120. 1 (633D–636A), p. 75.

121. 26 (1089B), p. 259.

122. 4 (680D), p. 93.

First, the spiritual father to whom the monk confesses need not necessarily be a priest. In all the many passages in *The Ladder* where John refers to spiritual fatherhood, as also in the special treatise that he wrote on this subject, *To the Shepherd,* it is in fact nowhere specified that the spiritual father should be in priestly orders; and, as we have seen, there is no evidence that John himself was so ordained, although he certainly exercised the ministry of spiritual fatherhood.

Second, what the monk confesses to his spiritual father are not only his sins but also his doubts and temptations, and still more generally his "thoughts" (*logismoi*), which may be neutral or even God-inspired as well as sinful. In this disclosure of thoughts the spiritual child lays before his father, so far as he can, all the events that are occurring in his life, whether outward or inward, even those that seem to him insignificant; for the spiritual father may see in them a deeper meaning of which the disciple is himself unaware.

St. John Climacus implies that this confession to the spiritual father will if possible take place daily; and he mentions the practice of certain monks at Alexandria who wrote down their thoughts at once in a notebook hanging from their belt, which they later showed to the abbot.[123] Normally the disclosure of thoughts is in private, but the spiritual father may sometimes insist on a public confession, for the good of the disciple or perhaps of the community.[124] Whether the confession is private or public, the underlying principle is the same: "Nothing gives demons and evil thoughts such power over us as to nourish them and hide them in our hearts unconfessed."[125] But, once brought into the open, they become powerless. As one of the monks at Alexandria said to John, describing what had happened to him after "a bad spiritual failure":

> But since it was never my custom to conceal a snake in the hiding place of my heart I grabbed it forthwith by the tail—meaning that I ended the matter—and I revealed it at once to the healer. He gave me a light blow on the chin, smiled, and said to me, "All right, child, go back to your job and do not

123. 4 (701CD), p. 105.
124. 4 (681B), p. 93.
125. 23 (976D), p. 211.

be in the slightest way afraid." With heart on fire I did as I was told, and within a few days I knew I was cured.[126]

It is, however, sometimes unnecessary, and even unwise, to confess sins in detail, for fear of reviving the sinful impulse within us. This is the case in particular with sins against chastity: "Do not insist," John advises, "on confessing your carnal acts in detail, since you might become a traitor to yourself."[127] As St. Mark the Ascetic (*alias* Mark the Hermit or Monk) observes, "To recall past sins in detail inflicts injury on the man who hopes in God. . . . They pollute him again with the old defilement."[128]

In the passage quoted above, it is significant that the Alexandrian monk refers to his spiritual father as "the healer." This is characteristic of *The Ladder*. When speaking of confession, John employs by preference imagery that is therapeutic rather than juridical. Confession does not merely bestow absolution from guilt, understood in a formal and legalistic fashion, but on a deeper, more organic level it confers healing and restoration to wholeness. Sin is disease; to go to confession is to enter the hospital and to expose our wounds; the spiritual father is the doctor who makes us inwardly whole by prescribing medicines, by bandaging, cauterizing, amputating.[129]

In this relationship between patient and physician—between spiritual child and father—what is required first of all from the child is openness of heart. If this is lacking, if the disciple in disclosing his thoughts deliberately conceals or misrepresents, then obviously the whole object of the confession is frustrated; the doctor cannot help if the patient lies about his ailments.[130] Besides openness of heart, the spiritual child needs to show trust and faithfulness. Look carefully, John urges, before choosing your spiritual father; but, having once chosen him, remain with him permanently. Those who move light-

126. 4 (697A), p. 102.

127. 28 (1140A), p. 281.

128. *On those who think that they are made righteous by works*, § 139 (*PG* 65, 952B); ET *Phil.*, § 151, p. 138.

129. For such metaphors, see for example 4 (716A), p. 112; 5 (776C), p. 130; and above all *Past.* 2 (1168D–1169C), pp. 232–3. On confession as a form of healing, see K. Ware, "The Orthodox Experience of Repentance", *Sobornost* ii (1980), pp. 22–26.

130. *Past.* 7 (1184AB), p. 236.

mindedly from one confessor to another make no progress, and "deserve every punishment from God."[131] Even if your spiritual father is guilty of fornication, you should not leave him.[132] It is not for you to judge him and his actions:

> When the thought strikes you to judge or condemn your superior . . . give no trust, place, entry, or starting point to that snake. Say this to the viper: "Listen to me. . . . I do not judge him; he judges me."[133]

But of course on his side the spiritual father is responsible before God for the example that he sets his disciples: he should act with prudence, not revealing his own faults too readily, for fear of giving needless scandal.[134]

What does the spiritual father provide in return for this openness and trust? He is, as we have seen, the physician who makes us inwardly whole. This he does, not only by his words of advice, but by his life; not only by imparting rules or imposing penances, but by offering a personal relationship within which the disciple can grow to maturity. And this personal relationship is established above all through prayer. The spiritual father helps his children by interceding for them. This is clearly seen in *The Sayings of the Desert Fathers:* what you say when you visit your *abba* is "Pray for me." John also insists on this,[135] remarking that the obedient monk, even if he raises the dead, will nevertheless believe that it is the prayers of his spiritual father which have enabled him to do this.[136]

But the spiritual father is more than an intercessor. He is also, in John's words, a "mediator" between us and God, an "intermediary" (*mesitis*) who reconciles us to Him.[137] He is the friend of the Great King, who can plead on our behalf with boldness in the royal pres-

131. 4 (680D, 709D), pp. 92, 110.
132. 4 (724B), p. 117.
133. 4 (681A), p. 93.
134. *Past.* 8 (1184C), p. 237.
135. See for example 4 (677D), p. 91; 15 (893B), p. 180.
136. 4 (705D–708A), p. 107.
137. 1 (636A), p. 75.

ence.[138] This means, says John, that to sin against our spiritual father is in a sense worse than to sin against God:

> What I am going to say to you now must not shock you. . . . It is better to sin against God than against our father. If we make God angry, our director can reconcile Him to us. But if he is angry, then there is no one to speak up for us before God.[139]

The paradox is deliberate, but the point is clear. This mediation, furthermore, works in both directions. Not only does the spiritual father represent us to God, but he also represents God to us. His words have the value of God's words. As one of the monks at Alexandria said to John about the abbot:

> I thought of the shepherd as the image of Christ. . . . I thought of the command [that he gave me] as coming not from him but from God.[140]

Physician, intercessor, mediator—the spiritual father is all this. But John goes further still. He also describes the spiritual father as *anadochos,*[141] the term used for the sponsor or godparent at baptism, and so signifying one who takes responsibility for another. In John's view, the spiritual father does nothing less than assume responsibility for his disciple's sins, for which he will answer before God at the Last Judgment. Thus the disciple can face death without anxiety, "knowing with certainty that when it is time to go, not he but his spiritual director will be called to render an account."[142]

"I thought of the shepherd as the image of Christ," said the Alexandrian monk to John. As sponsor or *anadochos,* the shepherd of souls is called to be a living ikon of the unique Good Shepherd. He is to

138. *Past.* 3 (1172D), p. 233.
139. 4 (725D), p. 119.
140. 4 (692B), p. 99; cf. 4 (709A), p. 109.
141. *Past.* 10 (1185B), p. 237.
142. 4 (705B), p. 107.

show the same sacrificial love as the Savior displayed when dying on the Cross for the sins of the world:

> It is love that shows who is the true shepherd; for by reason of love the Great Shepherd was crucified.[143]

Among the many qualities that John mentions in his treatise on spiritual fatherhood *To the Shepherd*, this is the most important. The father should possess insight, discretion, dispassion, gentleness tempered by severity. But above all he needs to show self-emptying love, for without such love no one can be a shepherd after the image of Christ. He needs to have compassion, using this word in its true and full sense; he is required to lay down his life for his children, offering up on their behalf all that he has and all that he is. As John puts it, "spiritual responsibility (*anadochi*) in the proper sense . . . is a laying down of one's soul on behalf of the soul of one's neighbor in all matters."[144]

While every monk is called to bear the burdens of others, the burden-bearer *par excellence* is the spiritual father: "Let your father be the one who is able and willing to labor with you in bearing the burden of your sins."[145] By thus interpreting the spiritual father's role in terms of Galatians 6:2, St. John Climacus shows himself a true follower of the sixth-century school of Gaza—of St. Varsanuphius, St. John the Prophet, and St. Dorotheus—all of whom appeal to the same Pauline precept.[146] Applying their teaching, John gives an example from his own experience: for twenty years a monk had suffered from unspeakable and blasphemous thoughts, and could gain no relief. Eventually he wrote the temptation on a piece of paper, went to a holy man and gave him the paper. After reading it, the old man said: "My son, put your hand on my neck. . . . Now let this sin be on my neck. . . . From now on, ignore it." At once the brother was freed

143. *Past.* 5 (1177B), p. 234.

144. *Past.* 12 (1183B), p. 239.

145. 3 (665D), p. 87. Cf. 24 (984C), p. 217; *Past.* 2 (1169B), p. 233; 12 (1189BC), pp. 239–40.

146. Varsanuphius and John, *Correspondence*, ed. S. Schoinas (Volos 1960), §§ 168–9, 189, 191, 199, 203, 206, 239, 483; French trans. by L. Regnault (Solesmes 1972), §§ 72–73, 94, 96, 104, 108, 111, 239, 483, *et passim*. Dorotheus, *Instructions* iv (ed. L. Regnault, *Sources chrétiennes* 92 [Paris 1963], §§ 56–57, pp. 240–2); vi (§ 79, p. 288).

from the thoughts of blasphemy, nor did they trouble him subsequently.[147]

From all this it is abundantly clear how exacting, in the eyes of St. John Climacus, are the demands made upon the spiritual father. There can, indeed, be no earthly vocation higher than this:

> We can offer to God no gift so acceptable as to bring Him through repentance souls made in His image. The whole world is not worth so much as a soul.[148]

Prayer and Stillness: The Invocation of the Name

"Prayer," says St. John Climacus, "is by nature a dialogue and a union of man with God." As such, it is cosmic in scope, the foundation of the universe: "Its effect is to hold the world together."[149] It is the primary end for which the human person was created—"What higher good is there than to cling to the Lord and to persevere in unceasing union with Him?"[150]—and it constitutes the touchstone of a monk's entire existence: "Your prayer shows where you stand.... Prayer is a monk's mirror."[151] In the words of Bishop Theophan the Recluse: "Prayer is the test of everything.... If prayer is right, everything is right."[152]

Thanksgiving, penitence, petition—such is the basic sequence to be followed when praying:

> Heartfelt thanksgiving should have first place in our book of prayer. Next should be confession and genuine contrition of

147. 23 (980AB), p. 213. For parallels to this incident in other texts, see J. Gouillard, "Christianisme byzantin et slave", *Ecole pratique des hautes études. Ve section. Sciences religieuses. Annuaire* lxxxii (Paris 1974), pp. 215–17.

148. *Past.* 13 (1196D), p. 244. John refers to spiritual brotherhood as well as spiritual fatherhood: 15 (892C), p. 179; 26 (1057B), p. 244.

149. 28 (1129A), p. 274.

150. 28 (1136A), p. 278.

151. 28 (1136C), p. 278.

152. In Igumen Chariton of Valamo, *The Art of Prayer: An Orthodox Anthology* (London 1966), p. 51.

> soul. After that should come our request to the universal King.[153]

We are not to begin by confessing our sins. Before peering downward at our own ugliness, we are to gaze outward and upward at the beauty of God. So it is in the Divine Liturgy of St. John Chrysostom (not that St. John Climacus appeals to this particular example): we do not commence with an act of penitence but with a proclamation of divine glory, "Blessed is the Kingdom of Father, Son and Holy Spirit. . . ." Only after receiving a glimpse of this heavenly Kingdom can we begin to repent as we should. Otherwise penitence becomes a form of grumbling, an expression of bitterness or self-loathing rather than hope. Penitence, John adds, should accompany us throughout the journey of prayer: "Even if you have climbed the whole ladder of the virtues, pray still for the forgiveness of sins."[154]

John is categorical about the value of simplicity in our prayer. We are to avoid garrulousness, *polylogia*, multiplicity of words:

> Pray in all simplicity. The publican and the prodigal son were reconciled to God by a single utterance. . . . In your prayers there is no need for high-flown words, for it is the simple and unsophisticated babblings of children that have often won the heart of the Father in heaven. Try not to talk excessively in your prayer, in case your mind is distracted by the search for words. One word from the publican sufficed to placate God, and a single utterance saved the thief. Talkative prayer (*polylogia*) frequently distracts the mind and deludes it, whereas brevity (*monologia*) makes for concentration. If it happens that, as you pray, some word evokes delight or remorse within you, linger over it.[155]

While, then, it is necessary, at any rate in the earlier stages, to use words when we pray—"enclose your mind [*or* thought] within the *words* of your prayer," John urges[156]—these words should be as direct, concise and uncomplicated as possible.

153. 28 (1132A), p. 275.
154. 28 (1132B), p. 276.
155. 28 (1129D, 1132AB), pp. 275–6.
156. 28 (1132C), p. 276.

In thus recommending the use of short, simple prayers, it seems that John had in view various possible formulae: this is implied by the advice just quoted, "if . . . some word evokes delight or remorse within you, linger over it." Sometimes, like the Desert Fathers in fourth-century Egypt, he suggests the employment of a verse from the Psalms:

> Cry out to God, Who has the strength to save you. Do not bother with elegant and clever words. Just speak humbly, beginning with, "Have mercy on me, for I am weak" (Ps. 6:3).[157]

Elsewhere John proposes a series of different scriptural texts for the monk to ponder, leaving him free to choose which he prefers: for, as he puts it, "all the loaves of heavenly bread do not have the same appearance."[158]

There is, however, one type of simple prayer to which John attaches particular importance: the invocation or remembrance of the Name of Jesus, the Jesus Prayer.[159] It is true that he refers to it only three times[160] in the entire *Ladder*, so that it cannot be regarded as a dominant theme in his spiritual teaching as a whole. In this respect there is a marked contrast between John and his follower St. Hesychius of Sinai, who mentions the Jesus Prayer continually throughout his work *On Watchfulness and Holiness*. But the three passages in *The*

157. 15 (900D), p. 184. On the Egyptian practice, see Dom L. Regnault, "La prière continuelle 'monologistos' dans la littérature apophtegmatique", *Irénikon* xlvii (1974), pp. 467–93.

158. 27 (1116A), p. 272. Short prayers can be used in particular during the antiphonal recitation of the Divine Office, while the opposite side of the choir is singing: cf. 19 (937D), p. 195.

159. For Climacus' teaching on the Jesus Prayer, see "Un Moine de l'Eglise d'Orient" [Archimandrite Lev Gillet (1892–1980)], *La Prière de Jésus* (3rd ed., Chevetogne 1959), pp. 27–28; ET, "A Monk of the Eastern Church", *The Prayer of Jesus*, translated by "A Monk of the Western Church" (New York/Tournai 1967), pp. 28–29; I. Hausherr, *Noms du Christ et voies d'oraison (Orientalia Christiana Analecta* 157: Rome 1960), pp. 248–53; ET *The Name of Jesus*, translated by C. Cummings (*Cistercian Studies Series* 44: Kalamazoo 1978), pp. 280–6. Fr. Hausherr, while rightly protesting that too much should not be read into the short statements of Climacus, surely goes too far in the opposite direction, adopting an unduly "reductionist" view.

160. Possibly there is a fourth reference in 9 (841C), p. 153, where Climacus speaks of *Iisou i prosevchi;* but more probably this means the Lord's Prayer.

Ladder, since they have greatly influenced subsequent writers, deserve to be considered with particular care.

(1) In Step 15, when discussing the impure thoughts suggested to us by the demons immediately before we go to sleep, John says:

> Let the remembrance of death and the concise Jesus Prayer go to sleep with you and get up with you, for nothing helps you as these do when you are asleep.[161]

Note here, first of all, the words "Jesus Prayer" (*Iisou evchi*): St. John Climacus is, it seems, the earliest author to use this expression. At the same time, he describes the Jesus Prayer as "concise" or, more literally, as "monologic" (*monologistos*), a term that means "consisting in a single phrase": John seems to be once again the first author to apply this adjective to prayer. The epithet *monologistos* calls to mind the contrast, in the passage cited earlier,[162] between talkativeness (*polylogia*) and brevity (*monologia*); thus the Jesus Prayer is being commended as an example of short, simple prayer.

But what exactly does John intend by this term "single-phrase Jesus Prayer"? Nowhere in *The Ladder* does he give a specific formula. The same is true of John's follower Hesychius: while very frequently using the term "Jesus Prayer"—and on one occasion the phrase "*monologistos* prayer"[163]—he refrains from giving a precise form of words. It has been argued—in particular by Fr. Hausherr—that John merely envisages, in a general way, *any* brief prayer for help, not necessarily including the name of Jesus. But in that case why should John say, not just "single-phrase prayer," but "single-phrase *Jesus* Prayer"? Surely it is more probable that the prayer contained the actual word "Jesus" as part of the "single phrase." The second of our three passages, to be considered shortly, confirms this by explicitly mentioning the *name* of Jesus.

Yet, if our supposition is correct, it does not therefore follow that the "single-phrase Jesus Prayer" contains *only* the name of Jesus and nothing else. To judge from other writers prior to *The Ladder* or con-

161. 15 (889D), p. 178.

162. 28 (1132B), p. 275: see above, note 155.

163. *On Watchfulness and Holiness* ii, 72 (*PG* 93, 1536B); ET *Phil.*, § 174, p. 193 (the translators have added the word "Jesus" before "prayer").

temporary with it, we would expect the name to be combined with further words as well; for none of the early texts speaks of employing the invocation "Jesus" on its own. Diadochus of Photice, for example, advises the use of a prayer beginning "Lord Jesus . . .", apparently followed by something more, although he does not tell us what.[164] Varsanuphius and John of Gaza suggest various formulae, such as:[165]

> "Lord Jesus Christ, have mercy on me"
> "Lord Jesus Christ, save me"
> "Master Jesus, protect me"
> "Jesus, help me"

—but never "Jesus" alone. What in later Orthodox spirituality has become the standard form of the Prayer, "Lord Jesus Christ, Son of God, have mercy on me," is first found in *The Life of Abba Philemon,*[166] an Egyptian text perhaps more or less contemporary with *The Ladder.* It is probable, then, that the "single-phrase Jesus Prayer" contained more than the simple invocation of the name. John, however, does not tell us exactly what is in his "single phrase," and so it may be that, like Varsanuphius and John of Gaza, he envisages a variety of possible texts. Writing as he was at a time when the wording of the Jesus Prayer had not yet become stereotyped, he may have preferred to leave each reader free to make his own choice among the different forms.

Three matters strike us about the context of the Jesus Prayer in Step 15. First, it is linked with the remembrance of death. This suggests that John saw the Jesus Prayer as, among other things, a prayer of contrition and penitence. Probably, then, he expected the Prayer to include the words "have mercy on me" or the equivalent; as already noted, he recommends the use of Psalm 6:3, "Have mercy on me. . . ." Second, the Prayer is seen as a weapon against the demons. Third, its use is specially commended when on the threshold of sleep. On the

164. *Century* 59, 61: *Phil.*, pp. 270–1.

165. *Correspondence* (ed. Schoinas), §§ 39, 126, 255, 268, 446, 659; French trans. by Regnault, §§ 39, 175, 255, 268, 446, 659. See also Dorotheus, *Life of Dositheus* 10 (ed. Regnault, *Sources chrétiennes* 92, p. 138).

166. *Philokalia ton ieron niptikon* (Greek text), vol. ii (Athens 1958), p. 244. On the importance of this text, see B. Krivochéine, "Date du texte traditionnel de la 'Prière de Jésus' ", *Messager de l'Exarchat du Patriarche russe en Europe occidentale* 7–8 (1951), pp. 55–59.

second and the third point, John's approach resembles that of Diadochus.[167]

(2) The second of the three passages occurs in Step 21. John is discussing the childish fear that overcomes a monk at night when entering some dark place alone. The solution, he says, is to arm yourself with prayer:

> When you reach the spot, stretch out your hands and flog your enemies with the name of Jesus, since there is no stronger weapon in heaven or on earth.[168]

Here, certainly, John has in view not just any short prayer for help but specifically the invocation of the name "Jesus." As in Step 15, this is seen as a weapon against the demons. He further suggests a particular bodily posture, with the arms outstretched in the form of a cross. This he also recommends elsewhere, but without referring to the name of Jesus.[169]

(3) The third and most important passage comes in Step 27, on solitude or stillness:

> Stillness (*hesychia*) is worshipping God unceasingly and waiting on Him. Let the remembrance of Jesus be present with your every breath. Then indeed you will appreciate the value of stillness.[170]

There is no explicit reference here to "the Jesus *Prayer*" or to "the *name* of Jesus," but only to "the *remembrance* of Jesus." It may be, then, that in this passage John is not thinking of a short formula of prayer, frequently repeated, but of "keeping Jesus in mind" in a more diffused and general sense. But it is also possible that the "remembrance" is in fact the same as the "single-phrase Jesus Prayer"; and that is how most later readers of *The Ladder* have understood the text.

Three points of interest arise in this passage. First, John states that the remembrance of Jesus should be so far as possible uninterrupted. In the other two passages the Jesus Prayer or invocation of

167. *Century* 31: *Phil.*, pp. 261–2.
168. 21 (945C), p. 200.
169. 15 (900C), p. 184.
170. 27 (1112C), pp. 269–70.

the name is recommended for use in particular situations—when falling asleep, when alone in the dark—but in this third text John envisages something all-embracing and continuous. Once more, his teaching resembles that of Diadochus, who insists emphatically that the remembrance or invocation of Jesus shall be unceasing.[171]

Second, John says that the remembrance of Jesus is to "be present with your every breath"; a more literal translation would run, "be united with your breathing." The phrase has been variously interpreted. Some see in it no more than a metaphor: we should remember God as often as we breathe[172]—John is simply underlining his point about "worshipping God unceasingly." Others give the phrase a far more precise sense: in their view, John has in mind a physical technique whereby the "single-phrase Jesus Prayer" is linked with the rhythm of the breathing. Such a technique is certainly advocated in a Coptic source, not easily dated, but perhaps slightly later than John:

> Is it not easy to say with every breath, "Our Lord Jesus Christ, have mercy on me; I bless Thee, my Lord Jesus, help me"?[173]

In the Greek tradition, however, there are no clear and unambiguous references to a "breathing technique" until the late thirteenth and the early fourteenth century, in the works of St. Nicephorus of Mount Athos, St. Gregory of Sinai, St. Gregory Palamas, and others.[174]

Now it is true that St. John Climacus accepts the basic principle underlying the physical method propounded by these later writers;

---

171. *Century* 59, 85, 88, and especially 97: *Phil.*, pp. 270, 285, 287, 293–4.

172. Compare, for example, Gregory of Nazianzus, *Oration* 27, 4 (*PG* 36, 16B), and Nilus of Ancyra, *Letters* I, 239 (*PG* 79, 169D), where the meaning is apparently no more than metaphorical.

173. "The Virtues of St. Macarius", ed. E. Amélineau, *Histoire des monastères de la Basse-Egypte* (Annales du Musée Guimet xxv: Paris 1894), p. 161; cited in J. Gouillard, *Petite Philocalie de la prière du coeur* (Paris 1953), p. 68; 2nd ed. (Paris 1968), p. 55. On the Jesus Prayer in the Coptic Macarian cycle, see A. Guillaumont, "Une inscription copte sur la 'Prière de Jésus' ", *Orientalia Christiana Periodica* xxxiv (1968), pp. 310–25; "The Jesus Prayer among the Monks of Egypt", *Eastern Churches Review* vi (1974), pp. 66–71. Professor Guillaumont dates the text quoted to the 7th–8th centuries.

174. See I. Hausherr, *La méthode d'oraison hésychaste (Orientalia Christiana* ix, no. 36: Rome 1927); J. Gouillard, "A Note on the Prayer of the Heart", in J.-M. Déchanet, *Christian Yoga* (Perennial Library: New York 1972), pp. 217–30; K. Ware, "The Jesus Prayer in St Gregory of Sinai", *Eastern Churches Review* iv (1972), pp. 14–16.

like them, he recognizes that the mind conforms to the body, that our outward posture influences our inward state.[175] But only in this one sentence in Step 27 does he refer specifically to the breathing in connection with the name of Jesus; the point is not developed, and it would be perilous to base too much on a single phrase. In default of further evidence, it seems wiser to interpret the words metaphorically. Probably the parallel phrase in Hesychius[176] should also be given a metaphorical sense; but Hesychius' wording is slightly more precise than John's, for he alters "remembrance of Jesus" to "Jesus Prayer," and when speaking elsewhere of the Jesus Prayer he makes a number of other references to the breathing.[177]

Third, in the passage quoted John indicates a connection between "the remembrance of Jesus" and the attitude of stillness (*hesychia*). Constantly to keep Jesus in remembrance is a way of attaining inner quiet: the Jesus Prayer helps to make the monk into a "hesychast," one who possesses silence of heart. *Hesychia*[178] is a key word in John's doctrine of prayer, and the step which he devotes to it has proved, with the possible exception of Step 7 on the gift of tears, the most influential in the whole of *The Ladder*. By "stillness" he means both an outward manner of life—that of the hermit or solitary, living in a cell on his own—and also an inner disposition of continual prayer, as in the passage under discussion: "Stillness is worshipping God unceasingly."[179]

It is the second sense that chiefly concerns John in Step 27—not

175. 15 (900C), p. 184; 26 (1000D–1001A), p. 227; 28 (1133B), p. 277; but in these passages there is no reference to the breathing. The allusion to "breathing God" in 4 (688C), p. 97, is surely metaphorical. But in 4 (724B), p. 117 and 14 (869A), p. 169, the sense is less clear: John may mean that the repetition of a short phrase from Scripture is to be linked with the rhythm of the breathing, but once more a metaphorical sense is possible.

176. "Let the Jesus Prayer cleave to your breath [*or* breathing]": *On Watchfulness and Holiness* ii, 80 (*PG* 93, 1537D): ET *Phil.*, § 182, p. 195.

177. *On Watchfulness and Holiness* i, 5; ii, 68, 85, 87 (1481D, 1533C, 1540CD); *Phil.*, §§ 5, 170, 187, 189 (pp. 163, 192, 195, 196). But in none of these passages is a metaphorical interpretation excluded.

178. See I. Hausherr, "L'hésychasme. Etude de spiritualité", in *Hésychasme et prière (Orientalia Christiana Analecta* 176: Rome 1966), pp. 163–237; K. Ware, "Silence in Prayer: the Meaning of Hesychia", in B. Pennington (ed.), *One yet Two (Cistercian Studies Series* 29: Kalamazoo 1976), pp. 22–47.

179. See note 170.

physical isolation but interior silence. Sometimes, certainly, he has in view both the outward and the inward at the same time:

> Close the door of your cell to your body, the door of your tongue to talk, and the gate within to evil spirits.[180]

But more often it is the inward level, "the gate within," of which he is speaking, as in his celebrated definition of the hesychast:

> Strange as it may seem, the hesychast is a man who fights to keep his incorporeal self shut up in the house of the body.[181]

The meaning here is, not that the hesychast dwells spatially separated from others in the desert, but that he confines within his body the powers of his soul, his thoughts, desires, imagination and the rest; he is not dispersed, but concentrated upon a single point. The hesychast's true journey is not outward and physical, into the wilderness, but inward and spiritual, into the sanctuary of the heart. John is saying the same as St. Basil the Great:

> When the intellect is no longer dissipated among external things or dispersed across the world through the senses, it returns to itself; and by means of itself it ascends to the thought of God.[182]

The hesychast is the one who has "returned to himself," who has, in St. Isaac the Syrian's phrase, "entered into the treasure house that is within."[183] He has constantly within him what John calls "unseen meditation,"[184] "mental prayer" or "noetic activity" (*noera ergasia*).[185]

Understanding stillness in this inward sense, we see that it is possible to be a hesychast even though committed to works of direct service to others: the hesychast is not just the solitary, but anyone who

180. 27 (1100A), p. 263.
181. 27 (1097B), p. 262.
182. *Letter* 2 (*PG* 32, 228A).
183. *Mystic Treatises*, ET Wensinck, p. 8 (adapted).
184. 3 (664B), p. 85.
185. 4 (685C), p. 96.

preserves interior silence amidst outward confusion.[186] This, indeed, is the highest form of *hesychia*. It is a great thing, says John, to achieve stillness in the isolation of a hermit's cell; but "it is incomparably greater to have no fear of turmoil, and to remain steadfast under its assault with a fearless heart, living outwardly with men but inwardly with God."[187]

Interpreted in this manner, as the hidden silence of the heart, *hesychia* signifies in *The Ladder* more particularly what Evagrius terms "pure prayer"—prayer, that is to say, unaccompanied by words, images or concepts. "Stillness means the expulsion of thoughts," writes John,[188] adapting a well-known phrase of Evagrius, "Prayer is the expulsion of thoughts."[189] But "expulsion" is perhaps too violent a word. John and Evagrius employ the term *apothesis*, which means "shedding," "putting aside": not a savage extirpation or brutal suppression of our thoughts, but a gentle yet persistent act of detachment or "letting go."

Heyschia or stillness, then, is the same as "the wordless prayer of the spirit,"[190] as distinguished from the singing of psalms and hymns, the liturgical prayer of the divine office. Evidently it is this "pure" or wordless prayer of stillness that John has in view when he describes prayer as "a turning away from the world, visible and invisible,"[191] or when he says, "Do not form sensory images during prayer."[192] Such remarks would not be applicable to all forms of praying.

We can now grasp more fully what John intends when, in Step 27, he connects the "remembrance of Jesus" with the state of stillness. The remembrance or invocation of Jesus is one of the ways—not necessarily the only one—whereby the aspirant upon the spiritual way is enabled to advance from oral to wordless prayer. Here, as so often in his teaching on the Jesus Prayer, John seems to be following Diadochus of Photice. The human intellect, so Diadochus observes, cannot rest inactive; if it is to be prevented from dispersing itself among a

---

186. 4 (700C), p. 103.
187. *Past.*, 9 (1185A), p. 237; cf. 27 (1097B), p. 262.
188. 27 (1112A), p. 269.
189. *On Prayer*, § 70 (*PG* 79, 1181C): ET *Phil.*, § 71, p. 64.
190. 19 (937D), p. 195: literally "non-material prayer."
191. 28 (1133C), p. 277.
192. 28 (1136D), p. 279.

multiplicity of sensory objects, it must be provided with some inner task to satisfy its "need for activity." This need, according to Diadochus, is met by the Jesus Prayer:

> For the complete fulfilment of its purpose we should give the intellect nothing but the prayer "Lord Jesus". . . . Let the intellect continually concentrate on these words within its inner shrine with such intensity that it is not turned aside to any mental images.[193]

The Jesus Prayer is in itself an oral prayer like any other; but, because the words are so very simple, the discipline of frequent repetition helps the intellect to gather itself together, to pass from multiplicity to unity, and so to reach out beyond all words into the pure prayer of stillness. Such is Diadochus' teaching. John is less explicit, but he seems to uphold the same standpoint: the invocation of the Holy Name forms the gateway to *hesychia*.

Stillness, as we have seen, is defined by John as the *unceasing* worship of God. For the true hesychast, inward prayer is not so much an occasional occupation as a continuous state; it is not merely one activity among others, but *the* activity of his whole life. He strives to fulfill the command, "Pray without ceasing" (1 Thess. 5:17). His prayer continues even in his sleep; as John puts it, "A hesychast is like an angel on earth . . . he says, 'I sleep, but my heart is awake' " (Song of Songs 5:2);[194] he is "at work not only when awake but also when he is asleep."[195] In the words of St. Isaac the Syrian, "Even when he is immersed in sleep, the perfumes of prayer will breathe in his soul spontaneously."[196] In this way the hesychast is not someone who *says* prayers from time to time, but someone who *is* prayer all the time. His prayer becomes in the true sense *prayer of the heart*, meaning by "heart" not only the emotions and affections but, as in Scripture, the totality of the human person dwelling in communion with God. In the words of *The Ladder*: " 'I cried out with all my heart,' said the

193. *Century* 59: *Phil.*, p. 270.
194. 27 (1100A), p. 263.
195. 27 (1116B), p. 272; cf. 20 (941C), pp. 197–8.
196. *Mystic Treatises*, ET Wensinck, p. 174.

psalmist (Ps. 118:145). He is referring to body, soul and spirit."[197] So the hesychast prays with his whole heart, with every aspect of his being, conscious, subconscious, supraconscious. He is identified with his prayer.

Divine Light and Divine Love

Such is the hesychast's aim as he mounts the unseen ladder: a direct touching, a simple gazing upon God that will be, so far as possible, continuous and free from mental pictures and discursive thought. And what lies beyond this? John is guarded. He does not use the language of "deification" or "divinization" (*theosis*), widespread among the Greek Fathers. But, while offering no detailed descriptions, he provides a few hints. The highest level of prayer, he says, is "rapture (*arpagi*) in the Lord,"[198] but he does not develop the point. Once he alludes to a visionary experience of his own;[199] evidently this was ecstatic in character, for he says, recalling St. Paul's words (2 Cor. 12:2), "and whether, during all this, I was in the body or out of it, I cannot rightly say." Yet in this vision it was not with Christ Himself that John spoke, but with an angel.

This is, moreover, an isolated passage; he does not speak elsewhere of receiving such visions. He does, however, refer in a number of places to experiences of light or illumination, although it is not easy to determine how far the language is intended to be more than metaphorical. The main passages are these:

(1) Overcome by chastity, the lust in our souls "receives that non-material (*aÿlon*) light which shines beyond all fire."[200]

(2) Purity of heart leads to "enlightenment" or "illumination." This "is something indescribable, an activity [*or* energy (*energeia*)] that is unknowingly perceived and invisibly seen."[201]

(3) "The truly obedient monk often becomes suddenly radiant and exultant during his prayers."[202]

197. 28 (1140B), p. 281. For this sense of "heart," as signifying the spiritual center of the human person, see A. Guillaumont, "Les sens des noms du coeur dans l'antiquité", in *Le Coeur (Etudes carmélitaines* xxix: Bruges 1950), pp. 41–81; "Le 'coeur' chez les spirituels grecs à l'époque ancienne", *DS* ii (1952), cols. 2281–8.

198. 28 (1132D), p. 276.

199. 27 (1109C), p. 268.

200. 7 (804C), p. 137. Cf.7 (808D), p. 140, referring to the "ineffable light" of God.

201. 7 (813B), p. 143.

202. 19 (937C), p. 195.

(4) On humility: "You will know that you have this holy gift within you . . . when you experience an abundance of unspeakable light."[203]

(5) "For the perfect there is increase and, indeed, a wealth of divine light. . . . A soul, freed of its old habits and also forgiven, has surely seen the divine light."[204]

(6) "In addition to these there is the way of rapture (*ekstasis*), the way of the mind mysteriously and marvellously carried into the light of Christ."[205]

(7) Some emerge from prayer "as if they were resplendent with light."[206]

(8) "When the heart is cheerful, the face beams, and a man flooded with the love of God reveals in his body, as if in a mirror, the splendor of his soul, a glory like that of Moses when he came face to face with God" (cf. Exod. 34:29–35).[207]

(9) Finally, there is a long passage at the end of the work *To the Shepherd*, in which the shepherd is likened to Moses:

> You have ascended to the heights, you have dispelled all manner of darkness and gloom and tempest—I mean the thrice gloomy darkness of ignorance. You have drawn nigh to that light which is far more awesome, brilliant and sublime than the flame in the bush. . . . While still in this life, you perhaps saw future things from behind (cf. Exod. 33:23)—I mean that illumination of knowledge which will come to pass in the last time. . . . You were glorified in the countenance of both your soul and your body.[208]

In all of these passages a figurative or metaphorical interpretation is by no means impossible. But, particularly in the first, the second and the eighth, John seems to intend something more than mere metaphor. The phrase "non-material light" in the first passage suggests that John has in view a light that is neither merely figurative,

203. 25 (996A), p. 223.
204. 26 (1033B), p. 242.
205. 26 (1065A), p. 249.
206. 28 (1137C), p. 280.
207. 30 (1157B), p. 288.
208. *Past.* 15 (1204C), p. 248.

nor yet physical and created, but spiritual and uncreated. In the second passage the words "invisibly seen," while they could apply to a metaphorical enlightenment of the mind, may also denote a higher, mystical illumination, whereby the initiate gazes—through his physical eyes, and yet in a manner that transcends them—not upon the material objects of normal sense-perception, but upon the "non-material" light of God. So far as the eighth passage is concerned, the glory shining from the face of Moses, as described in Exodus 34, is certainly not just metaphorical, for Moses has to place a veil over his face to protect the Israelites from its brightness. John seems to be thinking here of the occasions, frequently recorded in the lives of the saints, when the body of the holy man or woman shines visibly with divine light, as Christ's body shone at the transfiguration on Mount Tabor.[209] It is significant that in this passage the light is given an eschatological interpretation: it is an anticipation of "future things," a foretaste of the "illumination" that "will come to pass in the last time." According to the traditional teaching, the light of the age to come is an existent reality, not a mere metaphor.

With some hesitation, then, we may place St. John Climacus in the tradition of the "light mystics" of the Christian East, along with the *Homilies* attributed to St. Macarius (fourth-fifth centuries), with St. Symeon the New Theologian (eleventh century), and St. Gregory Palamas (fourteenth century). While John is far less explicit than they—and certainly we cannot find in *The Ladder*, in any clearly articulated form, the Cappadocian and Palamite distinction between God's essence and His energies[210]—yet John seems to agree with them in teaching that the Divinity is revealed as uncreated light, and that the human person can participate in this divine light not only metaphorically but literally, not only in the age to come but in this present life, and not only with the soul but with the body also.

There are, however, no traces in *The Ladder* of the parallel tradition of "darkness mysticism," represented by Philo the Jew (first century), St. Clement of Alexandria (third century), St. Gregory of Nyssa (fourth century), and St. Dionysius the Areopagite (fifth century). When, as in the ninth passage cited above, John refers to the

209. See K. Ware, "The Transfiguration of the Body", in A.M. Allchin (ed.), *Sacrament and Image* (The Fellowship of St. Alban and St. Sergius: London 1967), pp. 17–32.

210. But in 25 (993CD), p. 223, John uses the essence-energies distinction with reference to the sun.

darkness of Sinai, he takes this as signifying sinful ignorance, not divine transcendence and mystery. Unlike Philo, Clement, Gregory of Nyssa and Dionysius, John lays no particular emphasis upon the unknowability of God; the language of apophatic theology is largely absent from *The Ladder*. We are left with the impression that John does indeed regard God as beyond human understanding, but he does not discuss the matter in detail.

But, even though John has not followed Gregory of Nyssa in his interpretation of the darkness of Sinai, there is another idea, prominent in Gregory's *Life of Moses*, that appears also in *The Ladder:* the notion of unceasing advance, of perpetual progress through the infinite ages of eternity. John does not use Gregory's technical term *epektasis*,[211] but the concept itself is plainly present in his work. Virtue and love, he says, are things that have no limit or end-point, either in this life or in the age to come:

> There is no boundary to virtue. The psalmist says, "I have seen the end of all perfection, but Your commandment is very broad and is without limit" (Ps. 118:96). . . . And if it is true that "love never fails" (1 Cor. 13:8) . . . then love has no boundary, and both in the present and in the future age we will never cease to progress in it, as we add light to light. . . . Even the angels make progress . . . they add glory to glory and knowledge to knowledge.[212]

In the last step of all he returns to the idea that love has no limit: "It is the condition of angels, and *the progress of eternity*."[213]

In common, then, with St. Gregory of Nyssa, St. John Climacus has a strongly dynamic view of eternity. Movement and progress are the mark of life not only here below but in heaven, and this is true of angels as well as humankind. The essence of perfection consists paradoxically in the fact that we never become perfect, but advance unceasingly "from glory to glory." In John, as in Gregory, the reason

211. But see 29 (1148BC), p. 282, which uses the verb *epekteinomai* (cf. Phil. 3:14), shortly before a description of *apatheia* in terms of perpetual progress: ". . . the uncompleted perfection of the perfect." On *epektasis*, see Gregory of Nyssa, *The Life of Moses*, ET A.J. Malherbe and E. Ferguson (*The Classics of Western Spirituality:* New York 1978), esp. pp. 12–14.

212. 26 (1068AB), pp. 250–1.

213. 30 (1160B), p. 289. Cf. 28 (1129B), p. 274: prayer is "action without end."

for this view is that both of them envisage eternal life in terms of personal love.[214] Eternity is progress, because eternity is love: and a relationship of love between two persons is never static, never exhaustively explored, but implies always fresh growth, movement and discovery. So it is between human persons; so it is between the divine persons of the Holy Trinity; and so it is between the human soul and God.

John is most insistent about the primacy of love, agreeing here with his contemporary St. Maximus the Confessor. It is love, so John teaches, that makes the human person resemble God "insofar as this is humanly possible."[215] Love stands higher than any vision or ecstasy, higher than any mystical revelation. Evagrius, in his scheme of the spiritual ascent, regarded *gnosis* or knowledge as superior to love; but for John the summit of the ladder is love, and there can be nothing higher than this.

After all his negative words against sin, after all his austere demands for self-denial, St. John Climacus concludes the final chapter of *The Ladder* with words that are entirely positive: "Love is the greatest of them all."[216]

IV. SOURCES AND INFLUENCE

Personal Experience and Tradition

The Ladder is both a highly personal work, the fruit of creative originality, and at the same time a traditional work, drawing upon the past.

To St. John Climacus, as we have seen,[217] the Christian life was a matter of direct experience. It is not enough, he insists, for the spiritual teacher merely to repeat with accuracy things said by others; each must relive for himself what he has inherited from the past. *The Ladder* is therefore, as might be expected, strongly personal in character. John's approach is empirical. He often mentions things that he

214. In Gregory of Nyssa, *epektasis* is connected with apophatic theology as well as love: progress is infinite because God can never be known exhaustively. This apophatic aspect of *epektasis* is not brought out in *The Ladder*.

215. 30 (1156B), p. 286.

216. 30 (1160D), p. 290.

217. See above, pp. 7–8.

has himself seen and heard, and men whom he has himself met, such as John the Sabbaite[218] or George Arsilaites.[219] But, while John speaks about the experience of others, with the reticence characteristic of the Christian East he keeps silent, except on one occasion, about the events in his own inner life. In Step 28 on prayer, for example, we may be confident that he is speaking from direct experience, yet in fact he makes no such claim for himself.

At the same time throughout *The Ladder* personal experience is interwoven with past tradition. John appeals frequently to the authority of "the Fathers." When he wrote his book, monasticism had already existed as an established institution for more than three centuries. The golden age of the pioneers was long since over; there existed by John's day a mass of precedents, regulations and written texts. John is closely familiar with much of this earlier material; although insisting on his lack of learning, he is in reality far more widely read than he would have us believe. *The Ladder,* as well as being a work of personal experience, is a work of synthesis, presenting in summary form the monastic teachings of the past three hundred years, integrating into a single whole the many disparate strands of previous tradition. It is a first, and remarkably successful, attempt to produce a "directory" of monastic spirituality.

As a synthesizer, John Climacus resembles his contemporary Maximus the Confessor. What Maximus achieves in the field of Christology, John accomplishes in that of ascetic theology. Both lived in the days of Mohammed and witnessed the sudden Arab expansion that followed the Prophet's death. They both stood at a point of transition, at the end of an era, when the newly-established power of Islam was altering forever the face of the Eastern Mediterranean and of North Africa. Each in his own way gathered together the fruits of the past and transmitted them to a new age.

What are John's sources? This is not easy to determine; for, while he occasionally cites them by name, more often he borrows anonymously. It is at once clear that he is indebted first of all to the Bible, from which he quotes with great frequency. Next to Scripture his chief debt is to *The Sayings of the Desert Fathers*—known in Greek as the *Gerontikon* and in Latin as the *Apophthegmata Patrum*—which dates

218. 4 (720A–724B), pp. 115–7.
219. 27 (1112B), p. 269.

back substantially to the fourth and fifth centuries.[220] Even when he is not quoting directly from this, it has often influenced his style and presentation. At the same time, in *The Ladder* John draws together and unites the two major strands in the early spiritual tradition of the Christian East: the "intellectualist" approach exemplified by Evagrius of Pontus, and the "experiential" approach represented by the *Homilies* attributed to St. Macarius.

Although John mentions Evagrius only once, and then with disapproval,[221] and although he makes far less use of technical Evagrian terminology than Maximus does, yet traces of Evagrius' influence can be seen in many parts of *The Ladder*. John makes use of the basic distinction between the "active" and the "contemplative" life *(praxis/theoria)*,[222] although this is not followed out consistently in *The Ladder;* he derives from Evagrius much of his demonology and his analysis of the vices,[223] the close link between dispassion and love,[224] and the conception of prayer as the laying aside of thoughts.[225] But John discards altogether Evagrius' speculative cosmology; he is less systematic than Evagrius, and more concerned to emphasize the personal and conscious experience of grace.

Whether or not John was directly acquainted with the Macarian writings—for he never cites them explicitly—he agrees with them at many points, as for example in his view of the heart as the unifying

220. From the *Apophthegmata* Climacus derives his stories about Antony, Arsenius and others in 4 (717C), p. 114; 15 (885C, 889C, 892D), pp. 175, 178, 179; 19 (937D), p. 195; 25 (997C), p. 225; 27 (1112D), p. 270; 29 (1148CD), p. 283. He is also familiar with similar material in other early monastic texts: e.g. Pachomius, *First Greek Life* (27 [1117A], p. 273); Palladius, *The Lausiac History* (24 [984C], p. 217; 25 [997C], p. 225); John Moschus, *The Spiritual Meadow* (26 [1016B], p. 231); *The Story of Thais* (26 [1064C], p. 249). For detailed references, see the relevant footnotes below.

221. 14 (865A), p. 166.

222. See, for example, 4 (677D, 685A), pp. 91, 95; 26 (1021B, 1068B), pp. 235, 250; cf. above, p. 12. But John nowhere uses Evagrius' threefold scheme of *praktiki, physiki* ("natural contemplation"), and *theoria* of God.

223. See below, pp. 62–66. Climacus seems to be familiar with the work attributed to Nilus, but probably written by Evagrius, *On the Eight Spirits of Wickedness* (*PG* 79, 1145–64); also with another compilation circulating under the name of Nilus, *On the Eight Evil Thoughts* (*PG* 79, 1436–64), which is in fact a translation (in abbreviated form) from the Latin of St. John Cassian: see S. Marsili, "Résumé de Cassien sous le nom de saint Nil", *Revue d'ascétique et de mystique* xv (1934), pp. 241–5.

224. See above, p. 33.

225. See above, p. 52.

center of the human person, body, soul and spirit,[226] and in the primacy which he assigns to love. But he speaks far less than the *Homilies* do about the work of the Holy Spirit.

The Ladder is of course by no means the earliest work in which there is to be found a convergence between the Evagrian and the Macarian approaches. A similar *rapprochement* is already evident in two fifth-century writers, St. Mark the Ascetic and St. Diadochus of Photice. Even though John does not mention either of them by name, there can be little doubt that he is familiar with their writings. From Mark almost certainly he derives his analysis of temptation in Step 15.[227] Points of resemblance between Diadochus and John include their teaching on the invocation or remembrance of Jesus; a cautious attitude towards dreams;[228] the distinction between the two forms of the withdrawal of God's grace—between the temporary and providential abandonment permitted by God for our own good, and the far graver abandonment due to God's turning away from our sin;[229] and the belief that anger can be turned to good use.[230]

In his treatment of the Jesus Prayer, John is probably influenced also by the school of Gaza (early sixth century)—by St. Varsanuphius, St. John the Prophet, and their disciple St. Dorotheus—but once again he does not mention them by name. His understanding of spiritual fatherhood seems likewise to be indebted to the school of Gaza; and his moderate use of Evagrian terminology, in a not very systematic manner, resembles that found in Dorotheus. Another Palestinian writer, not explicitly cited, on whom John seems to draw is Abba Isaias (fifth century); both have similar views on what is "according to nature."[231]

---

226. See 28 (1140B), p. 281, quoted above, p. 53. Cf. 4 (700C), p. 103: the gateway of the heart; 7 (805A), p. 138: "Withdraw into your heart"; 15 (900C), p. 184: prayer of the heart; 28 (1137B), p. 280: watching over the heart. The phrase "perception (*aisthisis*) of the heart" occurs frequently.

227. See below, pp. 182–3 (with the notes). Mark is also cited, but not by name, in 23 (965D), p. 208.

228. 3 (669B–672B), pp. 89–90; cf. Diadochus, *Century* 36–38 (*Phil.*, pp. 263–4).

229. See 4 (708B), p. 108; 5 (777C), p. 129; 21 (948A), p. 200; 26 (1069A), p. 252; and in particular 7 (813C), p. 143; cf. Diadochus, *Century* 86 (*Phil.*, p. 286), using the same metaphor of a mother with her child.

230. 26 (1068D), p. 251; cf. Diadochus, *Century* 62 (*Phil.*, p. 272).

231. 26 (1068CD), p. 251; cf. Isaias, *Discourse* ii: ed. Avgoustinos (Jerusalem 1911), pp. 4–6; see also *Phil.*, p. 22.

Writers to whom John does refer by name include Origen (mentioned once, with disapproval),[232] St. Gregory of Nazianzus, the "Theologian" (cited several times),[233] St. John Cassian[234] and St. Ephraim the Syrian[235] (both cited once). He does not mention St. Dionysius the Areopagite, and it is not clear how far he is influenced by the Dionysian writings.

The Classification of the Vices

A particular problem arises over the classification of the vices in Steps 8–23 of *The Ladder*. Here, regarding blasphemy as a vice distinct from pride but treating sleepiness as an aspect of insensitivity, we have a list of fourteen vices. It is not at first sight clear how to relate this to the more usual list of eight "evil thoughts" found in Evagrius:[236]

gluttony
lust
avarice
dejection (*lypi*)
anger
despondency (*akidia*)
vainglory
pride

The order in which Evagrius lists the vices is deliberate. It reflects, first, the general development of the spiritual life: beginners contend against the grosser and more materialistic sins (gluttony, lust, avarice); those in the middle of the journey are confronted by the more inward temptations of discouragement and irritability (dejection, an-

232. 5 (780D), p. 131.

233. 15 (880C), note 64, p. 171; 22 (949A), p. 201—but this is possibly a reference to Pope Gregory the Great (see below, note 246); 26 (1064A), p. 248; 28 (1137C), p. 280.

234. 4 (717B), p. 114. For Climacus' debt to Cassian, and also for the manner in which he transforms what he borrows, see Archimandrite Sophrony, "De la nécessité des trois renoncements chez St. Cassien le Romain et St. Jean Climaque", *Studia Patristica* v (*Texte und Untersuchungen* 80: Berlin 1962), pp. 393–400.

235. 29 (1148D), p. 283, cited simply as "the Syrian."

236. *On the Eight Thoughts*, 1 (*PG* 40, 1272A). Evagrius is probably drawing upon Origen: see I. Hausherr, "L'origine de la théorie orientale des huit péchés capitaux", *Orientalia Christiana* xxx, no. 86 (Rome 1933), pp. 164–75.

ger, despondency); the more advanced, already initiated into contemplation, still need to guard themselves against the most subtle and "spiritual" of the vices, vainglory and pride. Secondly, the list of eight vices reflects the threefold division of the human person into the appetitive, the incensive and the intelligent aspect (*epithymitikon, thymikon, logikon*).[237] Gluttony, lust and avarice are more especially linked with the appetitive aspect; dejection, anger and despondency, with the incensive power; vainglory and pride, with the intelligent aspect.[238]

Evagrius' disciple, St. John Cassian, transmitted this list of the eight "thoughts" to the West, but made one change in the sequence: to make more evident the connection between dejection and despondency, he moved anger up to the fourth place, after avarice.[239] Further changes were made by St. Gregory the Great, Pope of Rome (590–604), known in the East as "Gregory the Dialogist." He set pride in a class on its own, as the source and mother of all other vices, and omitted dejection, regarding this as the same as despondency, while adding envy to the list. In this way he produced the catalogue of the "seven deadly sins," familiar to the Western Middle Ages:[240]

inanis gloria (vainglory)
invidia (envy)
ira (anger)
tristitia (dejection)
avaritia (avarice)
ventris ingluvies (gluttony)
luxuria (lust)

237. On this threefold division, see the note in *Phil.*, pp. 357–8. First formulated by Plato (see *Republic*, Book iv, 434D–441C), it is widely used by the Fathers: Evagrius, *Practicus* 89 (ed. A. Guillaumont, *Sources chrétiennes* 171 [Paris 1971], pp. 680–9), says that he has taken it from Gregory of Nazianzus (see his *Poems*, II, i, 47: *PG* 37, 1381A–1384A). For Climacus' use of the Platonic scheme, see for example *Past.* 15 (1205B), p. 249.

238. The vices are explicitly linked with the three aspects of the soul in John Cassian, *Conferences* xxiv, 15: Cassian gives a list of eighteen vices in all, including all eight from the Evagrian list. Couilleau, *DS* viii, col. 377, assimilates Climacus' list to that of Cassian, but the correspondence is by no means exact.

239. See *Institutes*, Books v–xii.

240. *Moralia* xxxi, 87 (*PL* 76, 621).

St. John Climacus does not follow any of these schemes exactly. He points out that sin, being by its very nature disordered and amorphous, cannot be classified with precision.[241] He is familiar with the eightfold scheme of Evagrius,[242] and like Evagrius he sometimes makes a distinction between the three chief sins of gluttony, vainglory and avarice, and the remaining five which spring from them.[243] But, alongside this eightfold scheme, John is also familiar with a sevenfold scheme, for which he expresses a preference: this treats vainglory and pride as a single vice.[244] In practice, however, he usually distinguishes between the two, discussing them separately in Steps 22 and 23; on the other hand he commonly omits dejection or gloom *(lypi)* from his list,[245] presumably because like Pope Gregory he considers this identical with despondency *(akidia);* and so, after all, he ends up with the number seven (for he omits envy, which figures on Gregory's list).[246] Thus in Step 29 he gives the following list:[247]

gluttony
lechery (lust)
cupidity (avarice)
despondency
anger
vainglory
pride

241. 26 (1021D), p. 235.

242. 13 (860C), p. 163; 17 (929B), p. 190.

243. 17 (929B), p. 190; 26 (1013A, 1021C), pp. 229, 235. For a somewhat different distinction between the five and the three, see 27 (1109A), p. 267.

244. 22 (948D–949A), p. 201.

245. *Lypi* is mentioned, however, in the list of the passions that assail the monk at different times of the day: 27 (1112C), p. 269.

246. Was Climacus aware of Pope Gregory's list? In 22 (949A), p. 201, when mentioning the sevenfold scheme as distinguished from the eightfold, he refers to "Gregory the Theologian" as one of those who prefer to reckon the vices as seven in number. Normally this would mean Gregory of Nazianzus; but I know of no such teaching in his works. John may therefore mean Pope Gregory; perhaps "Theologos" is a scribal error for "Dialogos" (cf. Couilleau, *DS* viii, col. 376). But John's list is not the same as Gregory the Great's: for, although both leave out dejection, John retains pride as one of the seven, and does not include envy.

247. 29 (1149AB), pp. 283–4.

Apart from the fact that dejection is omitted and that despondency precedes anger, these are the same as the eight "evil thoughts" of Evagrius, and are given in the same order.

In Steps 8–23, however, John expands Evagrius' list by adding seven further vices, dependent on the primary seven. In his list of the primary seven he follows Evagrius, except that he omits dejection; but he moves anger and despondency up to the beginning, thus placing the vices of the soul's incensive aspect before those of its appetitive aspect:

Evagrius	*Climacus*
	anger
	despondency
gluttony	gluttony
lust	lust
avarice	avarice
dejection	
anger	
despondency	
vainglory	vainglory
pride	pride

John is normally careful, in Steps 8–23, to point out how the dependent vices are linked with the primary seven: just as the virtues form a ladder, so the vices form a chain.[248] In detail his scheme takes this form:

anger (8)		
	dependent vices:	malice (9)

248. 9 (840D–841A), p. 152. Thus:
anger leads to malice: 9 (841A), p. 154;
malice leads to slander: 10 (845B), p. 155;
slander leads to talkativeness: 11 (852A), p. 158;
talkativeness leads to (1) falsehood: 12 (853D), p. 160;
(2) despondency: 13 (857D), p. 162;
despondency leads to lust: 26 (1109D), p. 268;
gluttony leads to (1) lust
(2) insensitivity: 14 (869D), p. 170; 17 (929B), p. 190;
insensitivity ("unbelief") and vainglory lead to fear: 21 (945B), p. 199;
vainglory leads to pride: 22 (949A), p. 201;
pride leads to blasphemy: 23 (976B), p. 211.

		slander (10)
		talkativeness (11)
		falsehood (12)
despondency (13)		
gluttony (14)		
lust (15)		
avarice (16)		
	dependent vices:	insensitivity (18)
		fear (21)
vainglory (22)		
pride (23)		
	dependent vice:	blasphemy (23)

John's classification of the vices, drawing as it does upon earlier authorities yet adhering slavishly to none of them, illustrates the way in which he combines tradition and personal originality in *The Ladder*. What he borrows he makes his own.

The Influence of The Ladder

Why should *The Ladder of Divine Ascent* have proved so remarkably popular?[249] Partly, no doubt, because of the striking symbol of the ladder, which binds together the whole book, and has caught the imagination of innumerable readers. More fundamentally, its popularity is surely due to the author's combination of shrewdness and humor, to his skill in drawing so many themes into a single synthesis, and above all to the depth of his spiritual insight.

The wide diffusion of *The Ladder* is reflected by the large number of surviving manuscripts, sometimes illustrated, and often including *scholia* or commentaries.[250] The respect felt for its author is evident from the unusual prominence that he enjoys in the ecclesiastical year. Besides having in the normal way an annual commemoration on March 30 in the calendar of fixed feasts, he is also commemorated on the fourth Sunday in Lent, and most of the liturgical texts on that day refer to him.[251] This Sunday commemoration in the Great Fast

249. On the influence of *The Ladder*, see M. Heppell, introduction to *The Ladder of Divine Ascent*, ET Archimandrite Lazarus, pp. 25–31; Couilleau, *DS* viii, cols. 382–8.

250. Some of these *scholia* appear in Rader's edition, and are reprinted in *PG* 88.

251. See *The Lenten Triodion*, ET Mother Mary and Archimandrite Kallistos Ware (London 1978), pp. 353–67.

marks John Climacus out as the ascetic author *par excellence,* whose writings provide a standard and model for the whole Church. As already mentioned, *The Ladder* is appointed to be read in Orthodox monasteries each year during Lent.

St. John Climacus' influence on later spiritual writers has been extensive. At Sinai itself his teaching on prayer and inward stillness was developed by Hesychius (?eighth-ninth century) and Philotheus (?ninth-tenth century). The first of these, in his work *On Watchfulness and Holiness,* takes up the scattered allusions in *The Ladder* to the Jesus Prayer and the invocation or remembrance of Jesus, and makes this his dominant theme. Although surprisingly *The Ladder* is nowhere cited in the vast eleventh-century anthology entitled *Evergetinos,* it was certainly read and valued by St. Symeon the New Theologian. Nicetas Stethatos, Symeon's biographer, recounts how, on a visit to his family home shortly before his profession as a monk, Symeon found the book in his father's library: "and, becoming closely familiar with it, like good earth he accepted the seed of the word in his heart."[252] *The Ladder*'s influence can be seen in particular in Symeon's teaching on the gift of tears, and in his picture of the spiritual father in the *Discourse on Confession.*

St. Peter of Damascus (twelfth century) quotes *The Ladder* at least thirteen times, and the fourteenth-century Hesychasts draw heavily upon it. There are thirteen citations from *The Ladder* in St. Gregory of Sinai—far more than from any other author—and, in his list of writers approved for monastic reading, Gregory puts first the name of John Climacus.[253] In the *Triads in Defense of the Holy Hesychasts* by St. Gregory Palamas, *The Ladder* is quoted some twenty-five times, and in the *Century* of St. Kallistos and St. Ignatios Xanthopoulos more than thirty times. The parts of *The Ladder* to which these fourteenth-century writers chiefly refer are Step 27 on *hesychia* and John's statements on the invocation of the name of Jesus.

The Ladder was soon translated into the other languages of the Christian East: into Syriac before the end of the seventh century,

252. *Life of St. Symeon the New Theologian* 6 (ed. I. Hausherr, *Orientalia Christiana* xii, no. 45 [Rome 1928], p. 12): Symeon was particularly helped by Step 13. *The Ladder* is cited twice in Symeon's *Catecheses* (4, lines 540–2; 30, line 141), although not apparently in his other writings; but Symeon hardly ever makes explicit citations from other writers.

253. *On Stillness and the Two Methods of Prayer* 11 (*PG* 150, 1324D).

within a few decades of John's death; into Arabic and Georgian by the tenth century, and also into Armenian; into Slavonic by the tenth century, and into Romanian early in the seventeenth century. Its influence in fifteenth-century Russia can be seen both upon the leader of the Non-Possessors, St. Nil Sorskii, and upon his chief opponent among the Possessors, St. Joseph of Volokalamsk. In the correspondence of Tsar Ivan IV, often styled "the Terrible," next to the Holy Scriptures the book most often quoted is *The Ladder.*[254] The anonymous Russian Pilgrim, in the middle of the nineteenth century, is also familiar with the work.[255]

In the West a first translation in Latin, perhaps only partial, was made in the eleventh century; a second version was made in the thirteenth or early fourteenth century by the Franciscan "spiritual" of the Strict Observance, Angelus Clarenus.[256] The first English translation appeared in 1858, the second in 1959 (revised edition, 1978);[257] the present English rendering, in the series *The Classics of Western Spirituality,* is thus the third.

"Ascend, my brothers, ascend eagerly."[258] *The Ladder* of St. John Climacus grew out of its author's living experience, and it requires from each reader a living, personal response. Read hastily, in a spirit of detached curiosity, the book is likely to prove a disappointment. But John never meant it to be read in that manner. He expected it to be pondered slowly, in a spirit of compunction, and with a sincere intention on the reader's part to change his way of life; and if the book has proved deeply influential, that is because so many have read it in precisely such a way, applying the words personally to their own situation. This is a ladder that we must each ascend for ourselves.

Bibliographical Note

(I) *The Greek Text.* There exists as yet no fully critical edition of the Greek text of *The Ladder* and *To the Shepherd.* The Greek is at present available in two independent editions:

(i) By Matthew Rader (Paris 1633). Twice reprinted:

(a) J.-P. Migne, *PG* 88 (Paris 1864), cols. 632–1208.

254. See HTM, p. xxvii.

255. *The Way of a Pilgrim,* ET R.M. French (London 1954), pp. 80, 82, 143, 191, 227.

256. See J. Gribomont, "La *Scala Paradisi,* Jean de Raïthou et Ange Clareno", *Studia Monastica* ii (1960), pp. 345–58.

257. For details, see below, "Bibliographical Note."

258. *Brief Summary* (1161A), p. 291.

(b) P. Trevisan, *Corona Patrum Salesiana*, series graeca 8–9 (2 vols., Turin 1941); includes some minor corrections of (a).

(ii) By the hermit Sophronios, monk of the Holy Mountain (Constantinople 1883); often superior to the text of Rader-Migne.

(II) *English Translations.*

(i) Father Robert, Monk of Mount St. Bernard's Abbey (Leicestershire, England), *The Holy Ladder of Perfection, by which we may ascend to heaven* (London 1858). Often more a paraphrase than an exact rendering. Omits most of Step 27 on stillness: "this Degree," says Father Robert, "as chiefly appertaining to solitaries, has been abridged by the translator" (p. 392).

(ii) Archimandrite Lazarus (Moore), *The Ladder of Divine Ascent*, with an introduction by M. Heppell (London 1959). Far more accurate than (i). Reissued in revised form by the Holy Transfiguration Monastery (Boston, Massachusetts 1978); this reissue includes, besides *The Ladder*, the work *To the Shepherd* (omitted in the 1858 and 1959 translations). As well as using the different printed editions of the Greek, the revisers consulted the ninth-century Sinai manuscript no. 421; but regrettably the helpful introduction by Dr. Heppell has been omitted.

(III) *Studies.* For a short but balanced survey of Climacus' life and teaching, with bibliography, see G. Couilleau, *DS* viii (Paris 1972), cols. 369–89.

Consult also:

M.O. Sumner, *St. John Climacus: the Psychology of the Desert Fathers* (The Guild of Pastoral Psychology, Guild Lecture no. 63: London 1950) (an attempt to understand Climacus in terms of Jungian analytical psychology; too brief to be fully convincing, but indicates an important field for further research).

J.R. Martin, *The Illustration of the Heavenly Ladder of John Climacus (Studies in Manuscript Illumination* 5: Princeton 1954) (on illustrated manuscripts of *The Ladder*).

I. Hausherr, "La théologie du monachisme chez saint Jean Climaque", in the collective volume *Théologie de la vie monastique* (Paris 1961), pp. 385–410.

W. Völker, *Scala Paradisi. Eine Studie zu Johannes Climacus und zugleich eine Vorstudie zu Symeon dem Neuen Theologen* (Wiesbaden 1968) (the fullest and most systematic existing study).

D. Bogdanović, *Jean Climaque dans la littérature byzantine et la littérature serbe ancienne* (Institut d'Etudes Byzantines, Monographies,

Fascicule 11: Belgrade 1968) (in Serbo-Croat, with summary in French on pp. 215–25; important).

C. Yannaras, "Eros divin et éros humain selon S. Jean Climaque", *Contacts* xxi (1969), pp. 190–204.

C. Yannaras, *I metaphysiki tou somatos. Spoudi ston Ioanni tis Klimakos* [*The metaphysics of the body. A study of John Climacus*] (Athens 1971) (helpful discussion of the body, *eros* and dispassion).

I have not been able to consult the unpublished Ph.D. dissertation of T.W. Blair, *Climacus and Christianity. A Study of the Effects of John Climacus' Conceptual Commitments on his Perception of Christianity* (Duke University 1977).

On monastic life in the Sinai peninsula, see H. Skrobucha, *Sinai* (London 1966), pp. 19–47; D.J. Chitty, *The Desert a City* (Oxford 1966), pp. 168–78 (scholarly and perceptive).

Bishop Kallistos

Llanfilo
Commemoration of the Holy Prophet Moses
4/17 September 1980

John Climacus

THE LADDER OF DIVINE ASCENT

THE CLASSICS OF WESTERN SPIRITUALITY

Step 1

ON RENUNCIATION OF LIFE

When writing to the servants of God, one should begin with our God and King Himself, the good, the supremely good, the all-good. Of all created and rational beings, endowed with the dignity of free will, some are friends of God, some are His true servants, some are useless servants (cf. Luke 17:10), some are entirely estranged, and there are some who, for all their weakness, take their stand against Him. We simple people assume that His friends, O holy Father, are properly speaking those intelligent and bodiless beings who surround Him. His true servants are all those who have done and are doing His will without hesitation or pause. His useless servants are those who think of themselves as having been worthy of the gift of baptism, but have not at all guarded their covenant with Him; while, it seems to us, the strangers from God, His opponents, are the unbelievers or heretics. His enemies are those who not only contravene and repudiate the commands of the Lord, but make stern war against all who obey Him.

Each of the above has his own special character and is deserving of fitting analysis. But for ignorant people like ourselves there is nothing to be gained by investigating these now. So, then, with unquestioning obedience let us reach out our unworthy hand to the true servants of God, to those who devoutly urge us on and in faith compel us by their commands. Let us make a treatise, with their knowledge as the implement of writing, a pen dipped in their subdued yet glorious humility, applied to the smooth white parchments of their hearts, or rather resting on the tablets of the spirit. Let us write on it divine words, or rather seeds,[1] and let us begin like this.

God is the life of all free beings. He is the salvation of all, of believers or unbelievers, of the just or the unjust, of the pious or the impious, of those freed from the passions or caught up in them, of monks or those living in the world, of the educated or the illiterate, of the healthy or the sick, of the young or the very old. He is like the outpouring of light, the glimpse of the sun, or the changes of the weather, which are the same for everyone without exception. "For God is no respecter of persons" (Rom. 2:11). An impious man is a rational being, one that must die, who willingly runs away from life, and refuses to believe in the existence of his own everlasting Creator. A transgressor is someone who observes the divine law only in his own depraved fashion and holds on to heretical belief in opposition to God. A Christian is an imitator of Christ in thought, word and deed, as far as this is humanly possible, and he believes rightly and blamelessly in the Holy Trinity. A friend of God is the one who lives in communion with all that is natural and free from sin and who does not neglect to do what good he can. The self-controlled man strives with all his might amidst the trials, the snares, and the noise of the world, to be like someone who rises above them. The monk finds himself in an earthly and defiled body, but pushes himself into the rank and status of the incorporeal angels. The monk clings only to the commandments and words of God in every season and place and matter. The monk is ever embattled with what he is, and he is the unfailing warder of his senses. The monk has a body made holy, a tongue purified, a mind enlightened. Asleep or awake, the monk is a soul pained by the constant remembrance of death. Withdrawal from the world is a willing hatred of all that is materially prized, a denial of nature for the sake of what is above nature.

All this is done by those who willingly turn from the things of this life, either for the sake of the coming kingdom, or because of the number of their sins, or on account of their love of God. Without such objectives the denial of the world would make no sense. God who judges the contest stands waiting to see how it ends for the one who has taken on this race.

The man turning away from the world in order to shake off the

1. The phrase "or rather seeds" only occurs in some texts.

burden of his sins should imitate those who sit by the tombs outside the city. Let him not desist from ardent raging tears, from the wordless moans of the heart, until he sees Jesus Himself coming to roll back the rock of hardness[2] off him, to free the mind, that Lazarus of ours, from the bonds of sin, to say to His ministering angels, "Loose him from his passions and let him go to blessed dispassion."[3] If it is not done thus, then it is all for nothing.

Those of us who wish to get away from Egypt, to escape from Pharaoh, need some Moses to be our intermediary with God, to stand between action and contemplation, and stretch out his arms to God, that those led by him may cross the sea of sin and put to flight the Amalek of the passions.[4] Those who have given themselves up to God but imagine that they can go forward without a leader are surely deceiving themselves. The fugitives from Egypt had Moses, while those escaping from Sodom had an angel for a leader. The former are like those who heal the passions of the soul by the care of doctors; they are the ones who have come out of Egypt. The latter long to shed the uncleanness of the wretched body, for which reason they need an angel or the help of some like being. We must have someone very skilled, a doctor, for our septic wounds.

Violence (cf. Matt. 11:12) and unending pain are the lot of those who aim to ascend to heaven with the body, and this especially at the early stages of the enterprise, when our pleasure-loving disposition and our unfeeling hearts must travel through overwhelming grief toward the love of God and holiness. It is hard, truly hard. There has to be an abundance of invisible bitterness, especially for the careless, until our mind, that cur sniffing around the meat market and revelling in the uproar, is brought through simplicity, deep freedom from anger and diligence to a love of holiness and guidance. Yet full of pas-

---

2. GK *poroseos.* Rader's text has *pyroseos,* "of burning."

3. Throughout this work "dispassion" translates the Gk *apatheia.* For St. John Climacus dispassion is the denial of the passions, not merely in a negative way by ascetic discipline, but by redirecting the natural impulses of the soul and body toward their proper goal. See the Preface, p. 32.

4. John is referring to Exod. 17:11–13 and applying to it an allegorical interpretation. In the battle against the Amalekites (the passions) the Israelites (souls under a spiritual director) prevailed as long as the arms of Moses (the guide) were held raised in prayer by Hur (action) on one side and Aaron (contemplation) on the other. Action (*praxis*) is the ascetic struggle to practice the virtues and overcome the passions. It is the necessary foundation for contemplation (*theoria*), which is the direct apprehension or vision of God by the intellect.

sions and weakness as we are, let us take heart and let us in total confidence carry to Christ in our right hand and confess to Him our helplessness and our fragility. We will carry away more help than we deserve, if only we constantly push ourselves down into the depths of humility.

Let all those coming to this marvelous, tough, and painful—though also easy—contest leap, as it were, into a fire, so that a nonmaterial flame may take up residence within them. But let each one test himself, draw food and drink from the bread of pain and the cup of weeping, lest he march himself to judgment.

If all are not saved who have been baptized, I will pass in silence over what follows.[5]

But to secure a rocklike foundation, those with a mind for the religious life will turn away from everything, will despise everything, will ridicule everything, will shake off everything. Innocence, abstinence, temperance—these make a fine thrice-firm foundation. Let all infants in Christ begin with these, taking real infants as their example; for among children no evil is found, nothing deceitful, no insatiable greed or gluttony, no flaming lust, but it seems that as you feed them more, they grow in strength until at last they come upon passion.

It is detestable and dangerous for a wrestler to be slack at the start of a contest, thereby giving proof of his impending defeat to everyone. Let us have a firm beginning to our religious life, for this will help us if a certain slackness comes later. A bold and eager soul will be spurred on by the memory of its first zeal and new wings can thus be obtained.

When the soul betrays itself, when that initial happy warmth grows cold, the reasons for such a loss ought to be carefully sought and, once found, ought to be combated with all possible zeal, for the initial fervor has to turn back through that same gate through which it had slipped away. The man who renounces the world because of fear is like burning incense, which begins with fragrance and ends in smoke. The man who leaves the world in hopes of a reward is like the millstone that always turns around on the same axis. But the man who leaves the world for love of God has taken fire from the start, and like fire set to fuel, it soon creates a conflagration.

5. I.e., if not all the baptized are saved, not all monks will reach their goal.

Some people when they build a house place bricks on top of rocks. Others raise columns up from the ground. Others still, when taking a walk, go slowly for a while, thus giving sinews and joints a warming up, and then stride out vigorously. Let the perceptive mind understand this analogy. Let us run our race eagerly as if summoned to it by our God and King. Our time is short. Let us not be found barren on the day of death and perish of hunger. Instead let us please the Lord as soldiers please the emperor; for at the end of the campaign we must give a good account of ourselves. We should be afraid of God in the way we fear wild beasts. I have seen men go out to plunder, having no fear of God but being brought up short somewhere at the sound of dogs, an effect that fear of God could not achieve in them.

We should love the Lord as we do our friends. Many a time I have seen people bring grief to God, without being bothered about it, and I have seen these very same people resort to every device, plan, pressure, plea from themselves and their friends, and every gift, simply to restore an old relationship upset by some minor grievance.

At the beginning of our religious life, we cultivate the virtues, and we do so with toil and difficulty. Progressing a little, we then lose our sense of grief or retain very little of it. But when our mortal intelligence turns to zeal and is mastered by it, then we work with full joy, determination, desire, and a holy flame.

All praise to those who from the beginning keep the commandments of God, and do so gladly and eagerly; and greatly to be pitied are those who after a long time in the ascetic life still keep them with great labor if they keep them at all. And let us not be horrified at or judge harshly those who renounce the religious life because of external circumstances. I have seen some men run away and accidentally meet the emperor, tarry with him, go to live in his palace, and take food with him. I have watched seed that accidentally fell into the ground bear much fruit again and again, though the opposite has also happened. I have seen someone go to a doctor for one kind of problem, and, because of that doctor's skill, be treated with an astringent and be cured of failing eyesight, for it often happens that very definite and lasting results emerge through chance rather than through the workings of prescience and planning. So let no one tell me that he is unfit for the monastic life because of the weight and number of his misdeeds, or that because of his addiction to pleasure he must be excused for remaining stuck in his sin. The more the putrefaction, the greater the need for treatment, if the uncleanness is to be done away with, for the healthy do not make their way to the doctor's surgery.

In this world when an emperor summons us to obedience, we leave everything aside and answer the call at once without delays or hanging back or excuses. We had better be careful then not to refuse, through laziness or inertia, the call to the heavenly life in the service of the King of kings, the Lord of lords, the God of gods. Let us not find ourselves unable to defend ourselves at the great tribunal of judgment. Someone caught up in the affairs of the world can make progress, if he is determined. But it is not easy. Those bearing chains can still walk. But they often stumble and are thereby injured. The man who is unmarried and in the world, for all that he may be burdened, can nevertheless make haste toward the monastic life. But the married man is like someone chained hand and foot.[6]

Some people living carelessly in the world put a question to me: "How can we who are married and living amid public cares aspire to the monastic life?"

I answered: "Do whatever good you may. Speak evil of no one. Rob no one. Tell no lie. Despise no one and carry no hate. Do not separate yourself from the church assemblies.[7] Show compassion to the needy. Do not be a cause of scandal to anyone. Stay away from the bed of another, and be satisfied with what your own wives can provide you. If you do all this, you will not be far from the kingdom of heaven."

Let us hasten with joy and trepidation to the noble contest and with no fear of our enemies. They are themselves unseen but they can look at the appearance of our soul. If they are really to see our spirits bowed down by fear, then indeed they will make a harsher sally against us, knowing how much we tremble. Let us courageously arm ourselves against them. No one goes to battle against a plucky fighter.

The Lord has wisely eased the struggles of novices, lest they be driven back into the world during their first battles. So then rejoice always in the Lord, all you servants of God. Recognize this first sign of the Lord's love. It is He Who has summoned you. He has often been known to act in the following way: when He sees courageous

6. Some versions add: "so when he wants to run he cannot."

7. Gk *ton synaxeon*. The synaxis was an assembly in church for the Office or the Eucharist. Here lay people are being told that they must not be absent from the weekly celebration of the Eucharist.

souls He permits them to be embattled from the very beginning, in order the sooner to reward them.

The Lord has concealed from those in the world the tough, but fine, nature of this struggle. Indeed, if people really understood it, no one would renounce the world. Still, offer your labors gladly to Christ in your youth and He will make your old age happy with abundant goodness.[8] The things which they have gathered in their youth will come to the support and encouragement of those worn down by age, so we should toil zealously when we are young and run our course with serious hearts. Death can come at any time, and we have countless hidden enemies—evil enemies, harsh, deceitful, wicked enemies with fire in their hands, wishing to set the Lord's temple alight with the flame that is in it. These enemies are powerful, unsleeping, incorporeal and unseen. No novice should heed the devilish words of his foes as they murmur: "Do not wear out your body, in case you fall prey to disease and weakness." Hardly anyone can be found in this day and age willing to bring low the body, although they may deny it the pleasure of abundant food. The aim of this demon is to make our entrance into the stadium weak and lethargic, and a fitting end will follow this beginning.

The real servants of Christ, using the help of spiritual fathers and also their own self-understanding, will make every effort to select a place, a way of life, an abode, and the exercises that suit them. Community life is not for everyone, because of gluttonous tendencies, and the solitary life is not for everybody, on account of the tendency to anger. Let each seek out the most appropriate way.

All monastic life may be said to take one of three forms. There is the road of withdrawal and solitude for the spiritual athlete; there is the life of stillness[9] shared with one or two others; there is the practice of living patiently in community. "Turn neither to right nor left," says Ecclesiastes (Prov. 4:27) but rather follow the royal way. The second of the three ways is said to be suitable for many people.

---

8. Gk *agatheias*, a *hapax legomenon;* the HTM reading is "dispassion," *apatheias.*

9. Stillness (*hesychia*) is a deep interior peace attained by those who practice the constant remembrance of God. It is the subject of Step 27. Although stillness is not impossible for monks living in community, solitude or near solitude is most conducive to it. According to the context, therefore, *hesychia* is sometimes translated as "solitude." Stillness is equivalent to contemplation, for "he who has achieved stillness has arrived at the very center of the mysteries" (27 [1100C], p. 264). See the Preface, pp. 50–53.

"Woe to the man living alone when he falls into despondency[10] or sleepiness, carelessness or despair, for then he has no one among men to lift him up." This is what Ecclesiastes says (Eccles. 4:10), and the Lord says: "Where two or three are gathered together in My name, I am there among them" (Matt. 18:20).

Who, then, is the faithful and wise monk? It is the man who has kept unquenched the warmth of his vocation, who adds fire each day to fire, fervor to fervor, zeal to zeal, love to love, and this to the end of his life.

This is the first step. Let him who has set foot on it not turn back.

---

10. Despondency (*akidia*) is a listlessness or torpor—"accidie"—that afflicts a monk when he relaxes his struggle to attain the virtues. It begins as a loss of a sense of purpose and ends in despair and spiritual death. See Step 13.

Step 2

ON DETACHMENT

If you truly love God and long to reach the kingdom that is to come, if you are truly pained by your failings and are mindful of punishment and of the eternal judgment, if you are truly afraid to die, then it will not be possible to have an attachment, or anxiety, or concern for money, for possessions, for family relationships, for worldly glory, for love and brotherhood, indeed for anything of earth. All worry about one's condition, even for one's body, will be pushed aside as hateful. Stripped of all thought of these, caring nothing about them, one will turn freely to Christ. One will look to heaven and to the help coming from there, as in the scriptural sayings: "I will cling close to you" (Ps. 62:9) and "I have not grown tired of following you nor have I longed for the day or the rest that man gives" (Jer. 17:16).

It would be a very great disgrace to leave everything after we have been called—and called by God, not man—and then to be worried about something that can do us no good in the hour of our need, that is, of our death. This is what the Lord meant when He told us not to turn back and not to be found useless for the kingdom of heaven. He knew how weak we could be at the start of our religious life, how easily we can turn back to the world when we associate with worldly people or happen to meet them. That is why it happened that when someone said to Him, "Let me go away to bury my father," He answered, "Let the dead bury the dead" (Matt. 8:22). There are demons to assail us after our renunciation of the world. They make us envy those who remain on the outside and who are merciful and compassionate. They make us regret that we seem deprived of these virtues. Their hostile aim is to bring us by way of false humility either to turn back to the world or, if we remain monks, to plunge down the cliffs of despair.

Conceit may lead us to disparage the secular life or secretly to despise those on the outside. We may act in this way in order to escape despair or to obtain hope. We should therefore heed the Lord when speaking to the young man who kept almost all the commandments: "You need one thing, to sell what you have and to give it to the poor" (Mark 10:21), for by making himself a pauper the young man would learn to accept the charity of others.

If we really wish to enter the contest of religious life, we should pay careful heed to the sense in which the Lord described those remaining in the world as living corpses (Matt. 8:22). What he said was, in effect, "Let the living dead who are in the world bury those dead in the body." Riches did not prevent the young man from coming to receive baptism, and it is quite wrong to say, as some do, that the Lord told him to dispose of his wealth so that he could be baptized. Let us be sure of this, and let us be satisfied with the promise of very great glory that goes with our vocation. We should investigate why those who have lived in the world, and have endured nightlong vigils, fasting, labors, and suffering, and then have withdrawn from their fellowmen to the monastic life, as if to a place of trial or an arena, no longer practice their former fake and spurious asceticism. I have seen many different plants of the virtues planted by them in the world, watered by vanity as if from an underground cesspool, made to shoot up by love of show, manured by praise, and yet they quickly withered when transplanted to desert soil, to where the world did not walk, that is, to where they were not manured with the foul-smelling water of vanity. The things that grow in water cannot bear fruit in dry and arid places.

If someone has hated the world, he has run away from its misery; but if he has an attachment to visible things, then he is not yet cleansed of grief. For how can he avoid grief when he is deprived of something he loves? We need great vigilance in all things, but especially in regard to what we have left behind.

I have observed many men in the world assailed by anxiety, by worry, by the need to talk, by all-night watching, and I have seen them run away from the madness of their bodies. They turned to the monastic life with totally free hearts, and still were pitiably corrupted by the stirrings of the body.

We should be careful in case it should happen to us that while talking of journeying along the narrow and hard road we may actually wander onto the broad and wide highway.

Mortification of the appetite, nightlong toil, a ration of water, a short measure of bread, the bitter cup of dishonor—these will show you the narrow way. Derided, mocked, jeered, you must accept the denial of your will. You must patiently endure opposition, suffer neglect without complaint, put up with violent arrogance. You must be ready for injustice, and not grieve when you are slandered; you must not be angered by contempt and you must show humility when you have been condemned. Happy are those who follow this road and avoid other highways. Theirs is the kingdom of heaven.

No one can enter crowned into the heavenly bridechamber without first making the three renunciations. He has to turn away from worldly concerns, from men, from family; he must cut selfishness away; and thirdly, he must rebuff the vanity that follows obedience. "Go out from among them," says the Lord. "Go apart from them. Do not touch the uncleanness of the age" (2 Cor. 6:17).

Who in the outside world has worked wonders, raised the dead, expelled demons? No one. Such deeds are done by monks. It is their reward. People in secular life cannot do these things, for, if they could, what then would be the point of ascetic practice and the solitary life?

Whenever our feelings grow warm after our renunciation with the memories of parents and of brothers, that is all the work of demons, and we must take up the weapons of prayer against them. Inflamed by the thought of eternal fire, we must drive them out and quench that untimely glow in our hearts. If a man thinks himself immune to the allurement of something and yet grieves over its loss, he is only fooling himself. Young men who still feel strongly the urge for physical love and pleasure and yet who also want to take on the regime of a monastery must discipline themselves with every form of vigilance and prayer, avoiding all dangerous comfort, so that their last state may not be worse than their first. For those sailing the tides of spirituality know only too well that the religious life can be a harbor of salvation or a haven of destruction, and a pitiable sight indeed is the shipwreck in port of someone who had safely mastered the ocean.

This is the second step, and if you take it, then do as Lot did, not his wife, and flee.

Step 3

ON EXILE

There is such a thing as exile, an irrevocable renunciation of everything in one's familiar surroundings that hinders one from attaining the ideal of holiness. Exile is a disciplined heart, unheralded wisdom, an unpublicized understanding, a hidden life, masked ideals. It is unseen meditation, the striving to be humble, a wish for poverty, the longing for what is divine. It is an outpouring of love, a denial of vainglory, a depth of silence.

For followers of the Lord, this manner of thinking operates abundantly at the beginning and they are greatly disturbed by it, as though by some holy fire. I mean separation from their relations for the sake of hardship and simplicity which drives on the lovers of this good. Yet for all that it is praiseworthy, it requires discretion, since not every kind of exile is good if taken to extremes.

The Lord says that every prophet is without honor in his own country (cf. John 4:44). If He is right, then we had better be careful that our act of renunciation is not for empty honor. Exile is a separation from everything, in order that one may hold on totally to God. It is a chosen route of great grief. An exile is a fugitive, running from all relationships with his own relatives and with strangers. Do not wait for souls enamored of the world when you are pressing on towards solitude and exile. In any case, death comes when least expected. Many set themselves the aim of rescuing the indifferent and the lazy—and end up lost themselves. The flame within them gets dim with the passage of time. So, if you have the fire, run, since you never know when it may be doused, leaving you stranded in darkness. Not all of us are summoned to rescue others. "My brothers, each one of us will give an account of himself to God," says the holy Apostle (Rom. 14:12). Again, he declares, "You teach someone else, but not yourself" (Rom. 2:21). It is as if he were saying, "I do not know about the others, but we have surely to look to what we must do ourselves."

If you choose to go into exile, then be on the watch for the demon of wandering and of pleasure, since there is an opportunity here for him.

Detachment is good and its mother is exile. Someone withdrawing from the world for the sake of the Lord is no longer attached to possessions, that he should not appear to be deceived by the passions. If you have left the world, then do not begin to reach out for it. Otherwise your passions will come back to you. Eve had no wish to be driven from Paradise, whereas a monk will abandon his homeland willingly; she would have wished again for the forbidden tree, but he has rebuffed the sure danger coming from the kinship of the flesh. Run from the places of sin as though from a plague. When fruit is not in plain sight, we have no great urge to taste it.

You have to beware the ways and the guile of thieves. They come with the suggestion to us that we should not really abandon the world. They tell us of the rewards awaiting us if only we stay to look on women and to triumph over our desire for them. This is something we must not give in to at all. Indeed, we must do the very opposite.

Then again we manage for some time to live away from our relatives. We practice a little piety, compunction, self-control. And then the empty thoughts come tramping toward us, seeking to turn us back to the places we knew. They tell us what a lesson we are, what an example, what a help to those who witnessed our former wicked deeds. If we happen to be articulate and well informed, they assure us that we could be rescuers of souls and teachers to the world. They tell us all this so that we might scatter at sea the treasures we have assembled while in port. So we had better imitate Lot, and certainly not his wife. The soul turning back to the regions from which it came will be like the salt that has lost savor, indeed like that famous pillar. Run from Egypt, run and do not turn back. The heart yearning for the land there will never see Jerusalem, the land of dispassion.[11]

11. "The land of dispassion" is an interpretation of the meaning of "Jerusalem."

Leaving home, some at the beginning are full of innocence. Their souls are clean. And then they want very much to go back, thinking, perhaps, that they might bring salvation to others, having attained it themselves. Moses, that man who saw God, returned. In his case it was to save the members of his tribe. Still, he ran into many dangers in Egypt and was caught up in the darkness of the world.

Offend your parents rather than God. He, after all, created and saved us, while they at times even killed the ones they loved, or handed them over to destruction.

A true exile, despite his possession of knowledge, sits like someone of foreign speech among men of other tongues.

If we have taken up the solitary life, we certainly ought not to abhor our own relations or our own places, but we ought to be careful to avoid any harm that may come from these. Here, as in everything, Christ is our teacher. It often looked as if He were trying to rebuff His earthly parents. Some people said to Him, "Your mother and your brothers are looking for you," and at once Christ gave an example of detachment that was nonetheless free from any harsh feelings. "My mother and my brothers are those who do the will of my Father in heaven," He said (Matt. 12:50). So let your father be the one who is able and willing to labor with you in bearing the burden of your sins, and your mother the compunction that is strong enough to wash away your filth. Let your brother be your companion and rival in the race that leads to heaven, and may the constant thought of death be your spouse. Let your longed-for offspring be the moanings of your heart. May your body be your slave, and your friends the holy powers who can help you at the hour of dying if they become your friends. "This is the generation of those who seek the Lord" (Ps. 23:6).

If you long for God, you drive out your love for family. Anyone telling you he can combine these yearnings is deceiving himself. "No one can serve two masters" (Matt. 6:24). "I did not come to bring peace on earth," says the Lord, knowing how parents would rise up against sons or brothers who chose to serve Him. "It was for war and the sword" (Matt. 10:34), to separate the lovers of God from the lovers of the world, the materially-minded from the spiritually-minded, the vainglorious from the humble.

Contradiction and dissent are pleasing to God when they arise from love of Him, but have a care that you do not find yourself swept away on a tide of sentiment while you are yet passionately attached to what was familiar to you. Do not let the tears of parents or friends fill you with pity, lest you find yourself weeping forever in the afterlife. When they circle around you like bees, or rather wasps, when they pour out their laments over you, do not hesitate at all but think at once of your death and keep the eye of your soul directed unswervingly to what it used to do, that you may be able to counteract one pain with another. Our kin, even our friends, make us false promises so as to restrain us from that noble contest and so as to draw us back to their own goal. We had better withdraw from our own locality. We had better flee to places which are less consoling and more conducive to lack of vanity and to humility. Otherwise we will take flight with our passions.

You are of noble birth? Hide the fact. You are famous? Do not discuss it. Otherwise your status and your deeds may come into conflict.

There is no greater example of renunciation than that great man[12] who heard the command, "Leave your country and your family and the house of your father" (Gen. 12:1). Obediently he went to a foreign country where the language was different. And so it is that anyone following this model of renunciation is glorified all the more by the Lord.

But even though this glory is given by God, it is still good to deflect it with the protective shield of humility. When demons or men lavish praise on us for our exile as if it were a great achievement, let us remind ourselves at once of Him Who came down from heaven for our benefit and exiled Himself to earth. Nothing we could ever do would match that.

An attachment to any of our relations or even to a stranger is hard enough to deal with. It can gradually pull us back toward the world and make cool the fire of our contrition. You cannot look to heaven and to earth at the same time; similarly, if you have not turned your back completely on your relatives and others in thought and in body, you cannot avoid endangering your soul.

To establish a good and firm character within ourselves is something very difficult and troublesome, and one crisis can destroy what we have worked so hard to set right. Bad, worldly and disorderly company destroys good character (cf. 1 Cor. 15:33). When a man has renounced the world and still returns to its affairs or draws near to it, he will either fall into its snares or will defile his heart with thoughts

12. Abraham.

of it. He may perhaps be uncorrupted himself. But if he comes to feel contempt for those who are corrupted, then assuredly he will join them in their corruption.

Concerning the dreams of novices

Our mind is the instrument of knowledge, but it is very imperfect and filled with all sorts of ignorance. This is a fact that cannot be disguised.

Now the palate discriminates between various kinds of food, the hearing distinguishes between the things it perceives, the sun shows up the weakness of the eyes, and words reveal the ignorance of a soul. Nevertheless, the law of love urges us to reach beyond ourselves, and so it seems to me—and I do not wish to be insistent—that, immediately after this discussion of exile, or rather, in the course of it, something ought to be said about dreams. For we should not be unaware of this type of deceit practiced by our wily enemies.

A dream is a stirring of the mind during the body's rest, while a fantasy is something that tricks the eyes when the intellect is asleep. Fantasy occurs when the mind wanders, while the body is awake. A fantasy is the contemplation of something that does not actually exist.

It must be clear why I have decided to speak here about dreams. After we leave home and family for the sake of the Lord, after we have gone into exile for the love of God, the demons try to shake us with dreams. They show us our relatives grieving, near death, poverty-stricken or imprisoned because of us. But the man who believes in dreams is like someone running to catch up with his own shadow.

The devils of vainglory do their prophecies in dreams. They guess the future and, as part of their deceit, they inform us of it so that we are astonished to discover our visions coming true. Indeed we get carried away with the notion that we are already close to the gift of foreknowledge.

To the credulous, a devil is a prophet; and to those who despise him, he is just a liar. Because he is a spiritual being, he knows what is happening in the lower regions, that someone is dying, for instance, so by way of dreams he passes the information on to the more gullible. However, demons lack actual foreknowledge. If they did not, these tricksters would be able to foretell our deaths.

Devils often take on the appearance of angels of light or martyrs and they appear to us in sleep and talk to us, so that they can push us into unholy joy and conceit when we wake up. But this very effect will reveal their trick, for what angels actually reveal are torments, judgments, and separation, with the result that on waking up we tremble and are miserable. And if we start to believe in the devils of our dreams, then we will be their playthings when we are also awake.

The man who believes in dreams shows his inexperience, while the man who distrusts every dream is very sensible. Trust only the dreams that foretell torments and judgment for you, but even these dreams may also be from demons if they produce despair in you.

* * *

This is the third step, equaling the number of the Three Persons. Whoever has reached it should look neither to right nor left.

Step 4

ON OBEDIENCE

It is right that our treatise should now deal with the warriors and athletes of Christ.

As flower comes before every fruit, so exile of body or will precedes all obedience. On these two virtues, as on two golden wings, the holy soul rises serenely to heaven. Perhaps it was of this the prophet sang when, filled with the Holy Spirit, he said, "Who will give me the wings of a dove?" and, "The active life will give me flight and I will be at rest in contemplation and lowliness" (Ps. 54:7).

We ought not omit in this treatise a clear description of the weapons of those noble fighters, the shield of faith which they hold up before God, and before their trainer, and with which they ward off, so to speak, all thought of unbelief or backsliding; the spiritual sword that is always drawn and lays low every selfish longing; the iron breastplate of meekness and patience to ward off every insult, every jab and missile; the protective prayer of their spiritual master which they have as a saving helmet. They do not stand with their feet close together, but one foot is advanced towards service, while the other stays firmly planted in prayer.

Obedience is a total renunciation of our own life, and it shows up clearly in the way we act. Or, again, obedience is the mortification of the members while the mind remains alive. Obedience is unquestioned movement, death freely accepted, a simple life, danger faced without worry, an unprepared defense before God, fearlessness before death, a safe voyage, a sleeper's journey. Obedience is the burial place of the will and the resurrection of lowliness. A corpse does not contradict or debate the good or whatever seems bad, and the spiritual father who has devoutly put the disciple's soul to death will answer for everything. Indeed, to obey is, with all deliberateness, to put aside the capacity to make one's own judgment.

The beginning of the mortification both of the soul's will and also of the body's members is hard. The halfway stage is sometimes difficult, sometimes not. But the end is liberation from the senses and freedom from pain.

The blessed living corpse grows sick at heart when he finds himself acting on his own behalf, and he is frightened by the burden of using his own personal judgment.

So you have decided to strip for the race of spiritual profession, to take Christ's yoke on your neck, to lay your own burden on the shoulders of another, to pledge your willing surrender to slavery? And for this you want it in writing that you get freedom in return, even when you swim across this great sea borne up on the hands of others? Very well, then. But you had better recognize that you have undertaken to travel by a short and rough road, along which there is only one false turning, that which they call self-direction[13] and if that is avoided—even in matters seemingly good, spiritual, and pleasing to God—then straightaway one has reached journey's end. For the fact is that obedience is self-mistrust up to one's dying day, in every matter, even the good.

When humbly and with true longing for salvation we resolve to bend the neck and entrust ourselves to another in the Lord, there is something to be done before we start. If there happens to be any cunning in us, any prudence, then we should question, examine, and, if I may say so, put to the test our master, so that there is no mistaking the sailor for the helmsman, the patient for the doctor, the passionate for the dispassionate man, the sea for the harbor—with the resulting shipwreck of our soul. But having once entered the stadium of holy living and obedience, we can no longer start criticizing the umpire, even if we should notice some faults in him. After all, he is human

13. "Self-direction" (*idiorythmia*), says scholion 2, Step 27 (1117B), "is to follow one's own regime and to satisfy one's own will." According to John it leads to hypocrisy (26 [1024B], p. 236).

and if we start making judgments, then our submissiveness earns no profit.

If we wish to preserve unshaken faith in our superiors, we must write their good deeds indelibly in our hearts and preserve them in our memories so that, when the demons scatter distrust of them among us, we can repel them by what we have retained in our minds. The more faith blossoms in the heart, the more the body is eager to serve. To stumble on distrust is to fall, since "whatever does not spring from faith is sin" (Rom. 14:23). When the thought strikes you to judge or condemn your superior, leap away as though from fornication. Give no trust, place, entry, or starting point to that snake. Say this to the viper: "Listen to me, deceiver, I have no right to pass judgment on my superior but he has the authority to be my judge. I do not judge him; he judges me."

The Fathers have declared the singing of psalms to be a weapon, prayer to be a wall, and honest tears to be a bath. To them, blessed obedience is confession of faith, without which no one subject to passions will see the Lord.

He who is submissive is passing sentence on himself. If his obedience for the Lord's sake is perfect, even when it does not appear to be so, he will escape judgment. But if in some things he follows his own will, then even though he thinks of himself as obedient, he takes the burden onto his own self. If the superior continues to rebuke him, then that is good; but if he gives up, I do not know what to say.

Those who submit to the Lord with simple heart will run the good race. If they keep their minds on leash they will not draw the wickedness of demons onto themselves.

Above all let us make our confession to our good judge, and to him alone, though to all if he so commands. Wounds shown in public will not grow worse, but will be healed.

In a monastery I once saw a judgment that was truly terrible. It was made by a superior who was good as a man and as a shepherd, and it happened while I was staying there. A robber sought admission to the monastic life, and that excellent superior, that man of healing, ordered him to take seven days of complete rest so that he might get to know the kind of life in the place. After a week the superior sent for him and asked him privately if he would like to live there among them. When the other man showed genuine enthusiasm for this, he asked him what wrong he had done in the world, and on observing the ready admission of everything, he tested him further. "I want you to tell this to the brethren," he said. Since the other man had really come to hate his wrongdoing and was not troubled by shame, he promptly agreed. "I will confess in the middle of Alexandria itself, if you wish," he said.

And so the superior gathered his flock into the church. There were 230 of them, and when the holy service was in progress, and the gospel had been read—for it was Sunday—this irreproachable convict was led out by some of the brethren who hit him, but lightly. He had his hands tied behind his back, he was wearing a hair shirt, and ashes had been sprinkled on his head. Everyone was amazed, and there were some shouts, for it was not clear what was happening. But when the robber appeared at the doors[14] of the church, that very charitable superior said loudly to him: "Stop! You are not worthy to come in here."

The robber was astounded by the voice of the superior coming from the sanctuary. (He swore afterwards that he thought he heard thunder and not a human voice.) At once he fell on his face and he trembled and shook with fear. While he lay on the ground, moistening the floor with his tears, the marvelous healer turned to him, trying everything so as to save him and to give everyone else an example of salvation and true humility. Before all, he exhorted him to describe in detail everything he had done. Terrified, the robber confessed all, sins of the flesh, natural and unnatural, with humans and with beasts; poisonings, murders, and many other deeds too awful to hear or to set down on paper. Everyone was horrified. But when he had finished his confession, the superior allowed him to be given the habit at once and to be included in the ranks of the brethren.

I was amazed by the wisdom of that holy man, and when we were alone I asked him why he had contrived such an extraordinary spectacle. "For two reasons," this true healer replied. "First, so that this man, having confessed now in shame, might in the future be spared fresh remorse for these deeds, which is what happened. He did not rise up from the floor, Brother John, until he had been granted forgiveness of all his sins. Have no doubt about this. Indeed one of the brethren who was present told me he saw a terrifying figure holding a book and a pen and crossing off each sin as it was confessed. Now this is quite probable if you bear in mind the words, 'I shall confess

14. Between the main body of the church and the narthex.

my wrongdoing to the Lord and You have taken away the wickedness of my heart' (Ps. 31:5). But there was a second reason. There are some among the brethren who have not confessed their sins and I want to encourage them to make their confession, for without this no one will be pardoned."

I saw many other wonders and marvels in the company of that unforgettable pastor and his flock, and I will try to tell you a great deal about them. For I stayed quite a while with this man, studying their way of life and being constantly amazed at how these men of earth succeeded in imitating heavenly beings.

An unbreakable bond of love joined these men together, and more wonderful was their freedom from all familiarity and idle chatter. Above all, they strove never to injure a brother's conscience. And if ever someone showed hatred of another, the shepherd banished him like a convict to the isolation monastery.[15] Once when a brother spoke ill of a neighbor, the holy man, on hearing him, had him expelled immediately. "I'm not having a visible devil here along with the invisible one," he said.

Among these holy fathers I saw things that were really profitable and worthy of admiration. I saw a fraternity assembled and united in the Lord and with a wonderful combination of action and contemplation. They were so taken up with the things of heaven and they practiced so much good that they had little need of the promptings of the superior, and it was out of their own goodwill that they stirred each to divine vigilance. They had certain holy and divine exercises that were laid down, studied, and established. If the superior was away and a brother began to resort to abusive language, criticism of others, or merely idle chatter, a discreet nod from another pulled him up short and quietly stopped him. If it happened that the brother did not notice, then the one who reminded him would prostrate himself before him and then go away.

If they had to speak, what they talked about all the time was the remembrance of death and the thought of everlasting judgment.

I must tell you about the astonishing achievement of the baker they had there. Noticing that during his work he preserved a totally recollected state and a capacity for tears, I asked him how he had managed to be granted such a grace. He answered me when I became

15. This is the "Prison" which is described in detail below (p. 105 and Step 5).

insistent: "It always seems to me that I serve God and not men," he said. "And so I judge myself to be undeserving of any rest. And this fire[16] here reminds me of the everlasting fire to come."

There is another achievement of theirs about which we should hear. Even in the refectory they did not cease from mental prayer,[17] and by secret signs and gestures these holy men reminded each other of it. And they did this not only in the refectory, but everywhere they met or assembled.

If one of them committed a fault, many of the brothers would seek his permission to take the matter to the shepherd and to accept both the responsibility and the punishment. When the great man found out that his disciples did this, he inflicted easier punishments, in the knowledge that the one punished was actually innocent. And he made no effort to discover the real culprit.

And what of idle talk and levity? Or if one of them started a row with a neighbor, a third who happened to pass by would undertake penance for it—and thus dissolve the anger. If he noticed that bad feeling somehow persisted among the disputants, he would report the matter to the father who was next to the superior and he would prepare for a reconciliation to be made before sundown. But if they persisted in their hard feelings, they would get no food until they had resolved their difference, or else they were driven from the monastery.

Praiseworthy sternness of this kind has reached a high point among them and bears plenty of fruit. Many of these holy fathers became experts in active life and in spirituality, in discernment and humility. Among them was the awful and yet angelic sight of men grey-haired, venerable, preeminent in holiness, still going about like obedient children and taking the greatest delight in their lowliness. I have seen men there who lived in total obedience for all of fifty years, and when I begged them to tell me what consolation they had won from so great a labor, some answered that having arrived thereby at the lowest depths of abasement they could repel every onslaught, while others declared that they had attained complete freedom from the senses and had obtained serenity amid every calumny and insult.

---

16. I.e., of the bakery.

17. By mental prayer (*noera ergasia*) John means a concentrated state of recollection in the depths of the heart. Elsewhere he says, "If you are careful to train your mind never to wander, it will stay by you even at mealtimes" (28 [1133A], p. 276).

I saw others among these wonderful fathers who had the white hair of angels,[18] the deepest innocence, and a wise simplicity that was spontaneous and yet directed by God Himself. The fact is that just as an evil person is two-faced, one thing in public and another in private, so a simple person is not twofold, but something whole.[19] There is no one among them who is silly and foolish in the way that some old men in the world are, as they say, senile. No indeed. They are openly gentle, kindly, radiant, genuine, without hypocrisy, affectation, or falsity of either speech or disposition—something not found in many. Spiritually, they are like children, with God and the superior as their very breath, and with the mind's eye on strict lookout for demons and the passions.

Holy Father and Brothers in God, a lifetime would not be enough to allow me to describe the virtue of those blessed men, or the heavenly life they lead. Still, their great struggles rather than my meager suggestions should adorn this treatise and should rouse you to be zealous in the love of God. After all, the lowly is adorned by the excellent, and I would only ask you to refrain from thinking that what I write is something made up, for a suspicion of this kind would only take away from its value.

So, then, let us resume.

In this monastery to which I have been referring, there was a man named Isidore, from Alexandria, who having belonged to the ruling class had become a monk. I met him there. The most holy shepherd, after having let him join, discovered that he was a troublemaker, cruel, sly, and haughty, but he shrewdly managed to outwit the cunning of the devils in him. "If you have decided to accept the yoke of Christ," he told Isidore, "I want you first of all to learn obedience."

"Most holy Father, I submit to you like iron to the blacksmith," Isidore replied.

The superior, availing of this metaphor, immediately gave exercise to the iron Isidore and said to him: "Brother, this is what I want you to do. You are to stand at the gate of the monastery, and before

18. White hair is often associated with angels (cf. *The Lives of the Desert Fathers* [*The Historia Monachorum in Aegypto*] II, 1, Abba Or). The monastic life is the angelic life on earth because those who have truly attained it are like the angels: servants of God and of men, free from sin, and as free as is humanly possible from material needs.

19. This sentence is missing in some versions.

everyone passing in or out you are to bend the knee and say, 'Pray for me, Father, because I am an epileptic.' " And Isidore obeyed, like an angel obeying the Lord.

He spent seven years at the gate, and achieved deep humility and compunction.

After the statutory seven years[20] and after the wonderful steadfastness of the man, the superior deemed him fully worthy to be admitted to the ranks of the brethren and wanted to ordain him. Through others and also through my feeble intercession, Isidore begged the superior many times to let him finish his course. He hinted that his death, his call, was near, which in fact proved to be so. The superior allowed him to stay at his place, and ten days later, humbly, gloriously, he passed on to the Lord. A week after his death the porter of the monastery was also taken, for the blessed Isidore had said to him, "If I have found favor in the sight of the Lord, you too will be inseparably joined to me within a short time." That is exactly what happened, in testimony to his unashamed obedience and his marvelous humility.

While he was still alive, I asked this great Isidore how he had occupied his mind while he was at the gate, and this memorable man did not conceal anything from me, for he wished to be of help. "At first I judged that I had been sold into slavery for my sins," he said. "So I did penance with bitterness, great effort, and blood. After a year my heart was no longer full of grief, and I began to think of a reward for my obedience from God Himself. Another year passed and in the depths of my heart I began to see how unworthy I was to live in a monastery, to encounter the fathers, to share in the divine Mysteries. I lost the courage to look anyone in the face, but lowering my eyes and lowering my thoughts even further, I asked with true sincerity for the prayers of those going in and out."

Once when I was sitting in the refectory with the superior, he asked me in a whisper if I would like to see holy prudence in someone very old. When I said I wished that very much, he summoned from the second table a man called Lawrence who had been about forty-eight years in the monastery and was second priest in the monastery.

20. No monastic rule laid down a seven year probation. But a seven years' penance was required by the Apostolic Canons for fornication. In view of the deacon Macedonius' reference to the "fornication of disobedience" (p. 101), it may be that the superior treated Isidore's haughtiness as fornication.

He came, genuflected before the abbot and received his blessing. When he stood up the abbot said nothing at all to him but left him standing beside the table and not eating. It was just the start of the midday meal so that he was left standing there a full hour, probably two. I was embarrassed to look this hard-working man in the face, for he was completely white-haired and all of eighty years. He stayed there until we had finished eating, and when we got up, the holy man sent him off to the great Isidore to recite to him the beginning of the thirty-ninth psalm.[21]

Being myself a bad character, I did not let slip the chance to tease the old man, so I asked him what he had been thinking about as he stood by the table. "I thought of the shepherd as the image of Christ," he said. "I thought of the command as coming not from him but from God. And so, Father John, I stood praying as if I were in front of the altar of God rather than the table of men; and because I trust and love my shepherd, I had no malevolent thoughts concerning him. It is said that love does not reckon up injury. But be sure of this much, Father, that anyone who freely chooses to be simple and guileless provides the devil with neither the time nor the place for an attack."

And the just Lord sent that shepherd of the holy flock someone just like himself to be bursar of the monastery. He was modest, like few others, and gentle as very few are. As a help to the others, the great elder once pretended to get angry with him in church and ordered him out before the usual time. Now I knew that he was innocent of the charge laid against him by the pastor, and when we were alone I started to plead with the great man on behalf of the bursar. But this is what the wise man said: "Father, I too know he is innocent. But just as it would be a pity and indeed quite wrong to snatch bread from the mouth of a starving child, so too the director of souls does harm to himself and to the ascetic if he denies him frequent opportunities to gain crowns such as the superior thinks he deserves at each hour, through having to put up with insults, dishonor, contempt, and mockery. Three things happen that are very wrong: first, the director misses the rewards due to him for making corrections; second, the director fails to bring profit to others when he could have done so through the virtue of that one person; but third, and worst, is that those who seem to be the most hard-working and obedient and hence confirmed in virtue, if left for any length of time without being

21. "I waited patiently for the Lord; He inclined to me and heard my cry."

censured or reproached by the superior, lose that meekness and obedience they formerly had. Good, fruitful, and fertile land, if left without the water of dishonor, can revert to being forest and can produce the thorns of vanity, cowardice,[22] and arrogance. The great Apostle understood this. Hence his instruction to Timothy: "Be insistent, criticize them, rebuke in season and out of season" (2 Tim. 4:2).

But when I argued the matter with that true director, reminding him of human frailty, I suggested that punishment, deserved or otherwise, might lead many to break away from the flock. That man, in whom wisdom had made a home, had this to say to me: "A soul bound in faith and love to the shepherd for Christ's sake does not go away, even when blood is spilt. He certainly does not leave if through the shepherd he has received the cure for his wounds, for he bears in mind the words, 'Neither angels, nor principalities, nor powers nor any other creature can separate us from the love of Christ' (cf. Rom. 8:38–39). If a soul is not attached, bound, and devoted to the shepherd in this fashion, it seems to me that the man should not be here at all; for what binds him to the shepherd is hypocrisy and false obedience." And the truth is that this great man is not deceived, for he has guided, led to perfection, and offered to Christ blameless sacrifices.

Let us listen to the wisdom of God found in earthen vessels and marvel at it.

While I was there I was astonished by the faith and the patience of the novices. With unshakable courage they accepted the criticisms of the superior and indeed of those far below him in rank.

For my own edification I put questions to one of the brothers, called Abbacyrus, who had lived fifteen years in the monastery and who, as I saw, was badly treated by nearly everyone. Those serving at table drove him out almost daily for being naturally unrestrained in his talk. "Brother Abbacyrus," I asked, "why do I see you thrown out of the refectory every day and going without supper to bed?"

"Father," he answered, "you may be sure that they are testing me to find out if I would ever make a monk. They do not really mean to be harsh. I know what the superior and they are trying to do, and so I put up with all this and do not become burdened by it. I have done it now for fifteen years. At the time I came into the monastery they told me that those who renounce the world are tested for thirty

22. In place of "cowardice" Rader's text has "lewdness" (*porneia*).

years. And they are right, Father John, for gold is not purified unless it has been tested."

This fine man Abbacyrus lived for two more years after my arrival at the monastery. Just before he passed on to the Lord, he said this to the fathers: "I thank the Lord and I thank you. For my own salvation you put me to the test, and for seventeen years now I have lived without being tempted by devils." And the just superior gave orders that he had earned the right to be buried as a confessor with the local saints.

Now I would do wrong to all those eager for perfection if I were to bury in the tomb of silence the achievement and the reward of Macedonius, the first of their deacons, a man zealous for God.

On one occasion, just two days before the feast of the Holy Theophany,[23] he asked the superior for permission to go to Alexandria for a certain personal matter. He promised to get back from the city in time for the preparation for the feast. The devil, however, who loathes everything good, contrived to put an obstacle in the way of the archdeacon, who, although permitted to leave the monastery, did not return for the holy feast at the time set by the superior. He came back a day late, was deposed from the diaconate by the pastor, and was put in the rank of the lowest novices. This good deacon[24] of obedience, this archdeacon of patience, accepted the decision of the father as calmly as though the punishment had been meted out to someone else. After forty days in that state, he was restored to his previous rank by the pastor; but scarcely a day later the archdeacon begged to be put back to his former condition of discipline and dishonor, saying, "I committed an unforgivable sin while I was in the city." This was untrue, and the holy superior knew it. The ascetic was looking for punishment for the sake of humility, and his wish was granted. Then came the spectacle of a white-haired elder passing his days as a novice, and sincerely begging everyone to pray for him. "I fell into the fornication of disobedience," he said, but secretly this great Macedonius explained to me, lowly that I am, why he had voluntarily adopted a humbled life of this kind. "I have never felt such absence of conflict within me, such sweetness of divine light, as now," he said. "It is said of angels that they do not, or, as some would

23. January 6.

24. "Deacon" means "servant" in Greek.

have it, that they cannot fall. But men fall, yet they can quickly rise again as often as this may happen to them. Devils, and devils only, never rise once they have fallen."

There was a brother there, the bursar of the monastery, who had this to say to me in confidence: "When I was young and had charge of the animals,[25] I had a very bad spiritual failure, but since it was never my custom to conceal a snake in the hiding place of my heart I grabbed it forthwith by the tail—meaning that I ended the matter—and I revealed it at once to the healer. He gave me a light blow on the chin, smiled, and said to me, 'All right, child, go back to your job and do not be in the slightest way afraid.' With heart on fire I did as I was told, and within a few days I knew I was cured; and so, with a mixture of joy and fear, I carried on."

They say that every creature has differences that mark it off from others. That is how it was in the assembly of the brothers, where differences of success and disposition were to be found. If the healer observed some showing off before visitors to the monastery from the outside world, he used to heap the worst insults on them in the presence of the visitors and used to send them off on the most humiliating jobs, with the result that they would hastily retreat, and the arrival of the secular visitors would turn out to be an opportunity for self-mastery. Thus there was to be seen the extraordinary spectacle of vanity chasing herself out of sight.

The Lord did not want to deprive me of the prayer of one of the holy fathers in the monastery. And so a week before I left He took to Himself a marvelous man called Menas, the second priest of the monastery, a man who for fifty-nine years had lived in the community and had served in every office. Three days after the death of this saintly monk, when we had finished with the customary rites, the place where he lay was suddenly filled with a great fragrance. We were allowed by the superior to open the coffin in which he lay, and when this was done we had sight of what seemed like two streams of myrrh flowing from his venerable feet. The teacher said to all of us: "Look, the sweat of his labors has been offered up as myrrh to God, and has been truly accepted."

The fathers of that place described many of the triumphs of this holy saint Menas. Among them were what follows. On one occasion the superior wanted to test his God-given patience. Coming in the

25. I.e., the beasts of burden belonging to the monastery (cf. 15 [885BC], p. 175).

evening to the abbot's cell he prostrated himself and, in the customary fashion, he asked for his instructions. However, the abbot left him on the ground until the time came for the Office and only then did he give him his blessing. But the holy man, knowing his heroic endurance, criticized him for self-display and impatience. He did it for the edification of everyone.

This story was confirmed by a disciple of the holy Menas. "I wanted to find out if he had fallen asleep while he was prostrate on the ground before the holy abbot. But he assured me that he had recited the entire psalter while lying down."

There is an emerald to adorn the crown of this discourse, and I must not forget to tell of it. For on one occasion I initiated a discussion of stillness among the most experienced elders there. They smiled and in their own cheerful way they spoke to me courteously as follows: "Father John, we are corporeal beings and we lead a corporeal life. Knowing this, we choose to wage war according to the measure of our weakness, and we think it better to struggle with men who sometimes rage and are sometimes contrite than to do battle with demons who are always in a rage and always carrying arms against us."

One of those memorable men showed me great love according to God. He was outspoken, and once, in his own kindly fashion, he said this to me: "Wise man, if you have consciously within you the power of him who said, 'I can do everything in Christ Who strengthens me' (Phil. 4:13), if the Holy Spirit has come upon you as on the Holy Virgin with the dew of purity, if the power of the Most High has cast the shadow of patience over you, then, like Christ our God, gird your loins with the towel of obedience, rise from the supper of stillness, wash the feet of your brethren in a spirit of contrition, and roll yourself under the feet of the brethren with humbled will. Place strict and unsleeping guards at the gateway of your heart. Practice inward stillness amid the twistings and the turbulence of your limbs. And, strangest of all perhaps, keep your soul undisturbed while tumult rages about you.

"Your tongue longs to jump into argument, but restrain it. It is a tyrant, and you must fight it daily seventy times seven. Fix your mind to your soul as to the wood of a cross, strike it with alternating hammer blows like an anvil. It has to be mocked, abused, ridiculed, and wronged, though without in any way being crushed or broken; indeed it must keep calm and unstirred. Shed your will as if it were some disgraceful garment, and having thus stripped yourself of it, go into the practice arena. Put on the breastplate of faith, which is so hard to come by, and let it not be crushed or damaged by distrust of your trainer. Let the rein of temperance curb the shameless onward leap of the sense of touch. With meditation on death bridle those eyes so ready to waste endless hours in the contemplation of physical beauty. Hold back your mind, so busy with its own concerns, so ready to turn to the reckless criticism and condemnation of your brother. Show instead every love and sympathy for your neighbor. Dearest father, all men will come to know that we are disciples of Christ if, as we live together, we have love for one another. Stay here with us, my friend, stay. Drink down ridicule by the hour, as if it were living water. David tried every pleasure under the sun, and at the end was at a loss saying, 'Behold, what is good or what is pleasant?' (Ps. 132:1). And there was nothing except that brothers should live together in unity. But if this blessing of patience and obedience has still not been given to us, then the best thing to do is, having discovered our weakness, to stay away from the athletes' stadium, to bless the contestants, and to pray that it might be granted to them to endure."

Such was the discourse of this good father and excellent teacher, who argued with me in an evangelical and prophetic way, like a friend. And I was persuaded, so that with no hesitation I agreed to give first place to blessed obedience.

When I have noted down a further profitable virtue of these blessed fathers, one that is surely from Paradise, I will come back to my own unlovely and useless briar patch.

The blessed pastor noticed that some continued to talk while the rest of us were standing at prayer. He made them stand in front of the church for a whole week and they had to make a prostration before everyone going in or out. And, what was even more surprising, he did it to people of clerical rank, that is, to priests.

I noticed one brother during the singing of the psalms. He showed more feeling than many of the others, and his movements and expressions were such as to make it look as though he were carrying on a conversation with someone. This was particularly so at the beginning of the hymns. I asked the holy man to explain this to me and because he knew it was to my advantage that he should not be reticent about it, he said this to me: "Father John, it is my custom at the very start to gather my thoughts, my mind and my soul. I call to them and cry out, 'Come! Let us worship and fall down before Christ, our King and God' " (cf. Ps. 94:6).

I also paid special attention to the brother in charge of the refectory. I noticed that he had a small book hanging in his belt, and I learned that every day he noted down his thoughts[26] in it and showed them to the shepherd. I found out that many of the brothers did this also as well as he, and I was told that this was on the instructions of the superior.

The shepherd once expelled a brother for having described a neighbor to him as a gossip and a blatherer. For an entire week the expelled monk remained at the gates of the monastery, begging entry and forgiveness. Now when that lover of souls discovered this, when he heard that the brother had eaten nothing for six days, he said to him: "If you really want to live in the monastery, I will put you down into the ranks of the penitents." The contrite monk gladly agreed, and the shepherd ordered him to be taken to the separate monastery for those who are in mourning for their failures. And so it was done.

But since I have mentioned this monastery I must say a few words about it.

A mile away from the great monastery was a harsh place called the Prison where smoke,[27] or wine, or oil for food or anything else was never seen, only bread and chopped vegetables. Here were shut up without permission to go out those who after entering monastic life had fallen into sin. Nor were they all together. Each had his own cell, or two at most might be together until the Lord gave the superior some assurance regarding each one of them. A great man named Isaac was in charge of them, and he demanded of them that they pray with scarcely an interruption. To ward off despondency they were given great quantities of palm leaves.[28] Such was their existence and rule, such their life-style, these men who truly sought the face of the God of Jacob!

It is a good thing to admire the labors of holy men; to imitate them procures salvation. But it is unreasonable and impossible to wish to imitate, on a sudden whim, every aspect of the way they live.

---

26. These thoughts (*logismoi*) are not simply reflections but inward promptings, some of which may be demonic. The superior would be able to discern which are helpful and which are not.

27. I.e., cooked food.

28. For making baskets and plaiting mats.

When we are bitten by rebukes, let us be mindful of our sins until the Lord, seeing the determination of our efforts, wipes away our sins and turns to joy that sadness eating our hearts. It is written: "Your consolations have gladdened my soul according to the number of my sorrows" (Ps. 93:19), and at the right time we should remember the words spoken to the Lord: "How many troubles and evils have You shown me, and You turned around to revive me. You brought me up from the depths of the earth when I had fallen" (Ps. 70:20).

Blessed is he who, slandered and despised every day for the Lord's sake, still restrains himself. He will be in the chorus of martyrs and will talk familiarly with angels. Blessed is the monk who thinks of himself by the hour as having earned all dishonor and contempt. Blessed is he who mortifies his will to the very end and who leaves the care of himself to his director in the Lord. He will be placed at the right hand of the Crucified. But he who refuses to accept a criticism, just or not, renounces his own salvation, while he who accepts it, hard or not though it may be, will soon have his sins forgiven.

Show God in your heart the faith you have in your spiritual father and the honest love you have for him. God in ways unknown will urge him to be well disposed to you and fond of you, just as you are well disposed toward him.

He who exposes every serpent shows the reality of his faith, while he who hides them still walks the trackless wastes.

A man will know that he truly loves his brother when he weeps for the sins of that brother and is delighted by his progress and by the gifts given to him.

A man should know that a devil's sickness is on him if he is seized by the urge in conversation to assert his opinion, however correct it may be. If he behaves this way while talking to his equals, then a rebuke from his seniors may heal him. But if he carries on in this way with those who are greater and wiser than he, his sickness cannot be cured by human means.

He who is not submissive in his talk will certainly not be so in what he does. To be unfaithful in the small things is to be unfaithful in the great, and this is very hard to bring under control. Such a monk labors in vain, and from holy obedience he will bring nothing but judgment on himself.

Someone with a totally clear conscience in the matter of being obedient to his spiritual father waits each day for death—as though it were sleep, or rather life; and he is unafraid, knowing with certainty that when it is time to go, not he but his spiritual director will be called to render an account.

If someone freely undertakes a task for his spiritual father and falls while doing it, he should blame not the father who gave him the weapon but himself. For it was he who accepted the weapon of battle against the enemy, but has turned it instead against his own heart. But if for the Lord's sake he compelled himself to accept the task, even though he first explained his own weakness to the spiritual father, then let him take heart. He may have fallen, but he is not dead.

One sweet loaf of virtue I have forgotten to set before you, my friends. I saw there servants of the Lord who subjected themselves to insult and contempt for God's sake, so that by this kind of preparation they would not falter beneath the insults coming from others.

Confession is like a bridle that keeps the soul which reflects on it from committing sin, but anything left unconfessed we continue to do without fear as if in the dark.

If we picture for ourselves the face of the superior whenever he happens to be away, if we think of him as always standing nearby, if we avoid every gathering, word, meal, sleep, or indeed anything to which we think he might object, then we have really learned true obedience. False children are glad when the teacher is away, but the genuine think it a loss.

I once asked a very experienced father how humility is achieved through obedience. This was his answer: "A wisely obedient man, even if he is able to raise the dead, to have the gift of tears, to be free from conflict, will nevertheless judge that this happened through the prayer of his spiritual director; and so he remains a stranger and an alien to empty presumption. For how could he take pride in something that, by his reckoning, is due to the effort not of himself but of his director?"

Now, of course, the practice of the above virtue is not something known to the hermit.[29] His conceit attributes his righteous acts to himself, suggesting that his achievements are the result of his own efforts. For the fact is that he who lives in obedience has eluded two snares[30] and remains an obedient servant of Christ for the future.

29. Gk *hesychastis*, one who practices stillness (cf. note 9), whether alone, with one or two others, or in community. The word is translated by "hermit" or "solitary" when the monk is clearly alone; otherwise the term "hesychast" is used.

30. I.e., disobedience and conceit.

The devil goes to battle with those in obedience. Sometimes he defiles them with bodily pollutions and hardheartedness or makes them more restless than usual, sometimes he makes them dry and barren, sluggish at prayer, sleepy and unilluminated. He does this to bring discouragement to their efforts, making them think that their obedience has brought no profit and that they are only regressing. He keeps them from realizing that very often the providential withdrawal of what seem to be our goods is the harbinger of our deepest humility.

That deceiver is often overcome by patient endurance, and yet while he is still talking there is another angel standing by to cheat us a little later in a different fashion.

I have known men living under obedience who, guided by their director, became contrite, meek, self-controlled, zealous, free of turmoil, fervent. Then came the demons. They suggested to them that they were now qualified for the solitary life, that as hermits they would win the ultimate prize of total freedom from passion. Thus fooled, they left harbor and put to sea, and when the storm lowered onto them, their lack of pilots left them pitifully exposed to disaster from this foul and bitter ocean.

This sea has to be stirred up, provoked and made angry so as to jettison onto dry land the wood, the hay, the corruption carried into it by the rivers of passion. Notice what happens in nature. After a storm at sea comes a deep calm.

The man who sometimes obeys his director and sometimes not resembles the person who puts into his eyes now medicine and now quicklime. It is said, "When one man builds and another pulls down, what has been the profit of their labor?" (Ecclus. 34:23).

Son, obedient servant of the Lord, do not be so fooled by the spirit of conceit that you confess your sins to your director as though they were someone else's. Lay bare your wound to the healer. Only through shame can you be freed from shame.[31] Tell him, and do not be ashamed: "This is my wound, Father; this is my injury. It happened because of my negligence and not from any other cause. No one is to blame for this, no man, spirit or body or anything else. It is all through my negligence."

At confession you should look and behave like a condemned man. Keep your head bowed and, if you can, shed tears on the feet of your

31. In HTM's text the sentence later in brackets is inserted here.

judge and healer, as though he were Christ. (Very often demons manage to persuade us either to omit confession, or else to confess as though the sins were committed by someone else or else to blame others as responsible for our own sins.)

Habit forms things and follows them. And it is particularly true that virtue depends on habit, and here God is the great collaborator.

My son, if at the very start you manage to allow your entire soul to suffer indignities, you will not have to struggle for many years in search of blessed peace.

You must not imagine that prostrating yourself in confession to your helper, as if he were God Himself, is in any way wrong. Condemned criminals, by their sorry looks, by earnest confession and pleadings, have softened the harshness of a judge and turned his rage to mercy. I have seen it happen. That is why John the Baptist demanded of those who came to him that they make their confession before baptism, not because he wanted to know their sins, but in order to bring about their salvation.

We ought not be surprised if the attacks continue to come even after confession. In any case, it is better to be battling with our thoughts[32] rather than our self-esteem.

Do not get excited or carried away by the stories concerning hesychasts and hermits. You are marching in the army of the First Martyr, and in the event of a fall you should remain on the practice ground, since then more than ever one needs a healer. He who strikes his foot against a rock while being helped would not only have stumbled unaided, but would have died.

It is when we are brought low that the demons quickly pounce. They suggest what looks like a reasonable pretext—though in fact it is not—to take up the life of solitude. Our enemies hope to wound us when we are committing sin.

When a doctor says he cannot help you, then you must go to another, since few are cured without one. Who, indeed, would disagree if I were to say that a ship wrecked while there was a skilled pilot aboard would quite certainly have been lost if there had been no pilot at all?

Humility arises out of obedience, and from humility itself comes dispassion, for "the Lord remembered us in our humility and saved us from our enemies" (Ps. 135:23–24). So we can rightly say that from

32. Rader's text reads "pollutions" (*molysmois*), not "thoughts" (*logismois*).

obedience comes dispassion, through which the goal of humility is attained. Humility is the beginning of dispassion, as Moses is the beginning of the Law, as the daughter completes the mother and Mary completes the synagogue.

The sick who try out a healer, receive help from him, and then, before being fully cured, jettison him for the sake of another deserve every punishment from God. Do not run from the hands of him who has brought you to the Lord, for never in your life again will you respect anyone as you did him.

It is not safe for an untried soldier to leave the ranks and take up single combat. Equally, it is dangerous for a monk to undertake the solitary life before he has had plenty of experience and practice in the battle with the passions of the soul. The one man jeopardizes his body, the other his soul. Now Scripture says, "Two are better than one" (Eccles. 4:9), meaning that it is better for a son to be with his father as, aided by the divine power of the Holy Spirit, he fights against his predispositions. He who deprives a blind man of his guide, a flock of its shepherd, a lost man of his counselor, a child of its father, a sick man of his doctor, a ship of its pilot, becomes a menace to everyone. And he who tries to fight unaided against the spirits gets himself killed by them.

Those entering a hospital for the first time should indicate where they hurt, and those entering on obedience should show their humility. Relief from pain is the sign of a return to health for the one, while increasing self-criticism is the sign for the other. Indeed, there is no clearer sign.

It is enough that your conscience should be the mirror of your obedience.

Those living in stillness and subject to a father have only demons working against them. But those living in a community have to fight both demons and human beings. The first kind keep the commands of their master more strictly since they are always under his scrutiny, while the latter break them to some extent on account of his being away. Still, the zealous and the hard-working more than compensate for this failing by their persistence, and accordingly they win double crowns.

We ought to be very careful to keep a watch on ourselves. When a harbor is full of ships it is easy for them to run against each other, particularly if they are secretly riddled by the worm of bad temper.

We should practice complete silence and ignorance in the presence of the superior, for a silent man is a son of wisdom and is always gaining great knowledge. I have watched while a monk anticipated the words of his superior, but I trembled for his obedience because I observed that this tendency led him to pride rather than lowliness.

Let us be all vigilance, care, and watchfulness as to when and in what form service should take precedence over prayer. For you cannot do all things all the time.

Watch yourself when you are in the presence of your brothers and under no circumstances should you put yourself forward as being better than they. For if you do, then you will be doubly in the wrong, provoking them with your fake zeal and stirring yourself up to presumption.

Be zealous within your soul, but do not give the slightest sign, word, or hint of it outwardly; and you will manage this as soon as you stop looking down on your neighbor, something you may be inclined to do. And if so, then become like your brethren in order not to differ from them solely by the measure of your conceit.

I once saw an inexperienced disciple who used to boast in certain quarters about the achievement of his teacher. He imagined that in this way he would win glory for himself from another's harvest. But he only got a bad name for himself, for everyone put this question to him: "How then could a good tree grow such a dead branch?"

We do not get the name of being patient when we bravely endure the derision of our father, but only when we endure it from every kind of person. For we put up with our father out of respect and because it is our duty.

Drink deeply of scorn from every man, as though it were living water handed you to cleanse you from lust. Then indeed will a deep purity dawn in your soul and the light of God will not grow dim in your heart.

If someone observes that his brothers are satisfied with him, let him not start boasting to himself. There are thieves all around. Remember the warning: "When you have done all that was laid on you to do, say, 'We are unprofitable servants. We did only what we had to' " (Luke 17:10). We will find out at the time of death what judgment has been passed on us.

A monastery is heaven on earth, so let us tune our hearts like angels serving the Lord. It happens occasionally that those living in this heaven possess hearts of stone. Yet by means of compunction they acquire consolation so that they escape from conceit, and they lighten their labors with their tears.

A small fire can soften a great lump of wax, and a small indignity will often ease, sweeten, and wipe away all the heart's harshness, insensibility and hardness.

I once saw two people sitting out of sight and watching the toils and hearing the groans of the ascetics. One did this so as to be able to imitate them. But the other did it so that when the time came he could laugh at God's laborer and get in the way of his good work.

Do not become silent in an unreasonable way that causes disturbance and hard feeling in others, and do not let your behavior and progress slow down when you have been told to hurry. Otherwise you will be worse than the possessed and the rebellious. I have often seen such things as these, as Job says (cf. Job 13:1), that is, souls burdened sometimes by slowness of character and sometimes by excessive eagerness. I was astounded by the variety of evil.

He who is in the company of others can get more benefit from prayer than from singing the psalms, for the confusion of voices makes the psalms indistinct.

Fight always with your thoughts and call them back when they wander away. God does not demand of those under obedience that their thoughts be totally undistracted when they pray. And do not lose heart when your thoughts are stolen away. Just remain calm, and constantly call your mind back.

Whoever has secretly vowed not to give up the struggle until his very last breath, to endure a thousand deaths of body and soul, will not fall easily into any of these difficulties, for it is inconstancy of heart and unfaithfulness to one's place that bring about stumblings and disasters. Those who readily go from monastery to monastery are totally unfit since nothing is more conducive to barrenness than impatience.

If you come upon a doctor and a hospital hitherto unknown to you, behave like a passerby and quietly examine the expertise of those living there. But if you discover that the doctors and the workers in that place can cure you of your ailments and, especially, of the spiritual pride that weighs you down, then go to them, buy your healing with the gold of humility, and write your terms in letters of service on the parchment of obedience, and let the angels be your witnesses as you tear up before them the book of your willfulness.

If you wander from place to place, you fritter away the gold with which Christ ransomed you. So let the monastery be for you a tomb before the tomb. No one can come out of the tomb before the general resurrection, and if there be monks who have gone out, then they are really dead. Let us beg the Lord not to let this happen to us.

When the more lazy find orders heavy, they decide that prayer is better for them. But when they are given something easy to do they run from prayer as if from a conflagration.

Imagine a particular task. Some leave it aside for the sake of a brother's peace of mind, some leave it because they are lazy; but then some stay with it out of vainglory and some stay with it out of zeal.

If, having bound yourself to certain obligations, you become aware of the fact that your soul's eye has made no progress, do not seek permission to quit. The authentic monk will persevere anywhere and the converse is also true.

In the world, slander has caused many a breakup, but in monastic communities it is gluttony that brings about all the falls and transgressions. Keep mistress gluttony under control and every abode will then give you dispassion, but let her take hold of you and every place outside the grave will be a menace to you.

The Lord, who makes wise the blind (cf. Ps. 145:8), opens the eyes of the obedient to the virtues of their spiritual director and blinds them to his faults, but does the opposite to the hater of what is good.

Let what we call quicksilver be a paradigm of perfect obedience. Roll it with any substance you wish, and it will nevertheless run to the lowest place and mix with nothing defiled.

The zealous should be especially careful not to condemn the easygoing in case they draw down a worse sentence on themselves. That, I think, was why Lot was justified. Despite the sort of people he lived with, he never seems to have condemned them.

On every occasion, but especially during the singing of hymns, we should be still and undistracted, for it is by means of distractions that devils try to make our prayers useless.

A servant of the Lord[33] stands bodily before men, but mentally he is knocking at the gates of heaven with prayer.

Insults, belittlings, and such like have the bitterness of wormwood for the soul of the novice; praise, honor, approval, are like hon-

33. I.e., a deacon in church (cf. note 24, p. 101).

ey and give birth to every kind of sweetness in pleasure lovers. But we should remember the nature of each of them. Wormwood purifies all internal filth, while honey increases gall.

Regarding those who have undertaken to care for us in the Lord, we should trust them completely, even when they order us to do something that looks like being contrary to our salvation. That is the time when our faith in them is tested as in a furnace of humiliation, and the sign of the most genuine faith is when we obey our superiors without hesitation, even when we see the opposite happening to what we had hoped.

From obedience comes humility, as we have already said. And from humility comes discernment. That is what the great Cassian has said in that marvelously philosophic and sublime chapter of his on discernment.[34] From discernment comes insight, and from insight comes foresight. And who would not run this fine race of obedience when such blessings are there ahead of him? The good psalmist had this great virtue in mind when he said: "O God, in Your goodness You have made ready Your presence in the heart of the poor obedient soul" (Ps. 67:10).

As long as you live, remember that great athlete who for eighteen whole years never heard with his outward ears his superior say to him, "May you be saved." Yet within him each day he heard from the Lord not just, "May you be saved," an uncertain wish, but, "You are saved," definite and sure.[34a]

There are some living in obedience who, on noticing the kindness and indulgence of their superior, seek his permission to follow their own wishes. They ought to know that if they get this, they deprive themselves completely of their confessor's crown. Obedience is foreign to hypocrisy and willfulness.

A monk was given an order once. He saw that the intention behind it was that no pleasure would come to him through having carried it out. So he asked to be excused. Another monk understood the intention but obeyed at once. The question is: Which of them acted more piously?

The devil cannot act contrary to his own will. Those living a negligent life, whether alone or in community, should convince you

34. John Cassian, *Second Conference*, ch. 10.

34a. John the Theban: *The Sayings of the Desert Fathers*, John the Theban.

of this. And if there is a temptation on us to move from a place, let that be proof that our life there is pleasing to God. War against us is proof that we are making war.

Now I will not be silent about something that should not be kept quiet. It would be against my fellowman to keep to myself what people should know.

The renowned John the Sabbaite[35] told me things well worth hearing. He was detached and was uncontaminated by any falsehood, evil word, or bad deed, as you yourself know, holy father, from personal experience.

This is what he told me: "In my monastery in Asia (this good man came from there), there was a certain elder who was extremely careless and undisciplined. I say this not to pass judgment on him, but merely to state the truth. He acquired a disciple—I could not say how—a young man called Acacius, good-hearted and sensible, who put up with so much from this elder that many will hardly believe it. He was tormented daily, not only with insults and indignities, but even with blows; and yet he accepted it, though not blindly. I would see him every day, and his condition was very bad, like that of the lowest slave. I often spoke to him when I met him. 'What is it, Brother Acacius? How is it with you today?' He would show me a black eye, or a bruised neck or head. Knowing that he was a worker, I used to say to him, 'Well done, well done. Put up with it, and it will be for your own good.' So for nine years he endured this pitiless elder, and then departed to the Lord. Five days after he had been buried in the cemetery of the fathers, Acacius's master went to a certain great elder living there, and said to him: 'Father, Brother Acacius is dead.' The old man answered: 'Elder, I assure you I do not believe it!' 'Come and see,' the other said. The elder immediately rose up and went to the cemetery with the master of the blessed ascetic. And he called to him who in death was truly alive, and he spoke to him as to a living being: 'Are you dead, Brother Acacius?' And this most obedient man, obedient even in death, answered the great elder: 'How could someone truly obedient die, Father?' The elder who had been Acacius's master

35. John, formerly of the monastery of St. Sabbas in Palestine, is an elder known to us from the narratives of Anastasius of Mount Sinai (see F. Nau, "Le texte grec des récits du moine Anastase sur les saints Pères du Sinai", *Oriens Christianus* ii [1902] pp. 58–89, §§ 6 and 34).

grew terrified and fell on his face weeping. Later he asked the abbot of the Laura[36] for a cell near the tomb. He lived devoutly there, and to the fathers he used to say: 'I have committed murder.' " And, Father John, I think that the one who spoke to the dead man was the great John himself. For that blessed soul told me another story as though about someone else, when in fact it was about himself, as I learned afterwards for sure.

"In the same monastery in Asia," said John, "there was someone who became a disciple of a monk who was very meek, gentle, and peaceable. When he realized that the elder respected him and cared for him, he decided, quite rightly, that this was something that could harm many. So he asked the elder to send him away, and this would cause no inconvenience since the elder had another disciple. He went away, therefore, and a letter from the elder got him into a monastery in Pontus. On his first night there he dreamed that his account was being made up, and after he had settled that dreadful reckoning he was still in debt to the extent of one hundred pounds of gold. He thought about this dream after he had awakened and said, 'Poor Antiochus (for this was his name), you certainly are very far short of your debt.'

" 'And,' he continued, 'after living for three years in total obedience in this monastery, despised by everyone, insulted as a foreigner, for there was no other foreign monk there, then again I had a dream in which someone gave me a note crediting me with ten pounds of my debt. When I woke up I thought about my dream and said: "Only ten! When will I ever pay the rest?" After that I said, "Poor Antiochus! Still more hard work and dishonor for you!" Thereafter I pretended to be a fool,[37] though without neglecting anything of my service of everyone. When those pitiless fathers saw that I willingly served in the same status, they loaded all the heavy work of the monastery onto me. I spent thirteen years this way, and then in a dream I saw those who had appeared to me before, and they gave me a receipt to mark full payment of my debt. When, therefore, the monks imposed in any way on me, I remembered my debt and took heart.' "

---

36. A laura is technically a loose community of hermits whose cells open onto an alleyway. This laura, however, is under an abbot (*higoumenos*) and is referred to in the next paragraph as a cenobium.

37. Gk *exichon*. Not the technical word for someone who pretended to be a fool as an ascetic discipline (*salos*), but clearly in the same tradition (cf. Palladius, *The Lausiac History*, ch. 34).

So, Father John, the wise John said all this to me as if about someone else. That was why he changed his name to Antiochus.[38] But in fact it was he who cancelled the bond courageously by his patience (cf. Col. 2:14).

Let us hear what a gift of discernment this holy man obtained through his perfect obedience. While he was living in the monastery of Saint Sabbas, three young monks came to him wishing to be his disciples. He received them gladly and gave them generous hospitality, for he wanted to refresh them after their long journey. After three days he said to them: "Brothers, I am very inclined to fornication, and I cannot receive any of you as disciples." But they were not scandalized, for they knew the good work of the old man. Yet for all that they begged him, they still could not make him change his mind. Then, prostrating themselves before him, they begged him at least to provide them with a rule by which they might know how and where to live. He gave in to their pleas and, understanding well that they would accept a rule from him in all humility and obedience, he said to one of them: "My son, the Lord wants you to live in a solitary place under the guidance of a spiritual director." To the second he had this to say: "Go, sell off your will, hand it over to God, take up your cross, and persevere in a community and monastery of brothers. Then you will surely have treasure in heaven." To the third he said: "Draw in inseparably with your breathing the phrase which says, 'He who perseveres to the end will be saved' (Matt. 10:22).[39] Go now and find, if you can, the harshest and strictest trainer in the Lord, and persevering daily imbibe insult and scorn as if they were milk and honey." Then the brother said to the great John: "But if the trainer is somehow lax, what then?" This is what the elder replied: "Even if you see him fornicating, do not go away from him. Just say to yourself, 'Why are you here, friend?' (Matt. 26:50). Then you will see all pride abandon you and lust dry up."

Those of us who wish to fear the Lord should strive mightily to avoid picking up, in the school of virtue, malice and wrongdoing, cunning and craftiness, curiosity and anger. It can happen, nor is it surprising. When a man is just a private citizen, a sailor, a laborer on the land, the enemies of the King do not take up arms against him.

38. With a pun on *anti-ocheo*, "to bear adversities."

39. An early instance of linking prayer with breathing, but not yet cultivated as a technique.

But when they see him accept the King's seal,[40] the shield, the dagger, the sword, the bow, the uniform of a soldier, then they gnash their teeth and do all they can to destroy him. So let us not be caught napping.

I have seen innocent lovely children come to school for wisdom, education, and profit, and learn only cunning and vice through the contact they make with other students. The wise man will understand what I am saying.

Those striving completely to learn a craft make daily progress. It has to be so. But some know how they are progressing. Others, by divine providence, do not know. Now a good banker never lets an evening pass without his reckoning profit and loss. However, he can have no clear picture of this unless he makes hourly entries in his record books. For it is the hourly account that yields the daily account.

A silly person feels hurt when accused or shouted at. He tries to answer back or else at once apologizes to his accuser, not for reasons of humility but to put a stop to his reproaches. In fact you should be silent when ridiculed. Accept patiently these spiritual cauterizations, or rather, purifying flames. And when the doctor has done his work, ask him to forgive you, for he may not accept your apology when he is angry.

Those of us who live in community must fight by the hour against all the passions and especially against these two: a mania for gluttony and bad temper. There is plenty of food for these passions in a community.

The devil proposes impossible virtues to those who live under obedience, and unsuitable ideas to those living in solitude. If you look at the thinking of inexperienced novices living under obedience, you will find ideas out of step with one another—desire for stillness, for extreme fasting, for unbroken prayer, for total freedom from vanity, for continual remembrance of death, for unceasing compunction, for absolute release from anger, for deep silence, for outstanding purity. And should they happen by divine providence to be without these at the start, they rush vainly toward a different life because they have been deceived. The enemy persuades them to look too soon for these

40. Soldiers were branded or tattooed. The "seal" (*sphragida*) also alludes to the seal of baptism; cf. John Chrysostom, *Hom. 3, 7 in II Cor. (PG* 61, 418), where the comparison is made explicit.

virtues, so that they may not persevere and attain them in due time. And to those living in solitude, the deceiver heaps praise on the hospitality of those living under obedience, on their service, their brotherly love, their community living, their visits to the sick. What the devil is trying to do is to make both restless.

Very few are able to live in solitude. This is really so. Indeed only those can do so whose labors have been encouraged by God and whose struggles have received His help.

We should analyze the nature of our passions and of our obedience, so as to choose our director accordingly. If lust is your problem, do not pick for your trainer a worker of miracles who has a welcome and a meal for everyone. Choose instead an ascetic who will reject any of the consolation of food. If you are arrogant, let him be tough and unyielding, not gentle and accommodating. We should not be on the lookout for those gifted with foreknowledge and foresight, but rather for those who are truly humble and whose character and dwelling place match our weaknesses. And remember the example of the righteous Abbacyrus, mentioned above. Adopt the fine habit, so conducive to obedience, of always assuming that the superior is testing you, and you will not be far wrong. If you are constantly upbraided by your director and thus acquire great faith in him and love for him, then you may be sure that the Holy Spirit has taken up residence invisibly in your soul and the power of the Most High has overshadowed you. But you must not boast or celebrate when you manage to be brave under insults and indignities. Rather should you mourn for having earned criticism and for having stirred your director to anger against you. And what I am going to say to you now must not shock you. (In any case I have the support of Moses in this.) It is better to sin against God than against our father. If we make God angry, our director can reconcile Him to us. But if he is angry, then there is no one to speak up for us before God. And in any case, the two situations are really the same. Or so it seems to me.

Let us be vigilant and very carefully and prudently decide when we should gladly and silently endure accusations made against us to our pastor, and when we ought to speak up for ourselves to him. I think we should always be silent when some indignity is offered to us, since we can profit from that. But where another person is involved we should make a defense so as to keep unbroken the bond of love and peace.

Those who have broken away from obedience will insist on its value, for only then have they fully understood the heaven in which they were living.

He who strives for dispassion and for God considers lost any day on which he was not criticized. Like trees swayed by the wind and driving their roots deeper into the ground, those who live in obedience become strong and unshakable souls.

When a monk living in solitude has realized what his weak point is, and when he changes place and sells himself to obedience, then, blind as he was once, he recovers sight and can see Christ without difficulty.

So then, keep running, brother athletes, and again I say to you, keep running. Listen to the cry of wisdom: "The Lord has tried them like gold in a furnace," or, rather, in a community, "and he has received them as burnt offerings into his bosom" (Wisd. 3:6). Glory and eternal dominion are His, in company with the eternal Father and the holy and adorable Spirit. Amen.

This step is of equal number with the evangelists. Keep running, athlete, and do not be afraid.

Step 5

ON PENITENCE

Once John outran Peter, and now obedience is placed before repentance. For the one who arrived first represents obedience, the other repentance.[41]

Repentance is the renewal of baptism and is a contract with God for a fresh start in life. Repentance goes shopping for humility and is ever distrustful of bodily comfort. Repentance is critical awareness and a sure watch over oneself. Repentance is the daughter of hope and the refusal to despair. (The penitent stands guilty—but undisgraced.) Repentance is reconciliation with the Lord by the performance of good deeds which are the opposites of the sins. It is the purification of conscience and the voluntary endurance of affliction. The penitent deals out his own punishment, for repentance is the fierce persecution of the stomach and the flogging of the soul into intense awareness.

Come, gather round, listen here and I will speak to all of you who have angered the Lord. Crowd around me and see what he has revealed to my soul for your edification.

Let us give first place to the story of the dishonored workers—who still earned respect. Let us listen, take heed, and act—we who may have suffered an unexpected fall. Rise up and be seated, all you

41. In Rader's text this sentence is attached to the end of Step 4.

who have been laid low by your sins. Hear what I have to say, my brothers. Listen, all you who long to be reconciled with God again in a true conversion.

I, the weakling, heard that there was a great and strange way of life and lowliness for those living in a separate monastery called "The Prison." It was under the authority of that man, that light of lights, referred to above, and during my visit I asked the good man to let me see it. This great man, who wished never to cause grief to any soul, gave his permission.

I went therefore to that abode of penitents, to that place of true grief, and if I may be so bold as to say so, I actually saw what the eye of an inattentive man never saw, what the ear of a lackadaisical man never heard, what never entered the heart of a sluggard (cf. I Cor. 2:9). I saw things done and said that could only draw down the mercy of God, deeds and attitudes of body that quickly win His love for men.

I saw some of those accused yet innocent men stand all night until dawn in the open air, their feet never moving, pitifully pounded by the natural urge to sleep, giving themselves no rest, reproaching themselves, driving sleep away with abuse and insults.

Others raised their eyes to heaven, wept, cried, and implored help from there.

Others prayed with their hands tied behind their backs, like criminals, their faces blackened with grief and bent earthward, since they thought themselves unworthy to look up to heaven. Overcome by their reflections and the weight of conscience, they could not speak, could not pray to God, could not even make a beginning of prayer; and filled, as it seemed, with darkness and empty despair, they could offer God only a blank soul and a wordless mind.

Others sat in sackcloth and ashes on the ground, hiding their faces between their knees, striking the earth with their foreheads.

Others constantly beat their breasts, recalling their past lives and the condition of their souls. Some shed their tears on the ground, while others, unable to weep, struck themselves. Some raised over their own souls a lament for the dead, since the strength to bear their heart's grief had left them. Others moaned inwardly, stifling the sounds of their wailing until, unable to bear it any longer, they would suddenly cry out.

I saw men who in look and disposition seemed out of their minds, made dumb by the complete darkness of their despair, insensible to the life around them, their minds sunk in the depths of humility, their eyes' tears dried up in the fire of despondency.

Others sat in deep thought with gaze rooted to the earth. Their heads were moving constantly. Like lions they roared and moaned from their innermost depths. Some were full of hope as they begged complete forgiveness, while others, out of extreme humility, condemned themselves as being unworthy to be forgiven and wailed that it was not in their power to justify themselves before God. Some implored the Lord to punish them here and to show mercy in the next life. Others, weighed down by the burden of conscience, would say in all sincerity, "We are unworthy of heaven, but to be spared from future punishment will satisfy us."

I saw there humble and contrite souls who were saddened by the weight of their burden. The stones themselves would have been moved to pity by their voices and by their cries to God. Looking down to the ground, they would say this: "We know, we know that we deserve every punishment and every torment. Rightly so. How could we make up for all that we owe, even if we had the entire world there to weep for us? All we ask, all we pray for, all we implore is that 'in Your anger You do not rebuke us or chasten us in Your wrath' (Ps. 6:2). Be sparing. It is enough for us if You deliver us from Your great threat and from unknown and hidden torments. We dare not ask for complete forgiveness. How could we, when we have failed to keep our vow unstained, but after all Your past loving kindness and forgiveness have defiled it?"

The words of David could surely be seen to be fulfilled there, for there were men in hardship and bowed down to the end of their lives, going about each day in sadness, their bodies' wounds stinking of rottenness (Ps. 37:6–7) and yet unnoticed by them. They forgot to eat their bread; their drink was mixed with tears. They ate dust and ashes instead of bread; their bones stuck to their flesh and they were dried up like grass (Ps. 101:4–12). The only words you could hear from them were these: "Woe, woe, alas, alas! It is just, it is just. Spare us, spare us, O Lord." Some said, "Be merciful, be merciful"; others, more sadly: "Forgive us, Lord, forgive us if it is possible."

You could see the tongues on some of them dry and hanging from their mouths in the manner of dogs. Some punished themselves in the blazing sun, others tortured themselves in the cold, while others, again, drank only as much water as would keep them from dying of thirst. Some munched on a bit of bread, flung away what was left of it and proclaimed themselves unworthy to be fed like human beings since they had behaved like animals.

Would you witness any laughter among them? Idle talk? Irritation? Anger? No, indeed. They no longer knew what it was for a man to be angry, for grief had done away with their capacity for rage.

Where was quarreling among them? Or merrymaking? Or bold speech? Or concern for the body? Where among them was any trace of vanity, or longing for comfort, or the thought of wine, or the taste of fresh fruit, or the enjoyment of cooked food, or the pleasing of the palate? The fact was that even the hope of such things in this world had been extinguished in them.

Did any of them worry about earthly things? Or pass judgment on anyone? Certainly not.

These were the shouts and cries they raised to the Lord without ceasing. Striking their breasts, as though standing before the gates of heaven, some would say to God: "Open up to us, O Judge! Open up! We have shut ourselves out with our sins. Open up to us!" Others would say, "Just show the light of Your face and we will be saved" (Ps. 79:4). Another would say: "Give light to those sitting humbly in darkness and in the shadow of death" (Luke 1:79). Another would say, "Ah, Lord, let Your mercy go speeding before us (Ps. 78:8) for we have perished in despair and have fallen completely away." Some said: "Will the Lord ever again show the light of His face to us?" (Ps. 66:2) and others, "Will our souls survive the unbearable debt?" (Ps. 123:5), while yet others said, "Will the Lord be moved at last to have mercy on us? (Judges 2:18). Will we ever hear him say to those of us in endless bondage, 'Come forth' (Isa. 49:9) and to those of us in the hell of penance, 'Be forgiven'? Has our cry come to the ears of the Lord?"

All of them sat ceaselessly contemplating death, saying, "How will it go for us? What will be the verdict on us? How will life end for us? Will we receive pardon? Will there be forgiveness for those in darkness, for the lowly, for the convicted? Is our prayer vigorous enough to come before the face of the Lord, or has it been rejected—and rightly so—for being worthless and shameful? Or, if it came as far as the Lord, how much could it sway Him? Would it be successful? Powerful? Profitable? Effective? Coming as it does from unclean lips and bodies, it does not have much power. Would our prayer reconcile us completely with the Judge or only in part, only to the extent of half our wounds, which are very great and require much sweat and hard work? Are the guardian angels standing by us, or are they still at a great distance? For until they come close to us, our efforts are vain and futile. Our prayer has neither the power of access nor the wings of purity to reach the Lord, unless our angels draw near to us and take it and bring it to the Lord."

With failing confidence, they would often speak to one another as follows: "Brothers, are we getting anywhere? Will we be granted what we ask? Will the Lord accept us once more? Will He open up to us?" Others would answer: "As our brothers the Ninevites said, Who knows if God will change His mind (Jon. 3:9) and deliver us from mighty punishment? Let us do what we can. If He opens the door, well and good; if not, then blessed be the Lord God Who in His justice has shut the door on us. At least we should continue to knock at the door as long as we live. Maybe He will open to us on account of our persistence." And so they encouraged one another, saying, "We must run, brothers, we must run. We have to run very hard because we have fallen behind our holy company. So let us run, driving on this foul and wicked flesh of ours, killing it as it has killed us."

And that precisely is what these holy men who had been called to account were doing. With knees like wood, as a result of all the prostrations, with eyes dimmed and sunken, with hair gone and cheeks wasted and scalded by many hot tears, with faces pale and worn, they were no different from corpses. Their breasts were livid from all the beatings, which had even made them spit blood. There was no rest for them in beds, no clean and laundered clothing. They were bedraggled, dirty, and verminous. Compared with this, what are the sufferings of the possessed, of those mourning the dead, of the exiled, or of those condemned for murder? These are suffering involuntary torture and punishment. But this is nothing in comparison with sufferings deliberately sought.

Believe me, brothers, I am not making all this up.

Often they came to the great judge, to that angel among men—I mean the shepherd—and they would plead with him to put irons and chains on their hands and necks, to bind their legs in the stocks and not to release them until death—or even afterwards.[42]

I will certainly not pass over the marvelous humility of these

42. The body of a monk named Sarapion has been discovered in Egypt wearing a collar, belt, bracelets and anklets of iron (Palladius, *The Lausiac History*, ed. Butler, vol. ii, p. 215, note 69). Such practices, however, were unusual in Egypt, although common in early Syrian monasticism.

holy men, their contrite love for God, and their penance. When one of these good citizens of the land of repentance was about to die and to stand before the impartial Judge, when he saw that his end was near, he would implore the man in charge of them with oaths to intercede with the abbot on his behalf and to beg that he be denied human burial, but that he be flung into a river bed, like some dumb animal, or thrown to the wild beasts in the field. And often the abbot, that great discerning light, would give instructions that the dead be carried away without the singing of psalms or without any sort of respect shown.

The last hour of one of these was fearful to behold. When the penitents in the prison learned that one of their number was finishing his course and going on ahead of them, they would gather round while his mind was still working. Thirsty, tearful, and sad, they would look at him compassionately, shaking their heads, racked with tenderness, and they would speak to the dying man: "Brother and fellow penitent, how is it with you? What will you say? What are your hopes and expectations? Have you achieved what you worked for so hard, or have you not? Has the door been opened to you, or are you still under sentence? Did you reach your goal, or did you fail? Has any kind of assurance come to you, or are you still uncertain in your hopes? Are you free at last, or does darkness and doubt still hang over your thoughts? Have you sensed any illumination in your heart, or is it still in darkness and dishonor? Did you hear an inner voice saying, 'You are made whole' (John 5:14) or 'Your sins are forgiven you' (Matt. 9:2) or 'Your faith has saved you' (Mark 5:34)? Or did a voice say, 'Let sinners be cast into hell' (Ps. 9:18); 'Bind him hand and foot, and throw him into the darkness outside' (Matt. 22:13); 'Let the wicked man be expelled so that he may not see the glory of the Lord' (Isa. 26:10)? Can you say anything to us, brother? Please tell us, so that we may know how it will be for us. Your time is over and you will never have another chance." Some of the dying would answer: "Blessed be God Who has not turned away my prayer nor His mercy from me" (Ps. 65:20). Others would say, "Blessed be the Lord Who has not given us a prey to their teeth" (Ps. 123:6). But others would be sad and say: "Will our soul pass through the impassable water of the spirits of the air?" (Ps. 123:5). These would be unsure, and would be worried about the rendering of accounts after death. And more sadly yet, others would say: "Woe to the soul that has not kept its vow unblemished! In this hour, and in this one only, it will discover what is prepared for it."

I came close to despair when I had seen and heard all this among them and when I had compared my own indifference with what they went through. What a dreadful place they lived in! It was dark, stinking, filthy, and squalid. To call it a prison or house of convicts was an accurate description. Just the sight of it would teach you penitence and mourning.

Yet what for some is hard and unbearable is easy and tolerable for those who have fallen away from virtue and spiritual treasures. A soul that has lost its one-time confidence and abandoned its hope of dispassion, that has broken the seal of chastity, that has squandered the treasury of divine graces, that has become a stranger to divine consolation, that has rejected the Lord's command, that has extinguished the beautiful fire of spiritual tears[43]—and that is wounded and pierced by sorrow as it remembers all this—will not only take on the labors mentioned above with all eagerness, but will even decide devoutly to kill itself with penitential works. It will do so if there is in it only the tiniest spark of love or of fear of the Lord. And of such a kind were these blessed men. Remembering all this, thinking of the heights of virtue from which they had fallen, they would say: "We remember the old days (Ps. 142:5) and that fire of our zeal." Some would cry to God, "Where are Your old mercies, Lord, which in Your truth You would reveal to our souls? Remember the reproach and the hardship of Your servants" (Ps. 88:50–51). Another would say: "Ah, I wish I were back as I used to be in the months of the days when God watched over me, when the lamp of His light shone over the head of my heart" (Job 29:2–3).

They would think of their former achievements and, weeping for them as though they were children that had died, they would say: "Where is the purity of my prayer? The confidence that was in it? Where are the sweet tears, instead of these bitter ones? Where is that hope of perfect chastity and purification? Where is that expectation of blessed dispassion? Where is my faith in the shepherd? Where is the result of his prayer for us? It is all lost and gone, as though it had never appeared. It has vanished as though it had never been there."

Some prayed to be possessed by devils, others that they might be-

43. Some MSS omit "spiritual."

come epileptics. Some wished for blindness so that they might be a pitiful spectacle, others sought paralysis so that they might not have to suffer later. And I, my friends, was so pleased by their grief that I was carried away, enraptured, unable to contain myself. But I must return to my discourse.

For all that I am impatient by nature, I stayed thirty days in that prison before returning to the main monastery and to its great shepherd. He noticed that I was very much changed and that I had yet to recover my former self. He understood what the change meant, for he was a very wise man. "So, Father John," he said, "you saw how these men were struggling?"

"I saw them, Father, and I was amazed," I replied. "It seems to me that those who have fallen and are penitent are more blessed than those who have never fallen and who do not have to mourn over themselves, because through having fallen, they have pulled themselves up by a sure resurrection."

"That is how it is," he said, and he told me this true story: "I had a brother here about ten years ago, and he was very active and enthusiastic. When I saw how zealous he was, I really trembled for him in case the devil, in envy, should trip his foot against an obstacle as he sped along—something that can happen to those in a hurry. And in fact it happened that way. One evening, late, he came to me, showed me an open wound, looked for a dressing, requested cauterization, and was in a very alarmed state. The physician did not wish to make too deep an incision, for the man deserved sympathy. But when the brother saw this, he flung himself on the ground, clasped my feet, moistened them with copious tears, and asked to be shut up in the prison you have seen. 'It is impossible for me to avoid going there,' he cried, and—something most unusual among the sick—he pleaded with the physician to change his kindness to harshness, and he hurried off to become a companion and fellow sufferer among the penitents. The grief that comes from loving God pierced his heart like a sword, and on the eighth day he died, having asked not to be given burial. But I brought him here and had him buried among the fathers, as he had deserved, because after his week of slavery he had been freed on the eighth day. And let me tell you that someone surely knows that he did not rise up from my foul and wretched feet before he had won God's favor. It is not to be wondered at, for having received in his heart the faith of the gospel harlot, he moistened my humble feet with the same trust. Everything is possible for the believer, said the Lord (cf. Mark 9:23). I have watched impure souls mad for physical love but turning what they know of such love into a reason for penance and transferring that same capacity for love to the Lord. I have watched them master fear so as to drive themselves unsparingly toward the love of God. That is why, when talking of that chaste harlot, the Lord does not say, 'because she feared,' but rather, 'because she loved much' she was able to drive out love with love" (Luke 7:47).

Now I know well, my friends, that these labors I have described will seem unbelievable to some, unattainable to others, and be a source of despair to others still. Yet they will actually be an incentive to a brave soul, a fiery blast, so that he will go away with zeal in his heart, whereas the man who feels a great incapacity in himself will understand his own weakness, be humbled easily by the reproach he levels against himself, and will at least try to follow the soul who is brave. And I am not at all sure but that he may even overtake him. But the careless man had better stay away from my stories, for otherwise he may fall into despair, throw away the little he has achieved, and prove to be like the man of whom it was said: "From the man who has no eagerness, even that which he seems to have will be taken away" (cf. Matt. 25:29). It is impossible for those of us who have fallen into the sink of iniquity ever to be drawn out of it unless we also plumb the depths of the humility shown by the penitent.

The sad humility of penitents is one thing. The reproach of conscience of those who are still sinners is another. The blessed treasure of humility that, with God's help, the perfect manage to attain is yet another. And we should be in no hurry to find words adequate to this third kind of humility, for our effort will be useless. But a sign of the second kind is the perfect bearing of indignity.

An old habit often dominates even someone who mourns. No wonder, for the judgments visited by God and our own lapses make up a list hard to understand, and it is impossible to be sure which of our failings are due to carelessness, which are due to the fact that God permitted them, and which arise from God's having turned away from us. I have been told, however, that lapses occurring as a result of divine providence cause us to repent swiftly, since He Who delivers us does not permit us to be held captive for long. But above all we must fight off the demon of dejection whenever we happen to slip, for he comes right beside us when we are praying and reminds us of our former good standing with God and tries to divert us from our prayer.

Do not be surprised if you fall every day and do not surrender. Stand your ground bravely. And you may be sure that your guardian angel will respect your endurance. A fresh, warm wound is easier to heal than those that are old, neglected, and festering, and that need extensive treatment, surgery, bandaging, and cauterization. Long neglect can render many of them incurable. However, all things are possible with God (Matt. 19:26).

God is merciful before a fall, inexorable after—so the demons say. And when you have sinned, pay no attention to him who says in regard to minor failings: "If only you had not committed that major fault! This is nothing by comparison." The truth is that very often small gifts soften the great anger of the Judge.

He who really keeps track of what he has done will consider as lost every day during which he did not mourn, regardless of whatever good he may happen to have done.

Let no one who grieves for his sins expect reassurance at the hour of death. There can be no assurance about the unknown. "Spare me before I depart from here, unsure of my salvation" (Ps. 38:14).

Where the Spirit of the Lord is, there the chains of sin are let loose; where there is real humility, all bonds are made free; but those without the one or the other should not be deceived: they are in bondage. Those living in the world, and they alone, are without these two assurances, especially the first, unless, through almsgiving, some so run their race that they know at the moment of death how much they have gained.

He who weeps for himself will not be wrapped up in the grief, lapse, or reproach of someone else. A dog injured by a wild animal becomes all the more maddened against it and is driven to implacable rage by the pain of the injury.

We ought to be on our guard, in case our conscience has stopped troubling us, not so much because of its being clear but because of its being immersed in sin.

A proof of our having been delivered from our failings is the unceasing acknowledgement of our indebtedness.

Nothing equals the mercy of God or surpasses it. To despair is therefore to inflict death on oneself.

A sign of true repentance is the admission that all our troubles, and more besides, whether visible or not, were richly deserved.

After Moses had seen God in the bush, he went back to Egypt, that is, to the darkness and the brick making of Pharaoh, who is to be understood here in a spiritual sense. But he returned to the bush. And not only to the bush, but to the mountaintop. For anyone who has experienced contemplation will never despair of himself. The great Job became a beggar, but afterwards he became twice as rich.

If you have no courage, if you are lazy, then lapses that occur after entering religious life are hard to bear. They wipe out the hope of dispassion and they make us imagine that true blessedness is simply to rise from the pit of sin. But note well that we never return by the road on which we strayed, but rather by a different and a shorter route.

I saw two men traveling the same route to the Lord, and at the same time. One of them was older, and had worked harder. The other, his disciple, soon overtook him and was first to arrive at the sepulchre of humility.

All of us—but especially the lapsed—should be especially careful not to be afflicted with the disease of the godless Origen.[44] This foul disease uses God's love for man as an excuse and is very welcome to those who are lovers of pleasure.

In my meditation, or more accurately, in my acts of repentance, a fire of prayer will burn and will consume everything material. Let the holy prisoners, described above, be a rule for you, a pattern, a model, a true picture of repentance, so that for as long as you live you will have no need of a treatise; until at last Christ, the divine Son of God, will enlighten you in the resurrection of true repentance. Amen.

Through repentance you have reached the fifth step. You have, in this way, purified the five senses, and by choosing to accept punishment have thereby avoided the punishment that is involuntary.

44. I.e., that all would finally be saved. The teaching of Origen (*c.* 185–*c.* 254) on universal salvation was condemned at the Fifth Ecumenical Council (553).

Step 6

ON REMEMBRANCE OF DEATH

As thought comes before speech, so the remembrance of death and of sin comes before weeping and mourning. It is therefore appropriate to deal now with this theme.

To be reminded of death each day is to die each day; to remember one's departure from life is to provoke tears by the hour. Fear of death is a property of nature due to disobedience, but terror of death is a sign of unrepented sins. Christ is frightened of dying but not terrified, thereby clearly revealing the properties of His two natures.

Just as bread is the most necessary of all foods, so the thought of death is the most essential of all works. The remembrance of death brings labors and meditations, or rather, the sweetness of dishonor to those living in community, whereas for those living away from turbulence it produces freedom from daily worries and breeds constant prayer and guarding of the mind, virtues that are the cause and the effect of the thought of death.

Tin has a way of looking like silver but is of course quite distinct; and for those with some discernment, the difference between natural and contranatural fear of death is most obvious. You can clearly single out those who hold the thought of death at the center of their being, for they freely withdraw from everything created and they renounce their own will.

The man who lives daily with the thought of death is to be admired, and the man who gives himself to it by the hour is surely a saint. And yet not every desire for death is good. A habitual sinner prays humbly for death, but the man who does not want to change his ways may, in sheer despair, actually long for death. And there are some who out of conceit consider themselves to be dispassionate, and for a while they have no fear of death, while a rare few hunger to leave by the inspiration of the Holy Spirit.

Some, because they are puzzled, ask the following question: "If the remembrance of death is so good for us, why has God concealed from us the knowledge of when we will die?" In putting such a question, they fail to realize how marvelously God operates to save us. No one who knew in advance the hour of his death would accept baptism or join a monastery long before it, but instead would pass all his time in sin and would be baptized and do penance only on the day of his demise. Habit would make him a confirmed and quite incorrigible sinner.[44a]

When you are lamenting your sins, do not ever admit that cur which suggests that God is soft-hearted toward men. (Such a notion may on occasion be of help to you when you see yourself being dragged down into deep despair.) For the aim of the enemy is to divert you from your mourning and from that fear of God which, however, is free from fear.

The man who wants to be reminded constantly of death and of God's judgment and who at the same time gives in to material cares and distractions, is like someone trying at the same time to swim and to clap his hands.

If your remembrance of death is clear and specific, you will cut down on your eating; and if, in your humility, you reduce the amount you eat, your passions will be correspondingly reduced.

To have an insensitive heart is to be dulled in mind, and food in abundance dries up the well of tears. Thirst, however, and the keeping of vigils afflict the heart; and when the heart is stirred, then the tears may run. Now all this may sound disgusting to the gluttonous and unbelievable to the sluggish, but a man pursuing the active life will try this course and the experience will make him smile, whereas the one who is still casting about him will become even more depressed.

The Fathers assert that perfect love is sinless. And it seems to me that in the same way a perfect sense of death is free from fear.

44a. This sentence is not in Rader's text.

There are many things that the mind of a man leading the active life can do. One can think about the love of God, the remembrance of death, the remembrance of God, the remembrance of the kingdom, the zeal of the holy martyrs, the remembrance of the presence of God as described in the saying, "I saw the Lord before me" (Ps. 15:8), the remembrance of the holy and spiritual powers, the remembrance of death, judgment, punishment, and sentence. The list begins with the sublime and ends with that which never fails.

This is what an Egyptian monk once said to me: "If it ever happened that I was inclined to offer some comfort to this carcass of mine, the remembrance of death that had been so firmly established in my heart would stand before me like a judge; and—a wonderful thing—even if I wanted to push it aside, I simply could not do so." Another monk, this time an inhabitant of the place called Tholas,[45] would go into an ecstasy at the thought of death, and when the brothers found him they had to raise him up and carry him, scarcely breathing, like someone who had fainted or had suffered an epileptic fit. And I must certainly tell you about Hesychius the Horebite. All his life he was careless and he paid not the slightest attention to his soul. Then a very grievous illness came on him, so that he was for a whole hour absent from the body. After he had revived, he begged us all to go away at once, built up the door of his cell, and remained twelve years inside without ever speaking to anyone and taking only bread and water. He never stirred and was always intent on what it was he had seen in his ecstasy. He never moved and had the look of someone out of his mind. And, silently, he wept warm tears. But when he was on the point of death, we broke in and we asked him many questions. All he would say was this: "Please forgive me. No one who has acquired the remembrance of death will ever be able to sin." It astonished us to see the blessed change and transformation that had taken place in someone hitherto so negligent. We buried him reverently in the cemetery near the fort;[46] and, some days later, when we looked for his holy remains, we could not find them. Such had been the marvel of his repentance that the Lord demonstrated to us

45. At the foot of Mount Sinai about five miles from the fort, St. John Climacus spent forty years there as a solitary (see the Preface, pp. 4–5).

46. The fort was built in 556–7 to protect the monks of Sinai from desert raiders. It is the present-day monastery of St. Catherine.

that fact that He accepts those who wish to make amends, even after the most prolonged negligence on their part.

Just as some declare that the abyss is infinite, for they call it a bottomless pit, so the thought of death is limitless and brings with it chastity and activity. The saint mentioned above proved this. Men like him unceasingly pile fear on fear, and never stop until the very strength in their bones is worn out.

We may be sure that remembrance of death, like every other blessing, is a gift from God. How else can you explain the fact that often we can be dry-eyed and hard at a cemetery, yet full of compunction when we are nowhere near such a place?

The man who has died to all things remembers death, but whoever holds some ties with the world will not cease plotting against himself.

Do not search about for the words to show people you love them. Instead, ask God to show them your love without your having to talk about it. Otherwise you will never have time enough both for loving gestures and for compunction.

Do not deceive yourself, foolish worker, into thinking that one time can make up for another. The day is not long enough to allow you to repay in full its debt to the Lord.

Someone has said that you cannot pass a day devoutly unless you think of it as your last. Even the Greeks have said some such thing, because they describe philosophy as meditation on death.

This, then, is the sixth step. He who has climbed it will never sin. "Remember your last end, and you will never sin" (Ecclus. 7:36).

Step 7

ON MOURNING

Mourning which is according to God is a melancholy of the soul, a disposition of an anguished heart that passionately seeks what it thirsts for, and when it fails to attain it, pursues it diligently and follows behind it lamenting bitterly.

Alternatively, mourning is a golden spur within a soul that has been stripped of all bonds and ties, set by holy sorrow to keep watch over the heart.

Compunction is an eternal torment of the conscience which brings about the cooling of the fire of the heart through silent confession.

Confession is a forgetfulness of nature, since because of this a man forgot to eat his bread (cf. Ps. 101:5).

Repentance is a cheerful renunciation of every creature comfort.

Those making some progress in blessed mourning are usually temperate and untalkative. Those who have succeeded in making real progress do not become angry and do not bear grudges. As for the perfect—these are humble, they long for dishonor, they look out for involuntary sufferings, they do not condemn sinners and they are inordinately compassionate. The first kind are acceptable, the second praiseworthy, but blessed surely are those who hunger for suffering and thirst for dishonor, for they will be filled to abundance with the food that cannot satiate them.

If you are endowed with mourning, hold fast to it with all your strength, for it can easily be lost if it is not well secured. Like wax melting near fire, it can easily be dissolved by noise, worldly cares, and luxury, but, in particular, by garrulity and frivolity.

The tears that come after baptism are greater than baptism itself, though it may seem rash to say so. Baptism washes off those evils that were previously within us, whereas the sins committed after baptism are washed away by tears. The baptism received by us as children we have all defiled, but we cleanse it anew with our tears. If God in His love for the human race had not given us tears, those being saved would be few indeed and hard to find.

Groans and sadness cry out to the Lord, trembling tears intercede for us, and the tears shed out of all-holy love show that our prayer has been accepted.

If nothing befits mourning as much as humility, certainly nothing opposes it as much as laughter.

Hold fast to the blessed and joyful sorrow of holy compunction and do not cease laboring for it until it lifts you high above the things of the world to present you, a cleansed offering, to Christ.

Never stop imagining and examining the abyss of dark fire,[47] its cruel minions, the merciless inexorable judge, the limitless chaos of subterranean flame, the narrow descents down to underground chambers and yawning gulfs, and other such images. Then lust in our souls may be checked by immense terror, by surrender to incorruptible chastity, and receive that non-material light which shines beyond all fire.

When you pray and plead, tremble like a convict standing before a judge. The way you look and the disposition of your heart may overcome the anger of the just Judge. He will not turn away from the widowed soul standing before Him, burdened with sorrow and wearying the Tireless One (cf. Luke 18:5).

He who has the gift of spiritual tears will be able to mourn anywhere. But if it is all outward show, there will be no end to his discussion of places and means. Hidden treasure is more secure than that which is exposed in the marketplace. Ponder this, and apply it to yourself.

---

47. The flames of hell burn without light (cf. St. Basil, *Hom. in Ps. 33*, § 8 [PG 29, 372A]).

Do not imitate those who in burying the dead first lament them—and then go off to get drunk. Rather, be like those prisoners in the mines who are flogged every hour by their warders.

The man who mourns at one time and then goes in for high living and laughter on another occasion is like someone who pelts the dog of sensuality with bread. It looks as if he is driving him off when in fact he is actually encouraging him to stay by him.

When you are recollected do not show off. Withdraw into your heart, and remember that devils fear recollection as thieves fear dogs.

We have not been called here to a wedding feast. No indeed. He who has called us has summoned us to mourn for ourselves.

Blind tears are suitable only to irrational beings, and yet there are some people who try, when they weep, to stifle all thought. Tears are actually the product of thought, and the father of thought is a rational mind.

Think of your lying in bed as an image of the lying in your grave; then you will not sleep so much. When you eat at table, remember the food of worms; then you will not live so highly. When you drink water, remember the thirst of the flames; then you will certainly do violence to your nature.

When the father superior visits an honorable rebuke, reprimand, or punishment on us, let us not forget the fearful sentence of the Judge, so that with meekness and patience—a two-edged sword—we may kill the irrational sorrow and bitterness that will surely be sown in us.

Job says: "The sea wastes with time" (Job 14:11). And with time and patience, the things I have been talking about are gradually acquired and made perfect within us.

Let the thought of eternal fire lie down with you in the evening and get up with you in the morning. Then indolence will never overwhelm you when it is time to sing the psalms.

Wear something to encourage you in your mourning. Those who lament the dead wear black. And if you find yourself unable to mourn, then lament that very fact; but if you are able to mourn, be sure to lament that by your sins you have brought yourself down from a condition free from toil to one that is full of labor.

Regarding our tears, as in everything else about us, the good and just Judge will certainly make allowances for our natural attributes. I have seen small teardrops shed like drops of blood, and I have seen floods of tears poured out with no trouble at all. So I judge toilers by their struggles, rather than their tears; and I suspect that God does so too.

Theology and mourning do not go together, for the one dissipates the other. The difference between a theologian and a mourner is that the one sits on a professorial chair while the other passes his days in rags on a dungheap. This, I think, is the reason behind the answer given by David. Although he was a teacher and a wise man, when he was asked why he was in mourning he said: "How shall I sing the Lord's song in a strange land?" (Ps. 136:4). He means, of course, the land of the passions.

In thc domain of creation as in that of compunction, there is that which moves itself and that which is moved by some other agent. When the soul grows tearful, weeps, and is filled with tenderness, and all this without having striven for it, then let us run, for the Lord has arrived uninvited and is holding out to us the sponge of loving sorrow, the cool waters of blessed sadness with which to wipe away the record of our sins. Guard these tears like the apple of your eye until they go away, for they have a power greater than anything that comes from our own efforts and our own meditation.

A man misses the true beauty of mourning if he can mourn at will, rather than because he genuinely wants to, or, more accurately, because God wishes him to. The ugly tears of vainglory mingle frequently with mourning which is pleasing to God, as we shall discover by experience whenever we find ourselves mourning and yet doing wrong.

True compunction is pain of soul without any distraction. It offers itself no rest and thinks hourly of death. It stands in wait for the God Who brings comfort, like cool waters, to humble monks. And those gifted with the heart's depth of mourning regard their lives as detestable, painful, and wearying, as a cause of tears and suffering, and they turn away from their body as from an enemy.

If we observe anger and pride in those who have the appearance of mourning in a fashion pleasing to God, then such tears will seem contradictory to us."For what fellowship is there between light and darkness?" (2 Cor. 6:14). True compunction brings consolation while that which is bogus produces self-esteem. Like the fire that consumes the straw, so do real tears consume impurity of body and soul.

Many of the Fathers declare that this problem of tears, especially where it concerns beginners, is a very obscure matter and hard to analyze since tears can come about in various ways. Tears come from nature, from God, from suffering good and bad, from vainglory, from licentiousness, from love, from the remembrance of death, and from numerous other causes. Having trained ourselves in all these ways by the fear of God, let us acquire the pure and guileless tears that come with the remembrance that we must die. There is nothing false in these, no sop to self-esteem. Rather do they purify us, lead us on in love of God, wash away our sins and drain away our passions.

It is not to be wondered at if mourning begins with good tears and ends with bad, but it is admirable if ordinary and natural tears can be turned round to become spiritual. This is something that will be understood by those inclined to vainglory.

If your soul is still not perfectly pure, then be suspicious of your tears, for wine drawn straight from the presses cannot be trusted.

No one will deny that all tears that are pleasing to God are profitable. But only at death will we find out where the profit lies.

The man who mourns constantly in a way that pleases God does not cease to celebrate daily, but tears without end are in store for the man who does not abandon bodily celebrations.

There is no joy or pleasure to be had in prison, and genuine monks do not feast on earth. There, perhaps, lies the reason for the sad statement: "Lead my soul out of prison so that henceforth it may rejoice in Your ineffable light" (Ps. 141:8).

In your heart be like an emperor, seated high in humility, commanding laughter: "Go!" and it goes; and sweet weeping: "Come!" and it comes; and our tyrant and slave, the body: "Do this!" and it does it.

The man wearing blessed, God-given mourning like a wedding garment gets to know the spiritual laughter of the soul.

Has any one ever lived so piously under a monastic regime that he never missed a day or hour or moment, but spent all his time for the Lord? And remember that never in your life can you see the same day twice.

Blessed is the monk who can lift up the eyes of his soul to the powers of heaven. And truly safe from lapse is the man who remembers sin and death constantly and who moistens his cheeks with living tears from his bodily eyes. It seems to me that the second state must surely lead to the first.

I have seen petitioners and shameless beggars melt even the hearts of kings by the artful words they use. But I have also watched another kind of beggar, those poor in virtue, men who have no knack with words, who talk in humble, vague, and halting fashion, who are not ashamed to implore the King of heaven persistently from the depths of a desperate heart and who by their tenacity lay siege to His inviolable nature and His compassion.

The man who takes pride in his tears and who secretly condemns those who do not weep is rather like the man who asks the king for a weapon against the enemy—and then uses it to commit suicide.

God does not demand or desire that someone should mourn out of sorrow of heart, but rather that out of love for Him he should rejoice with the laughter of the soul. Take away sin and then the sorrowful tears that flow from bodily eyes will be superfluous. Why look for a bandage when you are not cut? Adam did not weep before the fall, and there will be no tears after the resurrection when sin will be abolished, when pain, sorrow, and lamentation will have taken flight.

I have seen mourning in some; in others I have watched mourning for the inability to mourn, for though they have it they act as if they did not, and through such splendid ignorance they remain inviolate. Regarding such, it was said: "The Lord makes wise the blind" (Ps. 145:8).

Silly men often take pride in their tears—hence the reason some are not granted the gift of mourning. And men of this kind, discovering that they cannot weep, think of themselves as wretched and give themselves over to sighs and lamentation, sorrow of soul, deep grief, and utter desolation, all of which can safely take the place of tears, though the men in question regard these as nothing and benefit accordingly.

Devils play cruel tricks on us, as we will discover if we are observant. When we have a full stomach they make us feel guilty. When we fast they harden our hearts with the result that we can deceive ourselves with spurious tears and then give ourselves over to high living, which is the mother of passions. So do not listen to them, and act in a way opposite to what they suggest.

As I ponder the true nature of compunction, I find myself amazed by the way in which inward joy and gladness mingle with what we call mourning and grief, like honey in a comb. There must be a lesson here, and it surely is that compunction is properly a gift from God, so that there is a real pleasure in the soul, since God secretly brings consolation to those who in their heart of hearts are repentant.

Listen to a story that is a sad one but beneficial to the soul. Listen to it, for it is an inducement to most valuable mourning and sorrow.

A man called Stephen once lived here as a solitary. He spent many years in the wrestling-school of monastic life. Tears and fasting adorned his soul, as did many other fine achievements. His cell was on the side of the sacred mountain where the holy prophet and seer of God Elijah had once lived. He became famous and later he decided to practice a vastly more effective, ascetic and strict life of penance, and so moved on to Siddim, an abode of hermits. He spent several years there and lived very strictly. It was a place lacking every comfort and was rarely visited, since it was about seventy miles from the fort. Near the end of his life, the old man returned to the holy mountain, to his cell of which two holy disciples from Palestine had taken care. After a few days he was stricken by the illness from which he would eventually die. On the day before his death, he went into ecstasy and began to look to the right and to the left of his bed. He seemed to be rendering an account to someone, and in the hearing of the bystanders he said: "Of course it is true. That was why I fasted for so many years." Or again: "Yes, that is correct, but I wept and served my brothers." Or again: "No. You are accusing me falsely." Or sometimes: "Quite right. No, I have no excuse. But God is merciful." This unseen and relentless interrogation was a truly awful and frightening spectacle. Worst of all was the fact that he was charged with offenses of which he was innocent, and, what is extraordinary, regarding some of them this hesychast and hermit would say: "I do not know how to answer." And yet he had been a monk for almost forty years and he had the gift of tears as well. Alas, alas! Where, then, was the voice of Ezekiel, to say to the tormentor: "I will judge you as I find you, says God" (Ezek. 33:13–20)? He was truly unable to say such a thing. And why was that? Glory to Him who alone knows, and this was a man who had reared a leopard by hand in the desert,[48] or so I was solemnly told. So there he was now, called to account, and he died while it was happening leaving us unsure of the judgment passed on him, of his final end or sentence or of the verdict rendered him.

Like the widow who has lost her husband and whose only son is the single comfort remaining to her after the Lord, the only comfort

48. Or: "fed a leopard from his hand." An Adamic closeness to animals was a charism of the Desert Fathers.

for a lapsed soul at the moment of death is the toil of fasting and of tears.

Such people never sing, never raise a loud song, for mourning would thus be lost. And if you think you can summon it in this fashion, you have a long way to go. Mourning, after all, is the typical pain of a soul on fire.

For many people, mourning prepared the way for blessed dispassion. It worked over, ploughed, and got rid of what was sinful. Someone well practiced in this said to me: "Very often when I was tempted to be vain, angry, or gluttonous, the thought of mourning within me would protest: 'Do not be vain or else I shall abandon you.' The same thing happened when other passions troubled me. I would declare: 'I shall never disobey you until you present me to Christ.' "

The depths of mourning have witnessed comfort, and enlightenment has followed on purity of heart. Enlightenment is something indescribable, an activity that is unknowingly perceived and invisibly seen. Comfort is the balm of a distressed soul, which at the same time both cries and shouts happily, just like a child. Divine help is the renewal of a soul bowed by grief in such a way that painful tears are marvelously transformed into painless ones.

Tears over our death produce fear, but when fear begets fearlessness, then what a joy comes dawning! When joy is without interruption, holy love comes blossoming forth.

Drive off with lowly hand every passing joy as something of which you are unworthy, for if you let it in, you may be admitting a wolf instead of a shepherd.

Do not hurry to contemplation at the wrong time. Rather, let it come to you, seeking out the beauty of your lowliness, ready to join you for all time in a spotless marriage.

When a baby starts to recognize its father, it is filled with happiness. If the father has to spend time away on business before returning home, it has its fill of joy and sadness—joy at seeing the one it loves, sadness at the fact of having been deprived so long of that same love. Sometimes a mother hides from her baby and is delighted to note how sadly the child goes about looking for her, because this is how she teaches the child to be always attached to her and stirs up the flame of its love for her. He who has ears to hear, let him listen, as the Lord has said (cf. Luke 14:35).

A man who has heard himself sentenced to death will not worry about the way theaters are run. Similarly, a man who is truly in mourning will never go back to high living, glory, anger, or irritability. Mourning is the kind of sorrow which belongs to the penitent soul whose pains multiply like those of a woman in childbirth.

The Lord is just and is holy (Ps. 144:17). He leads the inwardly silent man to inward compunction, and every day He brings joy to the one who is inwardly obedient. But he who does not practice compunction or submission with sincerity is deprived of mourning.

Drive far away that hound of hell which comes at the time of your deepest mourning and whispers that God is neither merciful nor compassionate. You will find, if you take the trouble, that before you sinned he was assuring you that God is loving, compassionate, and forgiving.

Meditation gives birth to perseverance, and perseverance ends in perception, and what is accomplished with perception cannot easily be rooted out. On the other hand, however exalted our style of life may be, we may label it stale and bogus if our heart is still without contrition; for, if I may so express the matter, it is absolutely essential that those who have lapsed after baptism should clean the pitch from their hands with continuous fire of the heart and with the oil of God.

I have seen men who reached the ultimate in mourning, with the blood of a suffering and wounded heart actually flowing out of their mouths, and I was reminded of the saying: "Like grass I am cut down and my heart is dried up" (Ps. 101:5).

Tears caused by fear give some protection, but tears produced by a love that, as may well happen, has not yet attained perfection can be easily stolen. Of course, the reminder of eternal fire can stir the heart at certain efficacious times, and this humbler way is, surprisingly, very often the safer way.

There are material substances that can dry up the sources of our tears, and there are others that can produce mud and reptiles. From the former came the unlawful intercourse of Lot with his daughters (cf. Gen. 19:30–38). From the latter came the devil's fall from heaven.[49]

The forces against us are so abominable that they can even turn the mothers of virtue into the parents of vice, and they can turn into pride those very things that should produce humility in us.

---

49. The material substances are those which cause drunkenness on the one hand and pride on the other.

It often happens that the very sight of our solitary dwellings can stir our minds to compunction. Joshua, Elijah, and John are proof of this, and yet they were accustomed to solitary prayer. I have seen men moved to tears in cities and among crowds so that the thought has come that great assemblies of people may actually do us no harm. Yet they may draw us back too close to the world, since the evil spirits are working hard to bring this about.

A single word has often dispelled mourning. But it would be strange indeed if a single word brought it back.

When we die, we will not be criticized for having failed to work miracles. We will not be accused of having failed to be theologians or contemplatives. But we will certainly have some explanation to offer to God for not having mourned unceasingly.

Such, then, is the seventh step. May he who has been found worthy of it help me too. He himself has already been helped, for by taking this seventh step he has washed away the stains of the world.

Step 8

ON PLACIDITY AND MEEKNESS

As the gradual pouring of water on a fire puts out the flame completely, so the tears of genuine mourning can extinguish every flame of anger and irascibility. Hence this comes next in our sequence.

Freedom from anger is an endless wish for dishonor, whereas among the vainglorious there is a limitless thirst for praise. Freedom from anger is a triumph over one's nature. It is the ability to be impervious to insults, and comes by hard work and the sweat of one's brow.

Meekness is a permanent condition of that soul which remains unaffected by whether or not it is spoken well of, whether or not it is honored or praised.

The first step toward freedom from anger is to keep the lips silent when the heart is stirred; the next, to keep thoughts silent when the soul is upset; the last, to be totally calm when unclean winds are blowing.

Anger is an indication of concealed hatred, of grievance nursed. Anger is the wish to harm someone who has provoked you.

Irascibility is an untimely flaring up of the heart. Bitterness is a stirring of the soul's capacity for displeasure. Anger is an easily changed movement of one's disposition, a disfigurement of the soul.

Just as darkness retreats before light, so all anger and bitterness disappears before the fragrance of humility.

Some unfortunate people, who have a tendency to anger, neglect the treatment and cure of this passion and so give no thought to the saying, "The moment of his anger is his downfall" (Ecclus. 1:22).

A quick movement of a millstone can grind in one moment and do away with more of the soul's grain and fruit than another crushes in a whole day. So we must be understanding and we must pay attention, for a strong sudden wind may fan a blaze that will cause more damage to the field of the heart than a lingering flame could ever manage to achieve. Let us not forget, my friends, that evil demons sometimes leave us unexpectedly, with the result that we may become careless about these strong passions within us, thinking them to be of no consequence, and become, therefore, incurably ill.

Take a hard stone with sharp corners. Knock it and rub it against other stones, until its sharpness and hardness are crushed by the knocking and rubbing and, at last, it is made round. So too, take a soul that is rough and abrupt. Put it into the community and company of tough, short-tempered men. One of two things must happen: Either it learns through patience to cure its wound, or it will run away and, by so doing, it will learn its weakness, its cowardly flight showing it up as if in a mirror.

An angry person is like a voluntary epileptic who, through an involuntary tendency, breaks out in convulsions and falls down.

Nothing is quite so out of place in a penitent as an unruly spirit, for conversion requires great humility, and anger is an indication of all kinds of presumptuousness.

A sign of utter meekness is to have a heart peacefully and lovingly disposed toward someone who has been offensive, and a sure proof of a hot temper is that a man, even when he is alone, should with word and gesture continue to rage and fulminate against some absent person who has given offense.

If it is true that the Holy Spirit is peace of soul, as He is said to be and as, indeed, He is, and if anger is disturbance of the heart, as it really is and as it is said to be, then there is no greater obstacle to the presence of the Spirit in us than anger.

We know that the fruits of anger are abundant and unacceptable, yet we recognize that one of its involuntary offspring, though unlawful, is nevertheless quite useful. I have seen people delivered from passion by the very fact that they had flared up and then poured out their long-stored grievance and, in addition, they got from their offender either some reparation or some explanation for what had caused the long-standing grievance. On the other hand, I have seen men who appeared to be displaying stolid patience, but who, in reality, were silently harboring resentment within themselves. These, it seems to me, were much more to be pitied than the men prone to explosions of temper, because what they were doing was to keep away the holy white dove with that black gall of theirs. So this is a serpent that has to be handled carefully, for, like the snake of sensuality, it has nature for an ally.

I have seen angry men push food away out of sheer bitterness. And yet by this kind of unreasonable abstinence they merely added poison to poison. I have seen others who on being offended for some apparently justifiable reason gave themselves over to stuffing themselves, so that from the pit of anger they fell headlong over the precipice of gluttony. But others, again, I have seen who were intelligent about this matter and, like good doctors, they mixed both, and from moderate consolation they got very great profit.

Singing, in moderation, can occasionally ease bad temper. But if it is untimely and immoderate, it may open the path to pleasure. We should therefore set specific times for singing and make good use of it.

Once, while engaged on some task, I happened to be sitting outside a monastery and near the cells of those living in solitude. I could overhear them raging alone in their cells and in their bitter fury leaping about like caged partridges, leaping at the face of their offender as if he were actually there. My humble advice to them was to abandon solitary living in case they be turned from human beings into devils.

I have also noticed that people who are sensual and corrupt at heart are often meek. They manifest a kind of flattery, a display of familiarity, a love of beautiful faces. To these I gave the advice that they should undertake the solitary life, using it like a scalpel to cut away sensuality and corruption of the heart. Otherwise they might turn from being rational beings into pitifully irrational animals.

But, again, some told me that they were completely in the grip of anger and sensuality. I therefore forbade them to live as they wished and, in my concern for them, I suggested to their superiors that they should allow them sometimes to live one way, sometimes the other, but always in complete subjection to those in charge of them. There is the risk that a sensual person may harm himself and perhaps a close friend as well; while the angry person, like a wolf, often disturbs the entire flock and causes offense and discouragement among many souls.

The eye of the heart should not be troubled by anger. Remember the saying: "My eye is troubled from anger" (Ps. 6:8). Worse, however, is to give way to harsh words which reveal the upheaval in one's soul. But actually to start fighting is completely inimical to and at variance with the monastic, angelic, and divine life.

You wish, or rather, have decided, to remove a splinter from someone? Very well, but do not go after it with a stick instead of a lancet for you will only drive it deeper. Rough speech and harsh gestures are the stick, while even-tempered instruction and patient reprimand are the lancet. "Reprove, rebuke, exhort," says the Apostle (2 Tim. 4:2), not "batter." And should a beating be necessary, make sure this does not happen often and get someone else to do it instead of you.

You will note that many irritable persons practice vigils, fasting, and stillness. For the devils are trying to suggest to them, under cover of penance and mourning, what is quite likely to increase their passion.

If what I said above is true, namely, that a single wolf, helped by a demon, can trouble an entire flock, then surely a single very wise brother, helped by an angel, may calm the waves and make a smooth path for the ship by pouring a good skin full of oil on the waters. And as the sentence on the one will be heavy, so the reward for the other from God will be very great, and he will become an edifying example to everyone.

The first stage of blessed patience is to accept dishonor with bitterness and anguish of soul. The intermediate stage is to be free from pain amid all such things. The perfect stage, if that is attainable, is to think of dishonor as praise. Let the first rejoice and the second be strong, but blessed be the third, for he exults in the Lord.

Angry people, because of their self-esteem, make a pitiable sight, though they do not realize this themselves. They get angry and then, when thwarted, they become furious. It was amazing to see one fall punished by another and I was full of pity for them as I saw them taking revenge on sin by sin. The trickery of devils frightened me and I came close to despair for my own life.

Someone who notices that he is easily overcome by pride, a nasty temper, malice, and hypocrisy, and who thinks of defending himself against these by unsheathing the double-edged sword of meekness and patience, such a man if he wishes to break free entirely from these vices ought to go live in a monastery, as if it were a fuller's shop of salvation. In particular, he should choose the most austere place. He will be spiritually stretched and beaten by the insults, injuries, and rebuffs of the brothers. He may even be physically beaten, trampled on, and kicked, so that he may wash out the filth still lying in the sentient part of his soul. There is an old saying that reproof is the washtub for the soul's passions, and you ought to believe it, for people in the world who load indignities onto someone and then boast about it to others like to say, "I gave him a good scrubbing." Which, of course, is quite accurate.

The absence of a tendency to anger when it is found in novices and is the result of mourning—this is one thing; the peace found in the perfect is something else. In the one, tears, acting like a bridle, hold in the anger; but, among the perfect, anger has been mortified by mastery of the passions, like a snake killed by a sword.

I once saw three monks receive the same type of injury at the same time. The first felt it keenly, but did not speak; the second was delighted by the thought of the reward the injury would bring him and he felt compassion for the wrongdoer; the third wept fervently at the thought of the harm his offending neighbor was suffering. At work, then, were fear, the sense of a reward due, and love.

The fever suffered by the body is a single symptom but has many causes. Similarly, the seething movement of our anger and of our other passions arises for many different reasons, so that the same cure cannot be offered for all of them. Hence I would propose that each sick man should very carefully look for his own particular cure, and the first step here is the diagnosis of the cause of the disease. When this is known, the patients will get the right cure from the hands of God and from their spiritual doctors. Those who wish to join us in the Lord should therefore come to the spiritual tribunal where we can be tested in various ways and find out about the passions referred to above as well as their causes.

So, then, anger the oppressor must be restrained by the chains of meekness, beaten by patience, hauled away by blessed love. Take it before the tribunal of reason and have it examined in the following terms: "Wretch, tell us the name of your father, the name of the mother who bore you to bring calamity into the world, the names of your loathsome sons and daughters. Tell us, also, who your enemies are and who has the power to kill you." And this is how anger replies: "I come from many sources and I have more than one father. My mothers are Vainglory, Avarice, Greed. And Lust too. My father is named Conceit. My daughters have the names Remembrance of Wrongs, Hate, Hostility, and Self-justification. The enemies who have imprisoned me are the opposite virtues—Freedom from Anger and Lowliness, while Humility lays a trap for me. As for Humility, ask in due time who it was that bore her."

On the eighth step the crown is freedom from anger. He who wears it by nature may never come to wear another. But he who has sweated for it and won it has conquered all eight together.

Step 9

ON MALICE[49a]

The holy virtues are like the ladder of Jacob and the unholy vices are like the chains that fell off the chief apostle Peter. The virtues lead from one to another and carry heavenward the man who chooses them. Vices on the other hand beget and stifle one another. And because we have just heard senseless anger describe remembrance of wrongs as its offspring, we had better say something about it now.

Remembrance of wrongs comes as the final point of anger. It is a keeper of sins. It hates a just way of life. It is the ruin of virtues, the poison of the soul, a worm in the mind. It is the shame of prayer, a cutting off of supplication, a turning away from love, a nail piercing the soul. It is a pleasureless[50] feeling cherished in the sweetness of bitterness. It is a never-ending sin, an unsleeping wrong, rancor by the hour. A dark and loathsome passion, it comes to be but has no offspring, so that one need not say too much about it.

The man who has put a stop to anger has also wiped out remembrance of wrongs, since offspring can come only from a living parent.

A loving man banishes revenge, but a man brooding on his hatreds stores up troublesome labors for himself. A banquet of love does

49a. In this Step *mnisikakia* is rendered sometimes as "malice" and sometimes as the more specific "remembrance of wrongs."

50. Reading *anidonos* for Rader's *anodynos*, "painless."

away with hatred and honest giving brings peace to a soul,[50a] but if the table is extravagant then license is brought forth and gluttony comes jumping in through the window of love.

I have seen hatred shatter a lecherous relationship, and then afterwards remembrance of wrongs stood in the way of restoring the relationship. Now this is amazing, one devil cured by another. Still, this may be the work of divine providence rather than of demons.

Remembrance of wrongs is far removed from sturdy, natural love, but like a flea hidden on a dove, may live next door to fornication.

Let your malice and your spite be turned against the devils. Treat your body always as an enemy, for the flesh is an ungrateful and treacherous friend. The more you look after it, the more it hurts you.

Malice is an exponent of Scripture which twists the words of the Spirit to suit itself. Let the prayer of Jesus[51] put it to shame, that prayer which cannot be uttered in the company of malice.

If after great effort you still fail to root out this thorn,[52] go to your enemy and apologize, if only with empty words whose insincerity may shame you. Then as conscience, like a fire, comes to give you pain, you may find that a sincere love of your enemy may come to life.

A true sign of having completely mastered this putrefaction will come not when you pray for the man who offended you, not when you give him presents, not when you invite him to share a meal with you, but only when, on hearing of some catastrophe that has afflicted him in body or soul, you suffer and you lament for him as if for yourself.

A malicious hesychast is like a lurking snake carrying about its own deadly poison.

50a. The words "A banquet of love does away with hatred and honest giving brings peace to a soul" are not in Rader's text.

51. The words "prayer of Jesus" (*Iisou i prosevchi*) are sometimes understood as referring here to the Jesus Prayer, "Lord Jesus Christ, Son of God, have mercy on me." But more probably Climacus means the Lord's Prayer. The petition, "Forgive us our trespasses as we forgive those who trespass against us," is particularly apposite in the present context. See the Preface, pp. 45–53.

52. Or: "destroy this stumbling-block completely."

The remembrance of what Jesus suffered is a cure for remembrance of wrongs, shaming it powerfully with His patient endurance.

Worms thrive in a rotten tree; malice thrives in the deceptively meek and silent. He who has expelled malice has found forgiveness, but he who hugs it is deprived of mercy.

Some labor and struggle hard to earn forgiveness, but better than these is the man who forgets the wrongs done to him. Forgive quickly and you will be abundantly forgiven. To forget wrongs is to prove oneself truly repentant, but to brood on them and at the same time to imagine one is practicing repentance is to act like the man who is convinced he is running when in fact he is fast asleep.

I have seen malicious people recommending forgiveness to others and then, shamed by their own words, they managed to rid themselves of this vice.

Never imagine that this dark vice is a passion of no importance, for it often reaches out even to spiritual men.

Such is the ninth step. Let him who has taken it have the courage henceforth to ask Jesus the Savior to free him from his sins.

Step 10

ON SLANDER

I imagine that no one with any sense would dispute that slander is the child of hatred and remembrance of wrongs. Hence the need to discuss it next in the order after its forbears.

Slander is the offspring of hatred, a subtle and yet crass disease, a leech in hiding and escaping notice, wasting and draining away the lifeblood of love. It puts on the appearance of love and is the ambassador of an unholy and unclean heart. And it is the ruin of chastity.

There are girls who flaunt their shamelessness, but there are others who are much worse, for they put on the appearance of great modesty while secretly engaging in abominable behavior. So it is with shameful vices. And indeed there are numerous insincere maidens: hypocrisy, cunning, melancholy, brooding over past injuries, secret contempt for others. They put on a show of doing one thing—and then act otherwise.

I have rebuked people who were engaged in slander, and, in self-defense, these evildoers claimed to be acting out of love and concern for the victim of their slander. My answer to that was to say: "Then stop that kind of love, or else you will be making a liar out of him who declared, 'I drove away the man who secretly slandered his neighbor' (Ps. 100:5). If, as you insist, you love that man, then do not be making a mockery of him, but pray for him in secret, for this is the kind of love that is acceptable to the Lord. And remember—now I say this as something to be pondered, and do not start passing judgment on the offender—Judas was one of the company of Christ's disciples and the robber was in the company of killers. Yet what a turnabout there was when the decisive moment arrived!"

If you want to overcome the spirit of slander, blame not the person who falls but the prompting demon. No one wants to sin against God, even though all of us sin without being compelled to it.

I knew a man who sinned openly but repented in secret. I denounced him for being lecherous but he was chaste in the eyes of God, having propitiated Him by a genuine conversion.

Do not allow human respect to get in your way when you hear someone slandering his neighbor. Instead, say this to him: "Brother, stop it! I do worse things every day, so how can I criticize him?" You accomplish two things when you say this. You heal yourself and you heal your neighbor with the one bandage.

Do not make judgments, and you will travel no quicker road to the forgiveness of your sins. "Judge not, so that you may not be judged" (Luke 6:37).

Fire and water do not mix, neither can you mix judgment of others with the desire to repent. If a man commits a sin before you at the very moment of his death, pass no judgment, because the judgment of God is hidden from men. It has happened that men have sinned greatly in the open but have done greater good deeds in secret, so that those who would disparage them have been fooled, with smoke instead of sunlight in their eyes. So listen to me, all you accountants of other people's faults, listen well; for if, as is certain, it is true that "you shall be judged with the judgment you have used yourselves" (Matt. 7:2), then whatever sin of body or spirit that we ascribe to our neighbor we will surely fall into ourselves.

Those who pass speedy and harsh judgments on the sins of their neighbors fall into this passion because they themselves have so far failed to achieve a complete and unceasing memory of and concern for their own sins. Anyone untrammeled by self-love and able to see his own faults for what they are would worry about no one else in this life. He would feel that his time on earth did not suffice for his own mourning, even if he lived a hundred years, and even if a whole Jordan of tears poured out of his eyes. Mourning of that kind has, as I know, no trace in it of slander or harsh judgment.

It is the murdering demons who push us into sin. If they are balked here, they get us to pass judgment on those who are sinning, thereby smearing us with the stain we are denouncing in others.

You can always recognize people who are malicious and slanderous. They are filled with the spirit of hatred. Gladly and without a qualm they slander the teaching, the doings and the virtues of their neighbor. I have known men who secretly had committed very grave sins and had not been found out, yet cloaked in their supposed goodness they lashed out against people who had done something minor in public.

To pass judgment on another is to usurp shamelessly a prerogative of God, and to condemn is to ruin one's soul.

Self-esteem, even when there are no other attendant vices, can bring a man down. Similarly, if we have got into the habit of passing judgments, we can be destroyed completely by this alone, for the Pharisee was condemned for this very thing.

A good grape picker chooses to eat ripe grapes and does not pluck what is unripe. A charitable and sensible mind takes careful note of the virtues it observes in another, while the fool goes looking for faults and defects. It is of such a one that it was said, "They have searched out iniquity and died in the search" (Ps. 63:7).

Do not condemn. Not even if your very eyes are seeing something, for they may be deceived.

This is the tenth step, and he who succeeds in it has practiced love or mourning.

Step 11

ON TALKATIVENESS AND SILENCE

The brief discussion in the previous chapter was concerned with the great danger of passing judgment on others, or rather with being judged and being punished by one's tongue, and it touched on the fact that this vice can lay hold of the most apparently spiritual people.

The time has come now to indicate the cause of this vice and to give an adequate account of the door by which it enters—or, more accurately, by which it goes out.

Talkativeness is the throne of vainglory on which it loves to preen itself and show off. Talkativeness is a sign of ignorance, a doorway to slander, a leader of jesting, a servant of lies, the ruin of compunction, a summoner of despondency, a messenger of sleep, a dissipation of recollection, the end of vigilance, the cooling of zeal, the darkening of prayer.

Intelligent silence is the mother of prayer, freedom from bondage, custodian of zeal, a guard on our thoughts, a watch on our enemies, a prison of mourning, a friend of tears, a sure recollection of death, a painter of punishment, a concern with judgment, servant of anguish, foe of license, a companion of stillness, the opponent of dogmatism, a growth of knowledge, a hand to shape contemplation, hidden progress, the secret journey upward. For the man who recognizes his sins has taken control of his tongue, while the chatterer has yet to discover himself as he should.

The lover of silence draws close to God. He talks to Him in secret and God enlightens him. Jesus, by His silence, shamed Pilate; and a man, by his stillness, conquers vainglory. Peter wept bitterly for what he had said. He had forgotten the one who declared: "I said: I will guard my ways so that I may not sin with my tongue" (Ps. 38:1). He had forgotten too the saying, "Better to fall from a height to the ground than to slip with the tongue" (Ecclus. 20:18).

I would prefer not to write too much about this, despite the urgings of my wily passions. Someone who had asked me once about stillness told me that talkativeness invariably results from one of the following causes: from a bad or relaxed life-style ("the tongue," he said, "is a member of the body, like the rest, and therefore needs to be trained in its habits"); or it comes from vainglory, a particular problem with ascetics; or it comes at times from gluttony, which is why many who keep a hard check on the stomach can more easily restrain the blathering tongue.

The man who is seriously concerned about death reduces the amount of what he has to say, and the man who has received the gift of spiritual mourning runs from talkativeness as from a fire.

The lover of stillness keeps his mouth shut, but the man who likes to ramble outside is driven from his cell by this passion.

The man who has known the odor of heavenly fire runs from a gathering of men, like a bee from smoke, since smoke drives off a bee just as company militates against a man.

It is hard to keep water in without a dike. But it is harder still to hold in one's tongue.

This is the eleventh step. He who succeeds in taking it has with one blow cut off a host of evils.

Step 12

ON FALSEHOOD

From flint and steel comes fire; from chatter and joking comes lying. Lying is the destruction of charity, and perjury the very denial of God.

No sensible man imagines that lying is a minor failing. Indeed the All-Holy Spirit pronounced the most dreadful sentence on this sin above all others; and if, as David says to God, "You will destroy everyone speaking a lie" (Ps. 5:7), what will happen to those who swear to their lies on oath?

I have seen men, proud of their ability to lie, and exciting laughter by their clowning and joking, who have miserably destroyed in their hearers the habit of mourning. But when the demons observe that we stay clear of the sallies of some outstanding wit, as though we were avoiding the plague, they try to catch us with two seemingly plausible thoughts, namely that we should not be offensive to the person telling the witty story and we should not give the appearance of loving God more than he does. Be off! Do not dawdle! Otherwise the jokes will start coming back to you when you are at prayer. But do not simply run away. Break up the bad company in a devout way by setting before them the thought of death and judgment, and if a few drops of vainglory fall on you, what harm? Provided of course, that you become a source of profit to many.

Hypocrisy is the mother of lying and frequently its cause. Some would argue that hypocrisy is nothing other than a meditation on falsehood, that it is the inventor of falsehood laced with lies.

The man gifted with fear of the Lord has given up lying, for within him he has conscience, that incorruptible judge.

Various kinds of harm can be observed in the passions, and lying is no exception. So one judgment awaits the man who lies out of fear, another the liar who has nothing at all to worry about. One man lies for the sheer pleasure of it, another for amusement, another to raise a laugh among bystanders, another to trap his brother and do him harm.

Magistrates can root out lying with tortures, though it is an abundance of tears that truly destroys it. A man may lie on the grounds of prudence, and indeed regards as an act of righteousness the actual destruction of his own soul. The inventor of lies declares that he is following the example of Rahab and maintains that his own destruction is the cause of salvation for others.[53]

Only when we are completely free of the urge to lie may we resort to it, and then only in fear and out of necessity. A baby does not know how to lie, and neither does a soul cleansed of evil.

A man drunk on wine unwittingly tells the truth about everything. And a man drunk with compunction cannot lie.

This is the twelfth step. The man who has taken it has obtained the root of all blessings.

---

53. Rahab lied to save the lives of her family. Cf. Joshua 2:1ff.

Step 13

ON DESPONDENCY

Despondency or tedium of the spirit,[54] as I have often said, is frequently an aspect of talkativeness and indeed is its first child. For this reason I have given it an appropriate place in the chain of vices.

Tedium is a paralysis of the soul, a slackness of the mind, a neglect of religious exercises, a hostility to vows taken. It is an approval of worldly things. It is a voice claiming that God has no mercy and no love for men. It is a laziness in the singing of psalms, a weakness in prayer, a stubborn urge for service, a dedication to the work of the hands, an indifference to the requirement of obedience.[55] An obedient person does not know such tedium, for he has used the things of the senses to reach the level of the spirit.

Tedium is rebuffed by community life, but she is a constant companion of the hermit, living with him until the day of his death, struggling with him until the very end. She smiles at the sight of a hermit's cell and comes creeping up to live nearby.

A doctor calls on the sick in the morning, but tedium visits the hermit at noon.[56]

---

54. *Akidia* (see note 10, p. 80).

55. Translating Rader's emendation, *en hypakoi adokimos*, although all MSS read *en hypakoi dokimos*, with the opposite sense.

56. The Fathers commonly attribute despondency to the noonday demon of Ps. 90:6.

Tedium loves to be involved in hospitality, urges the hermit to undertake manual labor so as to enable him to give alms, and exhorts us to visit the sick, recalling even the words of Him Who said, "I was sick and you came to visit me" (Matt. 25:36). Tedium suggests we should call on the despairing and the fainthearted, and she sets one languishing heart to bring comfort to another. Tedium reminds those at prayer of some job to be done, and in her brutish way she searches out any plausible excuse to drag us from prayer, as though with some kind of halter.

At the third hour, the devil of tedium causes shivering, headache, and vertigo. By the ninth hour, the patient has recovered his strength, and when dinner is ready, he jumps out of bed. But now when the time for prayer comes, his body begins to languish once more. He begins his prayers, but the tedium makes him sleepy and the verses of the psalms are snatched from his mouth by untimely yawns.

There is a particular virtue available to overcome all the other passions. But tedium is a kind of total death for the monk.

A brave soul can stir up his dying mind, but tedium and laziness scatter every one of his treasures.

Tedium is one of the eight deadly vices, and indeed the gravest of them all, and so I must discuss it as I did the others. Still, just note this much. When the psalms do not have to be sung, tedium does not arise, and the Office is hardly over when the eyes are ready to open again.

The real men of spirit can be seen at the time when tedium strikes, for nothing gains so many crowns for a monk as the struggle against this. Note how tedium hits you when you are standing, and if you sit down, it suggests that it would be a good thing to lean back. It suggests that you prop yourself up against the walls of your cell. It produces noise and footsteps—and there you go peeping out of the window.

The man who mourns for himself does not suffer from tedium. This tyrant should be overcome by the remembrance of past sins, battered by hard manual labor and brought to book by the thought of the blessings to come. And when led before the tribunal, let these be the questions put to him: "You there! You crass and sluggish creature, what was it that evilly begot the likes of you? Who are your children? Who are your enemies? Who can destroy you?" And tedium may be constrained to reply: "I cannot lay my head among those who are truly obedient, and I live quietly where I may. I have many mothers—

Stolidity of Soul, Forgetfulness of the Things of Heaven, or, sometimes, Too Heavy a Burden of Troubles. My children who live with me are Changing from Place to Place, Disobedience to One's Superior, Forgetfulness of the Judgment to Come, and sometimes, the Abandonment of One's Vocation. The singing of psalms and manual labor are my opponents by whom I am now bound. My enemy is the thought of death, but what really slays me is prayer backed by a firm hope in the blessings of the future. And as to who gave birth to Prayer, you must ask her."

This is the thirteenth victory. He who has won it is really outstanding in all virtue.

Step 14

ON GLUTTONY

In our self-criticism we must refer particularly to the stomach, and indeed I wonder if anyone breaks free of this mistress before he dies.

Gluttony is hypocrisy of the stomach. Filled, it moans about scarcity; stuffed, and crammed, it wails about its hunger. Gluttony thinks up seasonings, creates sweet recipes. Stop up one urge and another bursts out; stop that one and you unleash yet another. Gluttony has a deceptive appearance: it eats moderately but wants to gobble everything at the same time. A stuffed belly produces fornication, while a mortified stomach leads to purity. The man who pets a lion may tame it but the man who coddles the body makes it ravenous.

The Jew celebrates on Sabbaths and feast days. The gluttonous monk celebrates on Saturdays and Sundays.[57] He counts the days to Easter, and for days in advance he gets the food ready. The slave of the belly ponders the menu with which to celebrate the feast. The servant of God, however, thinks of the graces that may enrich him.

If a visitor calls, then the slave of gluttony engages in charitable acts—but for the reasons associated with his love of food. He thinks that by allowing relaxations for himself, he is bringing consolation to his brother. He thinks that the duties of hospitality entitle him to

---

57. On the prohibition of fasting on Saturdays and Sundays see John Cassian, *Institutes* II, 18.

help himself to some wine, so that while apparently hiding his virtuous love of temperance, he is actually turning into a slave of intemperance.

Vanity and gluttony sometimes vie with one another and they struggle for the poor monk as if he were an acquired slave. The one tells him he should take it easy and the other suggests that he ought to emerge virtuously triumphant over his urge to gratify his appetite. A sensible monk, however, will avoid both vices, using one to repulse the other.

As long as the flesh is in full vigor, we should everywhere and at all times cultivate temperance, and when it has been tamed—something I doubt can happen this side of the grave—we should hide our achievement.

I have seen elderly priests tricked by demons so that on feast days they dispensed the young men with a blessing, though they were not in their charge, from abstinence from wine and so on. Now if priests giving such permission are quite clearly holy men, we may indulge. But within limits. If such priests tend to be careless, then we should ignore the permission they give, and we should do so especially if we are in the thick of the fight against the flesh.

I remember the case of Evagrius,[58] whom an evil demon led to the notion that of all men he was the most sensible in all he thought and said. The poor man was quite mistaken, of course, and in this matter as in many others he proved himself outstandingly foolish. He says: "When our soul wants different foods, keep it on bread and water,"[58a] a statement that is like telling a child to climb the entire ladder in a single stride. So let us reject him and say: When our soul wants different foods, it is looking for what is proper to its nature. Hence, we have to be very cunning in the way we deal with this most skillful opponent. Unless we are caught up in some crisis or unless we happen to be doing penance for some particular failings, what we

58. Evagrius Ponticus (*c.* 345–399) left a promising ecclesiastical career in Constantinople to become a monk first in Palestine and then in Egypt, where he spent two years in Nitria and fourteen at the Cells. He became there the leading theoretical exponent of the monastic life. His Origenist cosmology led to his condemnation at the Fifth Ecumenical Council of 553. But his ascetic theology, with its sharp distinction between action and contemplation, its list of eight principal temptations, and its account of dispassion leading to love, remained fundamental for monasticism. Climacus, in spite of his abuse of Evagrius, is clearly much influenced by him (see the Preface, p. 60).

58a. Evagrius, *Practicus* 16 (ed. Guillaumont, *Sources chrétiennes* 171, p. 540).

ought to do is to deny ourselves fattening foods, then foods that warm us up, then whatever happens to make our food especially pleasant. Give yourself food that is satisfying and easily digestible, thereby counteracting endless hunger by giving yourself plenty. In this way we may be freed from too great a longing for food as though from a plague by rapid evacuation. And we should note too that most food that inflates the stomach also encourages desire.

Be sure to laugh at the demon who, when supper is over, says that in future you should eat later, for you may be sure that at the ninth hour he will change the arrangements made on the previous day.

There is one sort of temperance for those of good conduct and another for those inclined to particular weaknesses. Among the former any kind of bodily stirring evokes an immediate urge to restraint, while among the latter there is no relief or relaxation from such stirrings until the very day they die. The former strive always for peace of mind, but the latter try to appease God by their spiritual grief and their contrition.

Joy and consolation descend on the perfect when they reach the state of complete detachment. The warrior monk enjoys the heat of battle, but the slave of passion revels in the celebrations of Easter.[59]

In his heart, the glutton dreams only of food and provisions whereas all who have the gift of mourning think only of judgment and of punishment.

Control your appetites[60] before they control you, and shame will greatly help you to maintain such mastery. Those who have tumbled headlong into the pit of sin know what I am talking about, and indeed only the eunuch is without such knowledge.[61] So let us restrain our appetites with the thought of the fire to come. Some have been so mightily enslaved by their appetites that they actually cut off their own genitals, and thereby died twice over.[62] For the truth is, as one

59. Literally: "the Feast of feasts and Festival of festivals."

60. Literally: "the belly." Among the ascetic writers gluttony and lust are always closely connected.

61. "The eunuchs are those of whom the Lord said that they have made themselves eunuchs for the kingdom of heaven's sake (Matt. 19:12), and who are practicing a general abstinence. For the other kind of eunuchs do not differ at all from ordinary men as far as the passions into which they fall are concerned" (scholion 13 [876B]).

62. I.e., physically and spiritually; the 24th Apostolic Canon sentences a layman who mutilates himself to three years' deprivation of Communion.

will discover, that the belly is the cause of all human shipwreck.

A fasting man prays austerely, but the mind of someone intemperate is filled up with unclean imaginings.

A full stomach dries up one's weeping, whereas the shrivelled stomach produces these tears. And the man who looks after his belly and at the same time hopes to control the spirit of fornication is like someone trying to put out a fire with oil.

Begrudge the stomach and your heart will be humbled; please the stomach and your mind will turn proud. And if you watch yourself early in the morning, at midday, and in the hour before dinner, you will discover the value of fasting, for in the morning your thoughts are lively, by the sixth hour they have grown quieter and by sundown they are finally calm. If you can begrudge the stomach, your mouth will stay closed, because the tongue flourishes where food is abundant. Fight as hard as you can against the stomach and let your vigilance hold it in. Make the effort, however little, and the Lord will quickly come to help you.

If leather bottles are kept supple, they can hold more; but they do not hold so much if they are neglected. The man who stuffs food into his stomach expands his insides, whereas the man who fights his stomach causes it to shrink, and once it has shrunk there is no possibility of overeating, so that henceforth one fasts quite naturally.

Sometimes thirst quenches thirst, but it is difficult if not impossible to end hunger by means of hunger. And if the stomach triumphs over you, tame it with hard work, and if you are too weak for this, fight it by keeping vigil. If you find yourself getting sleepy, turn to manual work, but keep away from that if you happen not to be sleepy, for you cannot serve both God and Mammon.[63] That is to say, you cannot turn your attention at the same time to God and to the work of your hands.

You should remember that frequently a demon can take up residence in your belly and keep a man from being satisfied, even after having devoured the whole of Egypt and after having drunk all of the Nile. After we have eaten, this demon goes off and sends the spirit of fornication against us, saying: "Get him now! Go after him. When his stomach is full, he will not put up much of a fight." Laughing, the spirit of fornication, that ally of the stomach's demon, comes, binds us

63. Monks supported themselves by the sale of their handiwork.

hand and foot in sleep, does anything he wants with us, befouls body and soul with his dirty dreams and emissions.

It is truly astounding how the incorporeal mind can be defiled and darkened by the body. Equally astonishing is the fact that the immaterial spirit can be purified and refined by clay.

If you have promised Christ to travel the straight and narrow road, then keep your stomach in check; for if you give in to it, if you enlarge it, you are breaking your promise. Listen and hear the word of warning: "Wide and spacious is the road of gluttony. It leads to the catastrophe of fornication, and there are many who travel that way. The gate is narrow and the way of fasting is hard, that way leading to the life of purity, and there are few to make the journey" (cf. Matt 7:13–14).

The fallen Lucifer is prince of the demons, and gluttony is prince of the passions. So when you sit at a well-laden table, remember death and remember judgment, and even then you will only manage to restrain yourself a little. And when you drink, keep always in mind the vinegar and gall of your Lord. Then indeed you will be either temperate or sighing; you will keep your mind humble. For you must not fool yourself. You will not escape from Pharaoh and you will not see the heavenly Passover unless you constantly eat bitter herbs and unleavened bread, the bitter herbs of toil and hard fasting, the unleavened bread of a mind made humble. Join to your breathing the word of him who said: "When devils plagued me, I put on sackcloth, humbled my soul with fasting, and my prayer stuck to the bosom of my soul" (Ps. 34:13).

To fast is to do violence to nature. It is to do away what whatever pleases the palate. Fasting ends lust, roots out bad thoughts, frees one from evil dreams. Fasting makes for purity of prayer, an enlightened soul, a watchful mind, a deliverance from blindness. Fasting is the door of compunction, humble sighing, joyful contrition, and end to chatter, an occasion for silence, a custodian of obedience, a lightening of sleep, health of the body, an agent of dispassion, a remission of sins, the gate, indeed, the delight of Paradise.

Let us put a question to this enemy of ours, this architect of our misfortunes, this gateway of passion, this fall of Adam and ruin of Esau, this destroyer of the Israelites, this one who bares the shame of Noah, this betrayer of Gomorrah, this reproach of Lot, this killer of the sons of Eli the priest, this guide to every uncleanness. Let us ask her from whom she is born, who her children are, what enemy there is to crush her, who finally brings her low. Let us ask this bane of all men, this purchaser of everything with the gold coin of greed: "How did you gain access to us? To what does your coming lead? How do you depart from us?"

Angered by such abuse, raging and foaming, Gluttony answers us: "Why are you complaining, you who are my servants? How is it that you are trying to get away from me? Nature has bound me to you. The door for me is what food actually is, its character and quality. The reason for my being insatiable is habit. Unbroken habit, dullness of soul, and the failure to remember death are the roots of my passion. And how is it that you are looking for the names of my offspring? For if I were to count them, their number would be greater than the total of the grains of sand. Still, you may learn at least the names of my firstborn and beloved children. My firstborn son is the servant of Fornication, the second is Hardness of Heart, and the third is Sleepiness. From me flow a sea of Dirty Thoughts, waves of Filth, floods of unknown and unspeakable Impurities. My daughters are Laziness, Talkativeness, Breezy Familiarity, Jesting, Facetiousness, Contradiction, Stubbornness, Contempt, Disobedience, Stolidity of Mind, Captivity, Boastfulness, Audacity, Love of Worldly Things, followed by Impure Prayer, Distracted Thoughts, and sudden and often unexpected Catastrophes, with which is linked that most evil of all my daughters, namely, Despair. The thought of past failings is an obstacle to me, but hardly overcomes me. The thought of death is my enemy always, but nothing human can really wipe me out. He who has received the Paraclete prays to Him against me; and the Paraclete, when entreated, does not allow me to act passionately. But those who have never tasted Him inevitably seek pleasure in my sweetness."

Victory over this vice is a brave one. He who is able to achieve it should hasten towards dispassion and total chastity.

Step 15

ON CHASTITY

We have heard from that raving mistress gluttony, who has just spoken, that her offspring is war against bodies. And no wonder, for our ancient ancestor Adam also teaches us this. Indeed if he had not been overcome by the belly he would not have known what a wife was. Therefore those who keep the first commandment do not fall into the second transgression, but remain sons of Adam without knowing what Adam was. They were made a little lower than the angels (cf. Ps. 8:6) in being subject to death.[64] And this was to prevent evil from becoming immortal, as he who is called the Theologian says.[64a]

To be chaste is to put on the nature of an incorporeal being.[65] Chastity is a supernatural denial of what one is by nature, so that a mortal and corruptible body is competing in a truly marvelous way with incorporeal spirits. A chaste man is someone who has driven out bodily love by means of divine love, who has used heavenly fire to quench the fires of the flesh.

---

64. The words "in being subject to death" do not occur in some versions.

64a. St. Gregory of Nazianzus, *Or.* 45, 8 (*PG* 36, 633A).

65. Rader's text is translated here although a sentence has undoubtedly dropped out. HTM adds: "Purity is the longed-for house of Christ and the earthly heaven of the heart." Rader's own Latin translation reads: "Purity is the longed-for house of Christ and the earthly shield of the heart" (*PG* 88, 879D).

Chastity is a name common to all virtues.

A chaste man feels no stirrings or change within himself even when he is asleep. A chaste man is completely oblivious to the difference between bodies.

The rule and limit of absolute chastity is to have the same feelings regarding animate and inanimate beings, rational and irrational.

Anyone trained in chastity should give himself no credit for any achievements, for a man cannot conquer what he actually is. When nature is overcome, it should be admitted that this is due to Him Who is above nature, since it cannot be denied that the weaker always yields to the stronger.

The beginning of chastity is refusal to consent to evil thoughts and occasional dreamless emissions; the middle stage is to be free of dreams and emissions even when there are natural movements of the body brought on by eating too much; the completion of chastity comes when mortified thoughts are followed by a mortified body.

Truly blessed is the man totally unstirred by any body, any color or any beauty. The chaste man is not someone with a body undefiled but rather a person whose members are in complete subjection to the soul, for a man is great who is free of passion even when touched, though greater still is the man unhurt by all he has looked on. Such a man has truly mastered the fires of earthly beauty by his attention concentrated on the beauties of heaven. In driving off this dog by means of prayer he is like someone who has been fighting a lion. He who subdues it by resistance to it is someone still chasing an enemy. But the man who has managed to reduce its hold completely, even when he himself is still in this life, is someone who has already risen from the dead.

A sign of real chastity is to be unaffected by the dreams that come with sleep. Equally, a sign of complete sensuality is to be liable to emissions from bad thoughts when one is awake.

The man who struggles against this enemy by sweat and bodily hardships is like someone who has tied his adversary with a reed. If he fights him with temperance, sleeplessness, and keeping watch, it is as if he had put fetters on him. If he fights with humility, calmness, and thirst, it is as though he had killed the enemy and buried him in sand, the sand being lowliness since it does nothing to feed the passions and is only earth and ashes.

One man keeps this tormentor under control by struggling hard, another by being humble, another by divine revelation. The first man is like the star of morning, the second like the moon when it is full, the third like the blazing sun. And all three have their home in heaven. Light comes from the dawn and amid light the sun rises, so let all that has been said be the light in which to meditate and learn.

A fox pretends to be asleep; the body and the demons pretend to be chaste. The former is on the watch to seize a bird, the latter to catch a soul. So as long as you live, never trust that clay of which you are made and never depend on it until the time you stand before Christ Himself. And never imagine that abstinence will keep you from falling. It was a being who never ate that was nevertheless thrown out of heaven.

Some wise men have said that renunciation is hostility to the body and war against the stomach.

Among beginners lapses usually occur because of high living, something that, together with arrogance, brings down also those who have made some progress. But among those nearing perfection, a lapse is solely due to the fact of passing judgment on one's neighbor.

Some have praised those who are naturally eunuchs. They say of them that they have been freed from the martyrdom of the body. But as far as I am concerned my praise goes out each day to those who take the knife, so to speak, to their own evil thoughts.

I have seen men who lapsed against their will and I have seen men who would willingly lapse but are unable to do so. These I pity far more than the daily sinner, for though impotent they long for corruption.

Pity the man who falls, but pity twice over the man who causes another to lapse, for he carries the burden of both as well as the weight of pleasure tasted by the other.

Do not imagine that you will overwhelm the demon of fornication by entering into an argument with him. Nature is on his side and he has the best of the argument. So the man who decides to struggle against his flesh and to overcome it by his own efforts is fighting in vain. The truth is that unless the Lord overturns the house of the flesh and builds the house of the soul, the man wishing to overcome it has watched and fasted for nothing. Offer up to the Lord the weakness of your nature. Admit your incapacity and, without your knowing it, you will win for yourself the gift of chastity.

A victim of sensuality who had overcome his weakness told me once that within people of his kind there flourishes a yearning for bodies, a shameless and terrible spirit that asserts itself at the very heart's core. Sheer physical pain burns so fiercely in the heart that it is like being scorched by an open fire. The sufferer finds that because of this he has no fear of God, he spurns the thought of punishment, turns away from prayer, and the sight of a corpse moves him no more than if it were a stone. He is like someone out of his mind, in a daze, and he is perpetually drunk with desire for man or beast. And if a limit were not placed on the activities of this demon, no one would be saved, no one who is made of clay mingled with blood and foul moisture. How could they be saved? After all, everything created longs insatiably for its own kind, blood for blood, the worm for a worm, clay for clay. And what does flesh desire if not flesh?

Those of us who try to restrain nature and who long to take the kingdom of heaven by force (cf. Matt. 11:12) try various artifices against this demon. Lucky the man who has not experienced the kind of conflict I have been talking about! So let us pray that we may always escape from such a trial because those who slide into the pit fall far below those others climbing up and down the ladder.[66] And indeed they have to sweat copiously and practice extreme abstinence if they are ever to get far enough out of that pit to be able to start the climb again.

When our spiritual foes are drawn up to do battle with us, we should ponder what it is they can do, just as we would take precautions in a visible war. For those foes have their proper tasks, strange as this may seem. And whenever I thought about those who were tempted. I noted that their lapses were of varying seriousness. "He who has ears to hear, let him hear" (Matt. 11:15).

In his battle against ascetics and those leading the solitary life, the devil regularly uses all his force, zeal, and low skill, all his intrigue, cleverness, and evil designs to overpower them by means that are unnatural rather than according to nature. And so it happens that when ascetics meet women and find themselves assailed neither by desire nor by evil thoughts, they occasionally come to imagine that they have achieved true blessedness. Poor idiots! They do not realize that a smaller lapse was not required since a major fall had in fact been prepared for them.

Those accursed murderers, in my opinion, manage to attack us poor wretches and bring us down with unnatural sins for the follow-

---

66. I.e., the angels whom Jacob saw in his dream ascending and descending a ladder reaching up to heaven (Gen. 28:12).

ing two reasons: first, that everywhere we may have plenty of opportunity for lapses; and second, that we may receive greater punishment. The truth of all this was personally discovered by the man who formerly was in charge of donkeys but then wretchedly fell under the sway of wild donkeys and was deluded. He had once fed on the bread of heaven but now he lost it, and even after he had repented, our founder Antony said,[66a] with bitter lament, that a great pillar had fallen. That wise man drew a veil over the nature of the sin, and he knew well that the sin of fornication does not require the availability of another body.

We carry a sort of death within us, a sin that is catastrophic, always with us and especially when we are young. I have not the courage to describe it, for my hand is restrained by him who said it is a shame to talk of, write about, or hear of the things done by them in secret (cf. Eph. 5:12).

This flesh of mine, and yet not mine, this enemy and friend, was called death by Paul. "Who will deliver me from this body of death?" he asked (Rom. 7:24). Another theologian[67] described it as passionate, slavish and nocturnal. For a long time I wondered why they spoke this way. If, as was said above, the flesh is death, then whoever defeats it will surely not die. And yet, who is the man who will live and not see death in all the impurity of his body?

I ask you to consider who is greater, the man who dies and rises again, or the man who does not die at all. Those who would pick the latter are certainly wrong, for Christ Himself died and rose. But he who opts for the former suggests in effect that one should not despair over the dying, or, rather, the lapsing.

Our relentless enemy, the teacher of fornication, whispers that God is lenient and particularly merciful to this passion, since it is so very natural. Yet if we watch the wiles of the demons we will observe that after we have actually sinned they will affirm that God is a just and inexorable judge. They say one thing to lead us into sin, another thing to overwhelm us in despair. And if we are sorrowful or inclined to despair, we are slower to sin again, but when the sorrow and the despair have been quenched, the tyrannical demon begins to speak to us again of God's mercy.

66a. A reference to St. Antony the Great: *The Sayings of the Desert Fathers,* Antony 14.

67. St. Gregory of Nazianzus; cf. *Or.* 45, 15 (*PG* 36, 644AB).

The Lord, being incorruptible and incorporeal, rejoices in the purity and cleanliness of our bodies. As for the demons, nothing is said to please them more than the foul smell of fornication, and nothing delights them as much as the defilement of the body.

Chastity makes us as familiar with God and as like Him as any man may be.

The mother of sweetness is earth and dew. The mother of chastity is stillness and obedience. Often the dispassion of body attained by stillness has been disturbed whenever the world impinged on it. But dispassion achieved through obedience is genuine and is everywhere unshakable.

I have seen humility emerge from pride, and I thought of the man who said: "Who has fathomed the mind of the Lord?" (Rom. 11:34). The pit and the fruit of arrogance is a fall; but a fall is often an occasion of humility for those willing to profit by it.

The man who imagines he can conquer the demon of fornication by gluttony and by stuffing himself is quite like someone who quenches fire with oil. And the man who tries to put an end to this struggle by means of temperance only is like someone trying to escape from the sea by swimming with just one hand. However, join humility to temperance, for the one is useless without the other.

The man who observes himself succumbing to some passion should first of all fight against this, especially if it has made its abode with him, for until this particular vice is wiped out it will be useless for us to have mastered other passions. Kill this Egyptian and we will surely have sight of God in the bush of humility (cf. Exod. 2:12; 3:2).

In the season of temptation I had the feeling that this wolf was giving me joy, tears, and indeed consolation in my spirit. Of course I was being deceived when I childishly imagined that I was deriving benefit instead of harm from this.

Every other kind of sin is external to the body, but the sin of impurity is a sin against the body, since the very substance of the flesh is defiled by pollution in a way that cannot happen in the case of other sins. And a good question to ask is this: "Why do we normally say regarding every other kind of sin that so-and-so has slipped, whereas we say sorrowfully that someone has fallen when we discover that he has committed fornication?"

A fish turns swiftly from the hook. The passionate soul turns from solitude.

When the devil decides to forge some disgraceful bond between two people, he goes to work on the inclinations of each of them—and then lights the fire of passion.

It often seems that those who incline towards sensuality tend to be sympathetic, merciful, and possessed of compunction, while those eager for chastity appear to lack these capacities in some measure.

A very well-informed man once put this question to me: "Leaving aside murder and the denial of God, what is the most serious of sins?"

"To lapse into heresy," I replied.

"In that case," he said, "why does the Catholic Church readmit heretics who have honestly come to reject their beliefs? Why are they deemed fit to share in the holy Mysteries when, by contrast, a man who has committed fornication is excluded from these sacred Mysteries for a number of years, and this by the direct command of the Apostolic Canons, even though he may have not only confessed but even abandoned his sinful ways?" The question astonished me, and I still do not know the answer.[68]

During the singing of the psalms we should examine, consider, and observe what kind of sweetness comes to us from the devil of for-

68. When the same question was put to Timothy of Alexandria (archbishop 380–5) he replied: "Because the one, the sin of the heretic, is committed with the free co-operation of the will through ignorance; and so the Church's discipline is designed to make heretics more ready to return and fornicators less eager to sin" (*Resp. Can.* 20, in J.B. Pitra, *Iuris Ecclesiastici Graecorum Historia et Monumenta*, vol. i, p. 635). The canonical position seems to have been as follows. Exclusion from Communion was a penitential discipline for those who had sinned after baptism (i.e., for those who were already in the Church). The Apostolic Penitential Canons prescribed seven years' deprivation of Communion for fornicators. Heretics were deemed outside the Church. They were baptized and chrismated on reception and could then proceed to Communion without further delay (cf. Canon 7 of Laodicea). However, those heretics who had lapsed after receiving Catholic Baptism and who then returned to the Church had to spend three years in the catechumenate, followed by a further ten years without Communion unless their repentance was especially fervent (cf. Canon 12 of Nicaea). Heretics were therefore not treated so much more leniently than fornicators. The point was that the former, if they had not previously been Catholics, were not liable to disciplinary measures. The scholiast to account for the apparently more serious nature of fornication suggests the following: "Heresy is a deviation of the mind and a ministry of the tongue, whence comes error. Fornication seduces and transforms all the senses and faculties of the body and soul, changing them from the image and likeness and casting them into nothingness; therefore it is also called a fall. Heresy comes from presumption, while fornication comes from bodily comfort. Heretics therefore attain perfection through humiliation, sensualists through bodily affliction" (scholion 26 [912D–913A]).

nication and what kind comes to us from the words of the Spirit and from the grace and power which is in them. Know yourself well, young man. For in fact I have seen men pray earnestly for their loved ones, men who thought they were fulfilling the requirements of love, when in reality it was the spirit of fornication that was stirring them.

The body can be defiled by the merest touch, for of all the senses this is the most dangerous. So think of the man who wrapped his hand in an ecclesiastical garment when he was about to carry his sick mother.[68a] Let your hand be dead to everything natural or otherwise, to your own body or to that of another.

I do not think anyone should be classed as a saint until he has made holy his body, if indeed that is possible.

We have to be especially sober and watchful when we are lying in bed, for that is the time when our mind has to contend with demons outside our body. And if our body is inclined to be sensual then it will easily betray us. So let the remembrance of death and the concise Jesus Prayer go to sleep with you and get up with you, for nothing helps you as these do when you are asleep.

Some think that struggles with passion and ejaculations during sleep are caused solely by what we have eaten. Yet I have noticed that very sick people or strict practitioners of fasting can also fall prey to these defilements. I once asked a very experienced and celebrated monk about this, and the holy man clearly explained the matter to me. "Emissions during sleep are the result of eating too much and living too well," this famous man declared. "They come too when we get complacent or when we preen ourselves because a long time may have elapsed since we experienced such emissions. They come also if we start passing judgment on our neighbor. The last two problems can occur even among the sick, and perhaps all three." If someone discovers that he is untroubled by these, he is surely lucky to be free of such passions. And if ever he suffers it, the reason must lie in the jealousy of the demons, something God allows to happen for a while in order that this man, after such an accident, which of course is free from sin, may achieve the purest humility.

Never brood by day over the fantasies that have occurred to you

68a. Rosweyde, *Vitae Patrum* v, § 68, p. 572: *PL* 73, 873B; ed. Nau, § 15a: *Revue de l'Orient chrétien* xiii (1908), p. 52.

during sleep, for the aim of the demons is to defile us while we are still awake by causing us to harp on our dreams.

Let us pay attention to another trick of our enemies. Just as bad food makes one sick after some time or indeed after some days, the same can happen in the case of actions that defile the soul. I have seen men give way to soft living and not notice at once the onset of the enemy. I have seen others take a meal with women, talk to them, and all the time be unafflicted by bad thoughts of any kind. In this way they were deceived and encouraged to grow careless and to imagine that they were safe and at peace. Then came sudden destruction in their cells. What bodily and spiritual destruction afflicts us when we are alone? The man who suffers temptation knows well. And the man who goes about untempted has no need to know.

When temptation comes, our best weapons are sackcloth and ashes, all-night vigils standing up, hunger, the merest touch of water when we are thirsty, time passed among the burial places of the dead, and most important of all, humility of heart; and if possible a spiritual director or a helpful brother, old in wisdom rather than years, should also support us. Indeed it would come as a great surprise if anyone could, by his efforts alone, save his ship from the sea.

The same sin earns punishment a hundred times greater for one person rather than another, depending on character, place, progress, and much else besides.

I was told once about an astonishing level of chastity attained by someone. "There was a man[69] who, having looked on a body of great beauty, at once gave praise to its Creator and after one look was stirred to love God and to weep copiously, so that it was marvelous how something that could have brought low one person managed to be the cause of a heavenly crown for another. And if such a man feels and behaves in similar fashion on similar occasions, then he has already risen to immortality before the general resurrection."

The same guideline ought to direct us when we sing songs and hymns, for the lovers of God are moved to holy joy, divine love, and tears by songs both worldly and spiritual, just as lovers of pleasure are moved to the opposite.

Some solitary monks, as I have said already, have to face vastly

69. St. Nonnus, bishop of Heliopolis (Rosweyde, *Vitae Patrum* I, p. 377: *PL* 73, 665).

more dangerous attacks from the demons. And no wonder, since these are the places where the devils choose to lurk, because the Lord, out of concern for us, has driven them to desert places[70] and to the dark reaches of hell. The devils of fornication launch vicious attacks on solitary monks. They try to drive them back into the world, by making them think that their time in the desert has been wasted. Devils do not bother us when we are in the world, and this is because they think that, if we are not attacked there, we will continue to stay with worldly-minded people. The place of temptation is the place where we find ourselves having to put up a bitter fight against the enemy, and wherever we are not involved in a struggle is surely the place where the enemy is posing as a friend.

If we have to go out into the world on some legitimate task, we have the hand of God to guard us, probably because our spiritual director is praying that we may not be a cause of blasphemy against the Lord. Sometimes we are protected by our insensitivity or by the fact that long experience has exhausted for us the spectacle of the world, its sounds and all its works. But sometimes the reason lies in the fact that the devils have left deliberately so that only the demon of pride remains to take over from all of them.

But all of you who wish to practice purity and preserve it should listen now to another cunning stratagem of that deceiver, for I have been told by someone who had to suffer the experience that the demon of sensuality often hid himself completely. Then he would have a monk sit or talk with women. He would inspire him with great piety and even a flood of tears, and then suggest that he speak about the remembrance of death, judgment, and chastity. The unfortunate women, deceived by his words and spurious piety, would rush to him, thinking him to be a shepherd instead of the wolf he really was. Acquaintance would grow into familiarity, and the wretched monk would suffer his downfall.

We should strive in all possible ways neither to see nor to hear of that fruit we have vowed never to taste. It amazes me to think we could imagine ourselves to be stronger than the prophet David, something quite impossible indeed (cf. 2 Kings [2 Sam.] 11:2–4).

Purity deserves such great and mighty praise that some of the Fa-

70. It was a common idea that demons dwelt in the desert; solitaries went there partly to do battle with them.

thers have actually dared to call it freedom from passion. But there are some who would claim that anyone who has tasted sin can never be called pure. I disagree, and for the following reason. You can easily graft a good olive onto a wild olive if you so wish. Now if the keys of the kingdom had been given to someone who had lived always in virginity, the claim mentioned above might have some force. But let the proponents of the claim be silenced by the man who had a mother-in-law and who nevertheless received the keys of the kingdom after he had become pure.[71]

The serpent of sensuality has many faces. To those who have had no experience of sin he suggests the idea of trying it once and then stopping. Then the crafty creature, exploiting the recollection of having sinned once, urges them to try again. And many of the people without experience feel no conflict within themselves because they do not know what is evil, whereas the experienced, knowing the evil for what it is, suffer disturbance and conflict, though sometimes the opposite can happen too.

When we rise from sleep in a good and peaceful frame of mind, we may assume that this is a secret gift from the heavenly angels, particularly if we had gone to sleep after much prayer and vigil. Sometimes, however, we get up in a bad mood, and this is caused by bad dreams and fantasies. For "I have seen the enemy all puffed up, high and tossing in me like the cedars of Lebanon" (Ps. 36:35) and I passed by with temperance, and see, his rage was not as it had been before, and I looked for him with humble mind and no place or trace of him could be found in me.

To have mastered one's body is to have taken command of nature, which is surely to have risen above it. And the man who has done this is not much lower than the angels, if even that.

That spirit should fight with spirit is not surprising. The real wonder is that a man dwelling in his body, and always struggling against this hostile and canny matter, should manage to rout spiritual foes.

The great concern of the good Lord for us is shown by the fact that shyness acts as a curb on the shamelessness of women. For if the woman chased the man, no flesh would be saved.

Among the discerning Fathers, distinctions are recognized be-

71. Peter was married: see Matt. 16:19, Luke 4:38 and 1 Cor. 9:5.

tween provocation, coupling, assent, captivity, struggle, and the disease called passion, which is in the soul.[72] These blessed Fathers say that provocation is a simple word or image encountered for the first time, which has entered into the heart. Coupling is conversation with what has been encountered, whether this be passionately or otherwise. Assent is the delighted yielding of the soul to what it has encountered. Captivity is a forcible and unwilling abduction of the heart, a permanent lingering with what we have encountered and which totally undermines the necessary order of our souls. By struggle they mean force equal to that which is leading the attack, and this force wins or loses according to the desires of the spirit. Passion, in their view, is properly something that lies hidden for a long time in the soul and by its very presence it takes on the character of a habit, until the soul of its own accord clings to it with affection.

The first of these conditions is free of sin, the second sometimes, and the condition of the soul determines whether or not the third is sinful. Struggle can earn a crown or punishment. Captivity is judged in different ways, depending on whether it happens at the time of prayer or at some other time, whether it happens in regard to what is unimportant or in the context of evil thoughts. But passion is unequivocally denounced in every situation and requires suitable repentance or future punishment. From all of which it follows that he who regards the first encounter with detachment cuts off with one blow all the rest that follow.

The most exact of the spiritual Fathers point to another more subtle notion, something they call *pararripismos*, or disturbance[73] of the mind. What happens is this. In a moment, without a word being spoken or an image presented, a sudden passionate urge lays hold of the victim. It comes faster than anything in the physical world and is swifter and more indiscernible than any spirit. It makes its appearance in the soul by a simple memory, which is unconnected with anything, independent of time and inexpressible, and in some cases comes without the person himself realizing the fact. Someone who

---

72. See, for example, St. Mark the Ascetic, *On the Spiritual Law*, §§ 139–42 (*PG* 65, 921–4: ET *Phil.*, §§ 138–41, pp.119–20), and St. Maximos the Confessor, *On Love*, I 84, II 31 (*PG* 90, 980, 993: ET *The Philokalia*, vol. ii). There is a valuable analysis of the terms which Climacus uses in the Glossary of *The Philokalia*, vol. i, pp. 364–6.

73. This is an expression used by St. Mark the Ascetic, *Letter to Nicolas the Solitary*, *PG* 65, 1040B (ET *Phil.* p. 153).

has been able to detect such a subtlety, someone with the gift of mourning, may be able to explain how with the eye alone, with a mere glance, by the touch of a hand, through a song overheard, the soul is led to commit a definite sin of unchastity without any notion or evil thought.

Some say that it is the thought of fornication that introduces passion into the body, while others deny this, insisting that evil thoughts derive from the capacity of the body to experience things sensual. The former declare that if the mind had not taken the lead, the body would not have followed.[73a] But the latter maintain that their view is proved by the depravity of bodily passion, for, very often, a pleasing sight, a touch of the hand, the scent of perfume, or the sound of sweet voices can be enough to generate evil thoughts. If anyone can do so in the Lord, let him explain what really happens. It would greatly benefit those living actively to understand this, though this problem need not really concern those practicing virtue with simple hearts. Still, not everyone has the necessary degree of understanding and not everyone possesses the holy simplicity that is a breastplate against the cunning of evil demons.

Some passions enter the body by way of the soul, and some work in the opposite way, the latter affecting people living in the world, the former assailing those living the monastic life and, hence, lacking stimulus from the outside. All I can say here about it is that if you look for wisdom among evil men, you most certainly will not find it (cf. Prov. 14:6).

After we have fought long and hard against this demon, this ally of the flesh, after we have driven it out of our heart, torturing it with the stone of fasting and the sword of humility, this scourge goes into hiding in our bodies, like some kind of worm, and it tries to pollute us, stimulating us to irrational and untimely movements. This particularly happens to those who have fallen to the demon of vainglory, for since dirty thoughts no longer preoccupy their hearts they fall victim to pride. Such people can discover whether or not this is true if once they have attained a certain stillness they quietly take stock of themselves. For they will then discover that deep down in their hearts, like a snake in dung, is the notion that by their own efforts and enthusiasm they made great advances in purity. Poor wretches!

73a. See St. Mark the Ascetic, *On the Spiritual Law*, § 120 (*PG* 65, 920C: ET *Phil.*, § 119, p. 118).

They forget the saying: "What have you got that you did not receive as a gift either from God or as a result of the help and prayers of others?" (cf. 1 Cor. 4:7). Let them beware then. Let them with all zeal eject from their hearts the snake mentioned above. Let them kill it with great humility, so that when they have got rid of it they may be stripped of their garments of skin[74] and sing, like pure children, a triumphant hymn of chastity to the Lord. Only let us hope that when they are thus stripped, they may not find that they are bereft of the humility and freedom from malice so natural to children.

This demon is especially on the lookout for our weak moments and will viciously assail us when we are physically unable to pray against it.

The effort of bodily prayer can help those not yet granted real prayer of the heart. I am referring to the stretching out of the hands, the beating of the breast, the sincere raising of the eyes heavenward, deep sighs and constant prostrations. But this is not always feasible when other people are present, and this is when the demons particularly like to launch an attack and, because we have not yet the strength of mind to stand up against them and because the hidden power of prayer is not yet within us, we succumb. So go somewhere apart, if you can. Hide for a while in some secret place. If you can, lift up the eyes of your soul, but if not, the eyes of your body. Stand still with your arms in the shape of the cross so that with this sign you may shame and conquer your Amalek.[75] Cry out to God, Who has the strength to save you. Do not bother with elegant and clever words. Just speak humbly, beginning with, "Have mercy on me, for I am weak" (Ps. 6:3). And then you will come to experience the power of the Most High and with help from heaven you will drive off your invisible foes. The man who gets into the habit of waging war in this way will soon put his enemies to flight solely by means of spiritual resources, for this is the reward God likes to bestow on those who put up a good struggle, and rightly so.

---

74. The "garments of skin" allude to Gen. 3:21 and represent that which was added to human nature as a result of the fall, i.e., the passions, sexual stirrings and mortality. For a discussion of the patristic use of this expression see Gregory of Nyssa, *The Life of Moses*, ET Malherbe and Ferguson (*The Classics of Western Spirituality*), pp. 160–1, note 29.

75. Like Moses with his arms raised in the battle with the Amalekites (cf. Exod. 17:11).

I was once at a gathering of holy men and I noticed a zealous brother troubled by evil thoughts. There was no place where he could go aside for secret prayer, and so he went out, as if on a call of nature. There he armed himself with intense prayer against the enemy. I criticized him for having gone to an inappropriate place, but the answer he gave me was this: "I chose an unclean place in which to pray to be cleansed from filth, that I might drive out unclean thoughts."

All demons try to darken our minds so that they may then suggest to us what they want us to do, and so long as the mind stays awake we will not be robbed of our treasure. But the demon of fornication tries harder than all the others. First, by darkening our minds, which guide us, it urges and inclines us in the presence of other people to do things that only the mad would think of. Then when our minds are cleared we become ashamed of these unholy deeds, words, and gestures, not only before those who saw us but before ourselves, and we are astounded by this earlier blindness of ours. The result is that frequently as a consequence of realizing what had happened, men turn away from this particular evil.

Drive out that enemy which, after you have sinned, comes between you and your prayers, meditation, and vigil. Remember the saying: "Because the soul tormented by earlier sin is a burden to me, I will save it from its enemies" (cf. Luke 18:5).

Who has won the battle over the body? The man who is contrite of heart. And who is contrite of heart? The man who has denied himself, for how can he fail to be contrite of heart if he has died to his own will?

There is a kind of passionate person, more passionate than most, who confesses his defilements with pleasure and delight.

Dirty, shameful thoughts in the heart are usually caused by the deceiver of the heart, the demon of fornication, and only restraint and indeed a disregard for them will prove an antidote.

By what rule or manner can I bind this body of mine? By what precedent can I judge him? Before I can bind him he is let loose, before I can condemn him I am reconciled to him, before I can punish him I bow down to him and feel sorry for him. How can I hate him when my nature disposes me to love him? How can I break away from him when I am bound to him forever? How can I escape from him when he is going to rise with me? How can I make him incorrupt when he has received a corruptible nature? How can I argue with him when all the arguments of nature are on his side?

If I try to bind him through fasting, then I am passing judgment on my neighbor who does not fast—with the result that I am handed over to him again. If I defeat him by not passing judgment I turn proud—and I am in thrall to him once more. He is my helper and my enemy, my assistant and my opponent, a protector and a traitor. I am kind to him and he assaults me. If I wear him out he gets weak. If he has a rest he becomes unruly. If I upset him[76] he cannot stand it. If I mortify him I endanger myself. If I strike him down I have nothing left by which to acquire virtues. I embrace him. And I turn away from him.

What is this mystery in me? What is the principle of this mixture of body and soul? How can I be my own friend and my own enemy? Speak to me! Speak to me, my yoke-fellow, my nature! I cannot ask anyone else about you. How can I remain uninjured by you? How can I escape the danger of my own nature? I have made a promise to Christ that I will fight you, yet how can I defeat your tyranny? But this I have resolved, namely, that I am going to master you.

And this is what the flesh might say in reply: "I will never tell you what you do not already know. I will speak the knowledge we both have. Within me is my begetter, the love of self. The fire that comes to me from outside is too much pampering and care. The fire within me is past ease and things long done. I conceived and give birth to sins, and they when born beget death by despair in their turn. And yet if you have learned the sure and rooted weakness within both you and me, you have manacled my hands. If you starve your longings, you have bound my feet, and they can travel no further. If you have taken up the yoke of obedience, you have cast my yoke aside. If you have taken possession of humility, you have cut off my head."

This is the fifteenth reward of victory. He who has earned it while still alive has died and been resurrected. From now on he has a taste of the immortality to come.

76. Gk *sainomenos.* HTM reads *siainomenos,* "if I turn away in loathing."

Step 16

ON AVARICE

As most of the experts reckon the matter, the demon of avarice, that spirit of countless heads, comes next after the tyrant described above, and who am I to run counter to the sequence which these learned men suggest? Hence I follow the same practice, and after a few words on the disease would like to talk briefly about the remedy.

Avarice is a worship of idols and is the offspring of unbelief. It makes excuses for infirmity and is the mouthpiece of old age. It is the prophet of hunger, and the herald of drought.

The miser sneers at the gospel and is a deliberate transgressor. The man of charity spreads his money about him, but the man who claims to possess both charity and money is a self-deceived fool. The man who mourns for himself has renounced even his body and does not spare it in due season.

Do not say that you are interested in money for the sake of the poor, for two mites were insufficient to purchase the kingdom (cf. Luke 21:2).

A generous man met a miser, and the miser said the other man was without discernment.

The man who has conquered this vice has cut out care, but the man trapped by it can never pray freely to God.

The pretext of almsgiving is the start of avarice, and the finish is detestation of the poor. The collector is stirred by charity, but, when the money is in, the grip tightens.

I have seen the poverty-stricken grow rich and forget their want, through living with the poor in spirit.

The monk who is greedy for money is a stranger to tedium of the spirit. Always he turns over within himself the words of the Apostle: "The man who does not work does not eat" (2 Thess. 3:10) and, "These hands of mine have served me and those who were with me" (Acts 20:34).

Such then is the sixteenth contest, and the man who has triumphed in it has either won love or cut out care.

Step 17

ON POVERTY

The poverty of a monk is resignation from care. It is life without anxiety and travels light, far from sorrow and faithful to the commandments. The poor monk is lord of the world. He has handed all his cares over to God, and by his faith has obtained all men as his servants. If he lacks something he does not complain to his fellows and he accepts what comes his way as if from the hand of the Lord. In his poverty he turns into a son of detachment and he sets no value on what he has. Having withdrawn from the world, he comes to regard everything as refuse. Indeed he is not genuinely poor if he starts to worry about something.

A man who has embraced poverty offers up prayer that is pure, while a man who loves possessions prays to material images.

Those living in obedience to another are free of all cupidity, for when the body has been given up, what else is there to call one's own? The only way they can be harmed is by readily and easily moving from place to place. I have seen monks content to remain in one locality on account of material possessions, but my praise is for those who are pilgrims for the Lord.

The man who has tasted the things of heaven easily thinks nothing of what is below, but he who has had no taste of heaven finds pleasure in possessions.

A man who is poor for no good reason falls into a double misfortune. He goes without present goods and is deprived of these in the future.

We monks should be careful not to be less trusting than the birds, which are not anxious and do not gather into barns (cf. Matt. 6:26).

The man who gives up possessions for religious motives is great, but the man who renounces his will is holy indeed. The one will earn money or grace a hundred times over, but the other will inherit eternal life.

Waves never leave the sea. Anger and gloom never leave the miserly.

The man who thinks nothing of goods has freed himself from quarrels and disputes. But the lover of possessions will fight to the death for a needle. Sturdy faith cuts off cares, and remembrance of death denies the body. There was no trace of avarice in Job, and so he remained tranquil when he lost everything.

Avarice is said to be the root of all evil (1 Tim. 6:10), and it is so because it causes hatred, theft, envy, separations, hostility, stormy blasts, remembrance of past wrongs, inhuman acts and even murder.

A small fire can burn down an entire forest. But one virtue can help many to escape all the vices mentioned above. That virtue is detachment, which is a withdrawal from all evil desires, and which grows from an experience and taste of the knowledge of God and from a meditation on the account to be rendered at death.

The careful reader will recall the story of the mother of every evil.[76a] Listing her wicked and accursed offspring, she named the stone of insensitivity as her second child. The many-headed serpent of idolatry prevented me from giving it its own due place. The discerning Fathers, for reasons unknown to me, give it third place in the chain of eight capital sins.

I have said enough about avarice, and I plan to say something about insensitivity as the third infirmity, despite being born second. Then I will go on to discuss sleep, keeping vigil, as well as childish cowardly fear, all failings of beginners.

This is the seventeenth step. He who has climbed it is traveling to heaven unburdened by material things.

76a. See 14 (869D), p. 170.

Step 18

ON INSENSITIVITY

Insensitivity is deadened feeling in body and spirit, and comes from long sickness and carelessness. Lack of awareness is negligence that has become habit. It is thought gone numb, an offspring of predisposition, a trap for zeal, a noose for courage, an ignorance of compunction, the gateway to despair, the mother of forgetfulness giving birth to loss of fear of God and, in turn, to a deadened spirit, like a daughter bearing her own mother.

The insensitive man is a foolish philosopher, an exegete condemned by his own words, a scholar who contradicts himself, a blind man teaching sight to others. He talks about healing a wound and does not stop making it worse. He complains about what has happened and does not stop eating what is harmful. He prays against it but carries on as before, doing it and being angry with himself. And the wretched man is in no way shamed by his own words. "I'm doing wrong," he cries, and zealously continues to do so. His lips pray against it and his body struggles for it. He talks profoundly about death and acts as if he will never die. He groans over the separation of soul and body, and yet lives in a state of somnolence as if he were eternal. He has plenty to say about self-control and fights for a gourmet life. He reads about the judgment and begins to smile, about vainglory and is vainglorious while he is reading. He recites what he has learnt about keeping vigil, and at once drops off to sleep. Prayer he extols, and runs from it as if from a plague. Blessings he showers on obedience, and is the first to disobey. Detachment he praises, and he shamelessly fights over a rag. When he is angry he gets bitter, and then his bitterness makes him angry, so that having suffered one defeat he fails to notice that he has suffered another. He gorges himself, is sorry, and a little later is at it again. He blesses silence and cannot stop talking about it. He teaches meekness and frequently gets angry while he is teaching it. Having come to his senses, he sighs and shaking his head embraces his passion once more. He denounces laughter, and while lecturing on mourning he is all smiles. In front of others he criticizes himself for being vainglorious, and in making the admission he is looking for glory. He looks people in the eye with passion and talks about chastity. Out in the world he is full of praise for the solitary life and cannot see how much he is disgracing himself. He glorifies almsgivers and despises the poor. In everything he shows himself up for what he is, and does not come to his senses, though I would not say he was incapable of doing so.

I have seen such men weep as they hear of death and the dread judgment, and with the tears still in their eyes they rush off to dinner. And it amazed me to see how this stinking tyrant by means of complete insensitivity could even manage to overpower mourning.

I have described, as much as my poor talents permit, the wiles and the havoc wrought by this stony, stubborn, raging, ignorant passion, and I refuse to dwell on it. If there is anyone with the God-given skill to heal the sores, let him not shrink from the task. I am not ashamed to admit that my powers fail here, for I am very sorely tried by this vice and I would not have been able alone to analyze its wily ways if I had not laid hold of it, gripping it hard, examining it to discover what has been described above, scourging it with fear of the Lord and endless prayer. That is why this tyrannical evildoer said this to me: "Those who are under my sway laugh when they see the bodies of the dead. At prayer they are stony, hard, and blinded. In front of the altar they feel nothing. They receive the Holy Gift as if it were ordinary bread. And I laugh at people when I see them stirred by compunction. My father taught me to kill everything born of courage and love. I am the mother of Laughter, the nurse of Sleep, the friend of the Full Stomach. When I am found out I do not grieve, and I am the ally of Fake Piety."

Amazed by the words of this demented fury, I asked, in my astonishment, for the name of her father. "I was not born of just one parent," she said. "I am of mixed and uncertain origin. Big meals keep me going, time adds to my stature and bad habit fixes me in such a way that he who possesses me will never be rid of me. But if you are always on the watch and think of eternal judgment, maybe I shall let go of you to some extent. If you discover why I came to be within you, it will be possible for you to do battle with my mother, since she is not the same for all. Pray often where the dead are laid out and paint in your heart an indelible image of them, traced there with the brush of fasting. For otherwise you will never defeat me."

Step 19

ON SLEEP, PRAYER AND THE SINGING IN CHURCH OF PSALMS

Sleep is a natural state. It is also an image of death and a respite of the senses. Sleep is one, but like desire it has many sources. That is to say, it comes from nature, from food, from demons, or perhaps in some degree even from prolonged fasting by which the weakened flesh is moved to long for repose.

Just as too much drinking comes from habit, so too from habit comes overindulgence in sleep. For this reason one has to struggle against it especially at the start of one's religious life, because a long-standing habit is very difficult to correct.

Let us observe and we shall find that the spiritual trumpet[77] that summons the brethren together visibly is also the signal for the invisible assembly of our foes. Some stand by our bed and encourage us to lie down again after we have got up. "Wait until the first hymns are over," they say. "Then it will be time enough to go to church." Others get those at prayer to fall asleep. Still others cause bad and unusual stomachache, while others encourage prattle in the church. Some

77. The usual means of summoning monks to prayer was by a wooden gong or plank known later as the *talanton.* Jerome, however, says that Pachomian monks were summoned by the sound of a trumpet (*PL* 23, 69B).

inspire bad thoughts, others get us to lean against the wall as though we were weary or to start yawning over and over again, while still others cause us to laugh during prayer so as to provoke the anger of God against us. Some get us in our laziness to hurry up with the singing, while others suggest we should sing slowly in order that we may take pleasure in it. Others, by sitting on our mouths, shut them so that we can scarcely open them.

However, the man who considers with sensitivity of heart that he is standing before God will be an immovable pillar in prayer, and none of the demons mentioned above will delude him.

The truly obedient monk often becomes suddenly radiant and exultant during his prayers. He is like a wrestler who was earlier trained and made eager for his enterprise.

Everyone can pray in a crowd. For some it is a good thing to pray with a single kindred soul. But solitary prayer is only for the very few.

When chanting hymns with others it may be impossible to pray with the wordless prayer of the spirit. But your mind should meditate on the words being chanted or read. Or else you should have a set prayer to say while you are waiting for the alternate verse of the chant. But no one should undertake any additional task, or rather, distraction, during the time of prayer. This is something that Antony the Great learned clearly from his attendant angel.[77a]

A furnace tests gold. Prayer tests the zeal of a monk and his love for God.

To draw close to God, to drive out the demons—there is a task to be praised!

77a. *The Sayings of the Desert Fathers,* Antony 1.

Step 20

ON ALERTNESS

Some stand weaponless and without armor before the kings of earth, while others hold insignia of office, shields, and swords. The former are vastly superior to the latter since they are regularly the personal relations of the king and members of the royal household.

Let us see now what happens when we stand in prayer during the evening or throughout the day and night before God our King. Some keep nightlong vigil, their hands raised in prayer like spirits free of every burden. Others sing the psalms or read, while some, out of weakness, bravely fight sleep by working with their hands. Others think constantly of death and try in this way to obtain a contrite heart. Of all these types, the first and last persevere in nightlong vigil out of love for God, the second do what is appropriate for a monk, and the third travel the lowliest road. Still, God accepts and judges the offerings of each type in accordance with their intentions and their abilities.

Alertness keeps the mind clean. Somnolence binds the soul. The alert monk does battle with fornication, but the sleepy one goes to live with it. Alertness is a quenching of lust, deliverance from fantasies in dreams, a tearful eye, a heart made soft and gentle, thoughts restrained, food digested, passions tamed, spirits subdued, tongue controlled, idle imaginings banished.

The vigilant monk is a fisher of thoughts, and in the quiet of the night he can easily observe and catch them.

The bell rings for prayer. The monk who loves God says, "Bravo! Bravo!" The lazy monk says, "Alas! Alas!"

Mealtime reveals the gluttonous, prayer time the lovers of God. The former dance and the latter frown when the table is made ready.

Long sleep produces forgetfulness, but keeping vigil clears the memory.

The farmer collects his wealth on the threshing floor and in the winepress. Monks collect their wealth and knowledge during the hours of evening and night when they are standing at prayer and contemplation.

Excessive sleep is a bad companion, stealing half a lifetime or more from the lazy man.

The inexperienced monk is wide awake when talking to his friends but half asleep at prayer time. The lazy monk is a great talker whose eyes begin to shut when the sacred reading is started. When the trumpet sounds the dead will rise, and when idle talk begins the dozing wake.

The tyrant sleep is a cunning fiend who slips away from us when our stomachs are full and attacks strongly when we are hungry and thirsty. It proposes that we do manual work at prayer time, for in no other way can it interfere with the prayers of those who are keeping watch. Its first step is to attack beginners, trying to make them careless from their first day. Or it strives to prepare the way for the demon of fornication. Hence until we conquer it we ought never seek to be absent from common prayer, since shame at least may keep us from dozing off.

The demon of vainglory is the enemy of sleep, just as the hound is the enemy of hares.

At day's end the merchant counts his profits, and the monk does the same when psalmody is over.

When prayer is over, wait quietly and you will observe how mobs of demons, as though challenged by us, will try to attack us after prayer by means of wild fantasies. Watch carefully and you will note those that are accustomed to snatch away the first fruits of the soul.

It can happen that our meditation on the psalms may persist even into our time of sleeping. This can sometimes be caused by demons in order to lead us to vainglory. I would not have mentioned this had I not been compelled to do so. But in fact the soul endlessly preoccupied by day with the word of God will love to be preoccupied by it in sleep too. This second grace is properly a reward for the first and will help us to avoid spirits[78] and fantasies.

Such then is the twentieth step. He who has climbed it has received light in his heart.

78. Gk *pnevmaton.* HTM reads *ptomaton,* "falls."

Step 21

ON UNMANLY FEARS

If you pursue virtue in a monastery or in gatherings of holy men, you are unlikely to be attacked by cowardice. But if you pass your time in solitary abodes, you must strive not to be mastered by cowardice, the child of vainglory, the daughter of unbelief.

Cowardice is childish behavior within a soul advanced in years and vainglory. It is a lapse from faith that comes from anticipating the unexpected.

Fear is danger tasted in advance, a quiver as the heart takes fright before unnamed calamity. Fear is a loss of assurance.

A proud soul is the slave of cowardice. Trusting only itself, it is frightened by a sound or a shadow.

Those who mourn and those who are insensitive suffer no cowardice, but the fearful and the frightened often collapse and their minds are unhinged. Nor is this unreasonable. For the Lord rightly withdraws His protection from the proud so that the rest of us may not become vain.

While cowards are vainglorious, not everyone who is free from fear is also humble. Thieves and grave robbers may be untroubled by fear.

Do not hesitate to go in the dark of the night to those places where you are normally frightened. The slightest concession to this weakness means that this childish and absurd malady will grow old with you. So as you go where fright will lay hold of you, put on the armor of prayer, and when you reach the spot, stretch out your hands and flog your enemies with the name of Jesus, since there is no stronger weapon in heaven or on earth. And when you drive the fear away, give praise to the God Who has delivered you, and He will protect you for all eternity, provided you remain grateful. Just as one morsel will not fill your stomach, so you will not defeat fear in one move. It will fade in proportion to your mourning and the less we mourn the greater will be our cowardice.

"My hair and my flesh shuddered" (Job 4:15). These were the words of Eliphaz when he was talking about the cunning of this demon. Fear starts sometimes in the soul, sometimes in the body, and the one communicates the weakness to the other. But if your soul is unafraid even when the body is terrified, you are close to being healed.[79] However, it is barrenness of soul, not the darkness or the emptiness of places, which gives the demons power against us. And the providence of God sometimes allows this to happen so that we may learn from it.

The servant of the Lord will be afraid only of his Master, while the man who does not yet fear Him is often scared by his own shadow. The body is terrified by the presence of an invisible spirit. Yet when an angel stands nearby, the soul of the humble is exultant. So if we detect an angel by the effect he is producing, let us hasten to pray since our heavenly guardian has come to join us.[80]

79. HTM adds: "But actual freedom from cowardice comes when we eagerly accept all unexpected events with a contrite heart."

80. HTM adds: "He who has conquered cowardice has clearly dedicated his life and soul to God."

Step 22

ON VAINGLORY

Some would hold that vainglory is to be distinguished from pride, and so they give it a special place and chapter. Hence their claim that there are eight deadly sins. But against this is the view of Gregory the Theologian[81] and other teachers that in fact the number is seven. I also hold this view. After all, what pride remains in a man who has conquered vainglory? The difference is between a child and a man, between wheat and bread, for the first is a beginning and the second an end. Therefore, as the occasion demands, let us talk about the unholy vice of self-esteem, the beginning and completion of the passions; and let us talk briefly, for to undertake an exhaustive discussion would be to act like someone who inquires into the weight of the winds.

From the point of view of form, vainglory is a change of nature, a perversion of character, a taking note of criticism.[81a] As for its quality, it is a waste of work and sweat, a betrayal of treasure, an offspring

81. In fact Gregory the Great. The eight principal temptations of Evagrius were gluttony, lust, avarice, dejection, anger, despondency ("accidie"), vainglory and pride. Cassian introduced this list to the West. Pope Gregory the Great reduced the number to seven by amalgamating vainglory with pride and dejection with despondency and by introducing envy. Cf. the Preface, p. 63.

81a. The sense is not clear. One would expect the opposite to *paratirisis,* viz. "a *refusal* to take note of criticism," as in the Latin translation (*PG* 88, 950A).

of unbelief, a harbinger of pride, shipwreck in port, the ant on the threshing floor, small and yet with designs on all the fruit of one's labor. The ant waits until the wheat is in, vainglory until the riches of excellence are gathered; the one a thief, the other a wastrel.

The spirit of despair exults at the sight of mounting vice, the spirit of vainglory at the sight of the growing treasures of virtue. The door for the one is a mass of wounds, while the gateway for the other is the wealth of hard work done.

Watch vainglory. Notice how, until the very day of the burial it rejoices in clothes, oils, servants, perfumes, and such like.

Like the sun which shines on all alike, vainglory beams on every occupation. What I mean is this. I fast, and turn vainglorious. I stop fasting so that I will draw no attention to myself, and I become vainglorious over my prudence. I dress well or badly, and am vainglorious in either case. I talk or I hold my peace, and each time I am defeated. No matter how I shed this prickly thing, a spike remains to stand up against me.

A vainglorious man is a believer—and an idolator. Apparently honoring God, he actually is out to please not God but men. To be a showoff is to be vainglorious, and the fast of such a man is unrewarded and his prayer futile, since he is practicing both to win praise. A vainglorious ascetic doubly cheats himself, wearying his body and getting no reward. Who would not laugh at this vainglorious worker, standing for the psalms and moved by vainglory sometimes to laughter and sometimes to tears for all to see?

The Lord frequently hides from us even the perfections we have obtained. But the man who praises us, or, rather, who misleads us, opens our eyes with his words and once our eyes are opened our treasures vanish.

The flatterer is a servant of the devils, a teacher of pride, the destroyer of contrition, a vandal of excellence, a perverse guide. The prophet says this: "Those who honor you deceive you" (Isa. 3:12).

Men of high spirit endure offense nobly and willingly. But only the holy and the saintly can pass unscathed through praise. And I have seen men in mourning who, on being praised, reared up in anger, one passion giving way to another as at some public meeting.

"No one knows the thoughts of a man except the spirit within him" (1 Cor. 2:11). Hence those who want to praise us to our face should be ashamed and silent.

When you hear that your neighbor or your friend has denounced you behind your back or indeed in your presence, show him love and try to compliment him.

It is a great achievement to shrug the praise of men off one's soul. Greater still is to reject the praise of demons.

It is not the self-critical who reveals his humility (for does not everyone have somehow to put up with himself?). Rather it is the man who continues to love the person who has criticized him.

I have seen the demon of vainglory suggesting thoughts to one brother, revealing them to another, and getting the second man to tell the first what he is thinking and then praising him for his ability to read minds. And that dreadful demon has even lighted on parts of the body, shaking and stirring them.

Ignore him when he tells you to accept the office of bishop or abbot or teacher. It is hard to drive a dog from a butcher's counter.

When he notices that someone has achieved a measure of interior calm, he immediately suggests to him the need to return from the desert to the world, in order to save those who are perishing.

Ethiopians have one kind of appearance, statues another. So too is it the case that the vainglory of those living in community is different from that which obtains in the desert.

Vainglory anticipates the arrival of guests from the outside world. It prompts the more frivolous monk to rush out to meet them, to fall at their feet, to give the appearance of humility, when in fact he is full of pride. It makes him look and sound modest and directs his eye to the visitors' hands in the hope of getting something from them. It induces him to address them as "lords and patrons, graced with godly life." At table it makes him urge abstinence on someone else and fiercely criticize subordinates. It enables those who are standing in a slovenly manner during the singing of psalms to make an effort, those who have no voice to sing well, and those who are sleepy to wake up. It flatters the precentor, seeks the first place in the choir, and addresses him as father and master while the visitors are still there.

Vainglory induces pride in the favored and resentment in those who are slighted. Often it causes dishonor instead of honor, because it brings great shame to its angry disciples. It makes the quick-tempered look mild before men. It thrives amid talent and frequently brings catastrophe on those enslaved to it.

I have seen a demon harm and chase away his own brother. Visitors from the outside world came just at a moment when a brother got angry and the wretched man gave himself over to vainglory. He was unable to serve two passions at the one time.

The servant of vainglory leads a double life. To outward appearance, he lives with monks; but in his heart of hearts he is in the world.

If we really long for heavenly things, we will surely taste the glory above. And whoever has tasted that will think nothing of earthly glory. For it would surprise me if someone could hold the latter in contempt unless he had tasted the former.

It often happens that having been left naked by vainglory, we turn around and strip it ourselves more cleverly. For I have encountered some who embarked on the spiritual life out of vainglory, making therefore a bad start, and yet they finished up in a most admirable way because they changed their intentions.

A man who takes pride in natural abilities—I mean cleverness, the ability to learn, skill in reading, good diction, quick grasp, and all such skills as we possess without having to work for them—this man, I say, will never receive the blessings of heaven, since the man who is unfaithful in little is unfaithful and vainglorious in much. And there are men who wear out their bodies to no purpose in the pursuit of total dispassion, heavenly treasures, miracle working, and prophetic ability, and the poor fools do not realize that humility, not hard work, is the mother of such things. The man who seeks a *quid pro quo* from God builds on uncertainty, whereas the man who considers himself a debtor will receive sudden and unexpected riches.

When the winnower[82] tells you to show off your virtues for the benefit of an audience, do not yield to him. "What shall it profit a man to gain the whole world and destroy himself?" (Matt. 16:26).

Our neighbor is moved by nothing so much as by a sincere and humble way of talking and of behaving. It is an example and a spur to others never to turn proud. And there is nothing to equal the benefit of this.

A man of insight told me this: "I was once sitting at an assembly," he said. "The demon of vainglory and the demon of pride came to sit on either side of me. One poked me with the finger of vainglory and encouraged me to talk publicly about some vision or labor of mine in the desert. I shook him off with the words: 'Let those who wish me harm be driven back and let them blush' (Ps. 39:15). Then the demon on my left at once said in my ear: 'Well done! Well done!

---

82. I.e., the devil.

You have become great by conquering my shameless mother.' Turning to him I answered appropriately, making use of the rest of the verse: 'Defeat and shame on all who say, "Well done! Well done!" ' " And how is it, I asked him, that vainglory is the mother of pride. His answer was this: "Praise exalts and puffs me up, and when the soul is exalted, pride lifts it up as high as heaven—and then throws it down into the abyss."

But there is a glory that comes from the Lord. "I will glorify those who glorify Me," He says (1 Kings [1 Sam.] 2:30). And there is a glory that follows it which is contrived by the demons, for it is said, "Woe to you when all men shall speak well of you" (Luke 6:26). You can recognize the first kind of glory when you look on it as dangerous and run from it in every possible way, hiding your life-style wherever you are. And you may be certain of the other sort when you find yourself doing something, however small, with the hope that men may notice you.

Dread vainglory urges us to pretend that we have some virtue which does not belong to us. It encourages us with the text: "Let your light so shine before men that they will see your good deeds" (Matt. 5:16).

The Lord often humbles the vainglorious by causing some dishonor to befall them. And indeed the first step in overcoming vainglory is to remain silent and to accept dishonor gladly. The middle stage is to check every act of vainglory while it is still in thought. The end—insofar as one may talk of an end to an abyss—is to be able to accept humiliation before others without actually feeling it.

Do not conceal your sin because of the idea that you must not scandalize your neighbor. Of course this injunction must not be adhered to blindly. It will depend on the nature of one's sinfulness.

If ever we seek glory, if it comes our way uninvited, or if we plan some course of action because of our vainglory, we should think of our mourning and of the blessed fear on us as we stood alone in prayer before God. If we do this we will assuredly outflank shameless vainglory, that is if our wish for true prayer is genuine. This may be insufficient. In which case let us briefly remember that we must die. Should this also prove ineffective, let us at least go in fear of the shame that always comes after honor, for assuredly he who exalts himself will be humbled not only there but here also.

When those who praise us, or, rather, those who lead us astray, begin to exalt us, we should briefly remember the multitude of our sins and in this way we will discover that we do not deserve whatever is said or done in our honor.

Some of the prayers of the vainglorious no doubt deserve to win the attention of God, but He regularly anticipates their wishes and petitions so that their pride may not be increased by the success of their prayers.

Simpler people do not usually succumb to the poison of vainglory, which is, after all, a loss of simplicity and a hypocritical mode of behavior.

A worm, fully grown, often sprouts wings and can fly up high. Vainglory, fully grown, can give birth to pride, which is the beginning and the end of all evil.

Anyone free of this sickness is close to salvation. Anyone affected by it is far removed from the glory of the saints.

Such, then, is the twenty-second step. The man untouched by vainglory will not tumble into that senseless pride which is so detestable to God.

Step 23

ON PRIDE

Pride is a denial of God, an invention of the devil, contempt for men. It is the mother of condemnation, the offspring of praise, a sign of barrenness. It is a flight from God's help, the harbinger of madness, the author of downfall. It is the cause of diabolical possession, the source of anger, the gateway of hypocrisy. It is the fortress of demons, the custodian of sins, the source of hardheartedness. It is the denial of compassion, a bitter pharisee, a cruel judge. It is the foe of God. It is the root of blasphemy.

Pride begins where vainglory leaves off. Its midpoint comes with the humiliation of our neighbor, the shameless parading of our achievements, complacency, and unwillingness to be found out. It ends with the spurning of God's help, the exalting of one's own efforts and a devilish disposition.

Listen, therefore, all who wish to avoid this pit. This passion often draws strength initially from the giving of thanks, and at first it does not shamelessly urge us to renounce God. I have seen people who speak aloud their thanks to God but who in their hearts are glorifying themselves, something demonstrated by that Pharisee with his "O God, I thank You" (Luke 18:11).

Pride takes up residence wherever we have lapsed, for a lapse is in fact an indication of pride. And an admirable man said once to me:

"Think of a dozen shameful passions. Love one of them, I mean pride, and it will take up the space of all the other eleven."[82a]

A proud monk argues bitterly with others. The humble monk is loath to contradict them.

The cypress tree does not bend to the ground in order to walk, nor does the haughty monk in order to gain obedience.

The proud man wants to be in charge of things. He would feel lost otherwise.

"God resists the proud" (James 4:6). Who then could have mercy on them? Before God every proud man is unclean and who then could purify such a person?

For the proud correction is a fall, a thorn (cf. 2 Cor. 12:7) is a devil, and abandonment by God is madness. Whereas in the first two instances there are human cures available, this last cannot be healed by man.

To reject criticism is to show pride, while to accept it is to show oneself free of this fetter.

Pride and nothing else caused an angel to fall from heaven. And so one may reasonably ask whether one may reach heaven by humility alone without the help of any other virtue.

Pride loses the profits of all hard work and sweat. They clamored, but there was none to save them, because they clamored with pride. They clamored to God and He paid no heed since they were not really trying to root out the faults against which they were praying.

An old man, very experienced in these matters, once spiritually admonished a proud brother who said in his blindness: "Forgive me, father, but I am not proud." "My son," said the wise old man, "what better proof of your pride could you have given than to claim that you were not proud?"

A help to the proud is submissiveness, a tougher and humbler mode of life, and the reading of the supernatural feats of the Fathers. Even then there will perhaps be little hope of salvation for those who suffer from this disease.

While it is disgraceful to be puffed up over the adornments of others, it is sheer lunacy to imagine that one has deserved the gifts of

82a. St. Mark the Ascetic, *On the Spiritual Law*, § 136 (*PG* 65, 921C) (reading *dodeka*): ET *Phil.*, § 135, p. 119.

God. You may be proud only of the achievements you had before the time of your birth. But anything after that, indeed the birth itself, is a gift from God. You may claim only those virtues in you that are there independently of your mind, for your mind was bestowed on you by God. And you may claim only those victories you achieved independently of the body, for the body too is not yours but a work of God.

Do not be self-confident before judgment has been passed on you. Remember the guest at the marriage feast. He got there, and then, tied hand and foot, he was thrown into the dark outside (cf. Matt. 22:13). So do not be stiff-necked, since you are a material being. Many although holy and unencumbered by a body were thrown out even from heaven.

When the demon of pride finds a place for himself among his own, he appears to them, in sleep or awake, and he looks like a holy angel or martyr and he hints at mysteries to be revealed or spiritual gifts to be granted, that the wretches may be deceived and driven utterly out of their minds.

If we were to die ten thousand times for Christ, we would still not have repaid what we owe, for in value rather than physical substance there is no comparison between the blood of God and that of His servants.

We should always be on the lookout to compare ourselves with the Fathers and the lights who have gone before us. If we do, we will discover that we have scarcely begun the ascetic life, that we have hardly kept our vow in a holy manner, and that our thinking is still rooted in the world.

A real monk is one whose soul's eye is not haughty and whose bodily senses are unmoved.

A monk is one who fights his enemies, like the wild beasts that they are, and harries them as he makes his escape from them.

To be a monk is to know ecstasy without end and to grieve for life.

A monk is shaped by virtues in the way that others are shaped by pleasures.

A monk has an unfailing light in the eye of the heart.

A monk is an abyss of humility in which every evil spirit has been plunged and smothered.

Pride makes us forget our sins, for the remembrance of them leads to humility.

Pride is utter poverty of soul disguised as riches, imaginary light where in fact there is darkness. This abominable vice not only stops our progress but even tosses us down from the heights we have reached.

The proud man is a pomegranate, gone bad within, radiant outside.

A proud monk needs no demon. He has turned into one, an enemy to himself.

Darkness is alien to light. Pride is alien to every virtue.

Blaspheming words rise up in the hearts of the proud, heavenly visions in the hearts of the humble.

A thief hates the sun. A proud man despises the meek.

It happens, I do not know how, that most of the proud never really discover their true selves. They think they have conquered their passions and they find out how poor they really are only after they die.

The man ensnared by pride will need God's help, since man is of no use to him.

I captured this senseless deceiver once. It was rising up in my heart and on its shoulders was vainglory, its mother. I roped them with the noose of obedience and flailed them with the whip of humility. Then I lashed them and asked how they had managed to gain access to me. "We have no beginning and no birth," they said, "for we are the source and the begetters of all the passions. The strongest opposition to us comes from the contrition of heart that grows out of obedience. We can endure no authority over us, which is why we fell from heaven where we surely had authority. In short, we are the authors and the progenitors of everything opposed to humility, for everything that favors humility brings us low. We prevail everywhere except in heaven. So, then, where will you run to escape us? You will find us often where there is patient endurance of dishonor, where there is obedience and freedom from anger, where there is willingness to bear no grudge, where one's neighbor is served. And our children are the falls of those who lead the life of the spirit. Their names: Anger, Calumny, Spite, Irascibility, Yelling, Blasphemy, Hypocrisy, Hatred, Envy, Argumentativeness, Self-will, Disobedience.

"There is only one thing with which we cannot interfere, and the violence you do us will make us admit what this is. If you can honestly condemn yourself before the Lord, then indeed you will find us as flimsy as a cobweb. For, you see, Vainglory is pride's saddle-horse on which I am mounted. But holy Humility and Self-deprecation will laugh at the horse and its rider and will joyfully sing the song of triumph: 'Let us sing to the Lord, for He has been truly glorified. Horse and rider He has thrown into the sea' (Exod. 15:1), into the depths of humility."

Such is the twenty-third step. Whoever climbs it, if indeed anyone can, will certainly be strong.

Concerning unspeakably blasphemous Thoughts

As we have already heard, from a troublesome root and mother comes a most troublesome offspring. What I mean is that unspeakable blasphemy is the child of dreadful pride. Hence the need to talk about it, since it is no ordinary foe but is far and away the deadliest enemy of all. Worse still, it is extremely hard to articulate and to confess it and therefore to discuss it with a spiritual healer, and the result has been to cause frustration and despair in many people, for like a worm in a tree this unholy enemy gnaws away all hope.

This atrocious foe has the habit of appearing during the holy services and even at the awesome hour of the Mysteries, and blaspheming the Lord and the consecrated elements, thereby showing that these unspeakable, unacceptable, and unthinkable words are not ours but rather those of the God-hating demon who fled from heaven because, it seems, of the blasphemies he uttered there too against the Lord. It must be so, for if these dreadful and unholy words are my own, how could I offer humble worship after having partaken of the sacred gift? How could I revile and praise at the same time?

This deceiver, this destroyer of souls, has often caused men to go mad. And no other thought is as difficult to admit in confession, which is why so many are dogged by it all their days. In fact nothing gives demons and evil thoughts such power over us as to nourish them and hide them in our hearts unconfessed.

If you have blasphemous thoughts, do not think that you are to blame. God knows what is in our hearts and He knows that ideas of this kind come not from us but from our enemies.

Drunkenness leads to stumbling. Pride leads to unholy thoughts. The drunkard will be punished not for his stumbling but for his drunkenness.

Those unclean and unspeakable thoughts come at us when we are praying, but, if we continue to pray to the end, they will retreat, for they do not struggle against those who resist them.

This unholy demon not only blasphemes God and everything

that is divine. It stirs up the dirtiest and most obscene thoughts within us, thereby trying to force us to give up praying or to fall into despair. It stops the prayer of many and turns many away from the holy Mysteries. It has evilly and tyrannously caused the bodies of some to be worn away with grief. It has exhausted others with fasting and has given them no rest. It has struck at people living in the world, and also at those leading the monastic life, whispering that there is no salvation in store for them, murmuring that they are more to be pitied than any unbeliever or pagan.

Anyone disturbed by the spirit of blasphemy and wishing to be rid of it should bear in mind that thoughts of this type do not originate in his own soul but are caused by that unclean devil who once said to the Lord: "I will give you all this if only You fall down and adore me" (Matt. 4:9). So let us make light of him and pay no regard whatever to his promptings. Let us say: " 'Get behind me, Satan! I will worship the Lord my God and I will serve only Him' (Matt. 4:10). May your word and your effort rebound on you, and your blasphemies come down on your own head now and in the world to come." To tackle the demon of blasphemy in any way other than this is to be like a man trying to hold lightning in his hands. For how can you take a grip on, seize, or grapple with someone who flits into the heart quicker than the wind, talks more rapidly than a flash, and then immediately vanishes? Every other kind of foe stops, struggles a while, lingers and gives one time to grapple with him. But not this one. He hardly appears and is gone again immediately. He barely speaks and then vanishes.

This particular demon likes to take up residence in the minds of simpler and more innocent souls, and these are more upset and disturbed by it than others. To such people we could quite rightly say that what is happening to them is due not to their own undue self-esteem but to the jealousy of the demons.

Let us refrain from passing judgment or condemnation on our neighbor. If we do, then we will not be terrorized by blasphemous thoughts, since the one produces the other.

The situation here is like that of someone shut up in his own house who overhears but does not join in the conversation of passers-by. The soul that keeps to itself overhears and is disturbed by the blasphemies of devils who are merely transients.

Hold this foe in contempt and you will be liberated from its torments. Try cleverly to fight it and you will end up by surrendering, for the man who tries to conquer spirits by talk is like someone hoping to lock up the winds.

There was once a zealous monk who was badly troubled by this demon. For twenty years he wore himself out with fasting and vigils, but to no avail, as he realized. So he wrote the temptation on a sheet of paper, went to a certain holy man, handed him the paper, bowed his face to the ground and dared not to look up. The old man read it, smiled, lifted the brother and said to him: "My son, put your hand on my neck." The brother did so. Then the great man said: "Very well, brother. Now let this sin be on my neck for as many years as it has been or will be active within you. But from now on, ignore it." And the monk who had been tempted in this fashion assured me that even before he had left the cell of this old man, his infirmity was gone. The man who had actually experienced this told me about it, giving thanks to Christ.

He who has defeated this vice has banished pride.

Step 24

ON MEEKNESS, SIMPLICITY, GUILELESSNESS, AND WICKEDNESS

The light of dawn comes before the sun, and meekness is the precursor of all humility. So let us listen to the order in which Christ, our Light, places these virtues. He says: "Learn from Me, because I am meek and humble of heart" (Matt. 11:29). Therefore before gazing at the sun of humility we must let the light of meekness flow over us. If we do, we will then be able to look steadily at the sun. The true order of these virtues teaches us that we are totally unable to turn our eyes to the sun before we have first become accustomed to the light.

Meekness is a mind consistent amid honor or dishonor. Meekness prays quietly and sincerely for a neighbor however troublesome he may be. Meekness is a rock looking out over the sea of anger which breaks the waves which come crashing on it and stays entirely unmoved. Meekness is the bulwark of patience, the door, indeed the mother of love, and the foundation of discernment. For it is said: "The Lord will teach His ways to the meek" (Ps. 24:9). And it is meekness that earns pardon for our sins, gives confidence to our prayers and makes a place for the Holy Spirit. "To whom shall I look if not the meek and the peaceful?" (Isa. 66:2).

Meekness works alongside of obedience, guides a religious community, checks frenzy, curbs anger. It is a minister of joy, an imitation of Christ, the possession of angels, a shackle for demons, a shield against bitterness. The Lord finds rest in the hearts of the meek, while the turbulent spirit is the home of the devil. "The meek shall inherit the earth" (Matt. 5:5), indeed, rule over it; and the bad-tempered shall be carried off as booty from their land.

A meek soul is a throne of simplicity, but a wrathful mind is a creator of evil.

A gentle soul will make a place for wise words, since the "Lord will guide the meek in judgment" (Ps. 24:9), or rather, in discretion.

An upright soul is the companion of humility, but an evil one is the daughter of pride.

The souls of the meek shall be filled with wisdom, but the angry mind will cohabit with darkness and ignorance.

A bad-tempered man met a dissembler, and not an honest word passed between them, for if you open the heart of the one you will find frenzy, and if you examine the soul of the other you will see malice.

Simplicity is an enduring habit within a soul that has grown impervious to evil thoughts.

Evil is a deliberate kind of knowledge. Or, rather, it is a deformity of the devil. There is no truth in it. And it imagines it can avoid being detected by many.

Hypocrisy is soul and body in a state of opposition to each other, intertwined with every kind of invention.

Guilelessness is the joyful condition of an uncalculating soul.

Honesty is innocent thought, a genuine character, speech that is neither artificial nor premeditated.

Innocence is a soul as pure as the day it was created and always concerned for everyone.

Malice is honesty perverted, a deluded thought, a lying disposition, perjury, and ambiguous words. Malice is a false heart, an abyss of cunning, deceit that has become habitual, pride that is second nature. It is the foe of humility, a fake penitence, mourning depleted,[83] a refusal to confess, an insistence on getting one's own way. It is the agent of lapses, a hindrance to resurrection, a tolerance of wrongdoing, false grief, false reverence. It is life gone diabolical.

The evil man is the namesake and companion of the devil, which

---

83. Gk *mikrysmos.* HTM reads *makrysmos,* "an estrangement from mourning."

is why the Lord taught us to call the devil by that name, saying, "Deliver us from the Evil One" (Matt. 6:13).

Let us run from the precipice of hypocrisy, from the pit of duplicity. Let us heed the words of him who said: "The evildoers shall be destroyed" (Ps. 36:9); "like the grass they shall wither and like green herbs shall they fall away" (cf. Ps. 36:2). People of this kind are fodder for demons.

God is called uprightness just as He is called love. This is why in the *Song of Songs* the wise man says to the pure heart: "Uprightness has loved you" (Song of Songs 1:4). The father of the wise man says: "The Lord is good and upright" (Ps 24:8). He says that those who are God's namesakes are saved: "He saves the upright of heart" (Ps. 7:11). "His countenance sees and visits the honest and the just" (Ps. 10:8).

Unadorned simplicity is the first characteristic of childhood. As long as Adam had it, he saw neither the nakedness of his soul nor the indecency of his flesh.

Good and blessed is that simplicity which some have by nature, but better is that which has been goaded out of wickedness by hard work. The former is protected from much complexity and the passions, while the latter is the gateway to the greatest humility and meekness. There is not much reward for the one and no end of reward for the other.

If you wish to draw the Lord to you, approach Him as disciples to a master, in all simplicity, openly, honestly, without duplicity, without idle curiosity. He is simple and uncompounded.[84] And He wants the souls that come to Him to be simple and pure. Indeed you will never see simplicity separated from humility.

The evil man is a false prophet. He imagines that from words he can catch thoughts, from appearances the truth of the heart.

I have seen good souls turn evil from the example of evil people, and it amazed me that they could so quickly shed their natural simplicity and innocence. But it is as easy for the honest to lapse as it is hard for evildoers to change their ways. Still, a genuine turning away from the world, obedience, and a guarding of the lips have often proved very effective and have wonderfully restored those who seemed to be beyond recall.

If knowledge can cause most people to become vain, perhaps ig-

84. Cf. St. Basil, *Adversus Eunomium* I, 23 (*PG* 29, 564A).

norance and lack of learning can make them humble. Yet now and again you find men who pride themselves on their ignorance.

Paul the Simple,[85] that thrice-blessed man, was a shining example to us. He was the measure and type of blessed simplicity, and no one has ever seen or heard or could see so much progress in so short a time.

A simple monk is like a dumb but rational and obedient animal. He lays his burden on his spiritual director. And like the animal who never answers back to the master who yokes him, the upright soul does not talk back to his superior. Instead, he follows where he is directed to go and will raise no protest even if sent to his death.

"It is hard for the rich to enter the kingdom" (Matt. 19:23). It is hard too for the foolishly "wise" to enter simplicity.

A lapse often saves the clever man, bringing him salvation and innocence in spite of himself.

Fight to escape from your own cleverness. If you do, then you will find salvation and an uprightness through Jesus Christ our Lord. Amen.

If you have the strength to take this step, do not lose heart. For now you are imitating Christ your Master and you have been saved.

85. Paul the Simple went off to join St. Antony in the desert after catching his wife in the act of adultery. St. Antony thought him too old to become a monk, but Paul submitted to the severest discipline with such unquestioning obedience that in a relatively short time he acquired spiritual powers even greater than those of St. Antony. See Palladius, *The Lausiac History*, ch. 22; *The Lives of the Desert Fathers*, ch. 24; *The Sayings of the Desert Fathers*, Paul the Simple.

Step 25

ON HUMILITY

Do you imagine that plain words can precisely or truly or appropriately or clearly or sincerely describe the love of the Lord, humility, blessed purity, divine enlightenment, fear of God, and assurance of the heart? Do you imagine that talk of such matters will mean anything to someone who has never experienced them? If you think so, then you will be like a man who with words and examples tries to convey the sweetness of honey to people who have never tasted it. He talks uselessly. Indeed I would say he is simply prattling. The same applies in the first instance. A man stands revealed as either having had no experience of what he is talking about or as having fallen into the grip of vainglory.

Our theme sets before us as a touchstone a treasure stored safely in earthen vessels, that is, in our bodies. This treasure is of a quality that eludes adequate description. It carries an inscription of heavenly origin which is therefore incomprehensible so that anyone seeking words for it is faced with a great and endless task. The inscription reads as follows: "Holy Humility."

Let all who are led by the Spirit of God come with us into this spiritual and wise assembly. Let them hold in their spiritual hands the tablets of knowledge inscribed by God Himself. We have come together. We have put our questions. We have searched for the meaning of this precious inscription.

"Humility is constant forgetfulness of one's achievements," someone says.

"It is the admission that in all the world one is the least important and is also the greatest sinner," another says.

"It is the mind's awareness that one is weak and helpless," a third says.

"It is to forestall one's neighbor at a contentious moment and to be the first to end a quarrel."

"It is the acknowledgement of divine grace and divine mercy."

"It is the disposition of a contrite soul and the abdication of one's own will."

I listened to all this and thought it over carefully and soberly, and was not able to grasp the sense of that blessed virtue from what I had heard. I was the last to speak; and, like a dog gathering crumbs from a table, I collected what those learned and blessed fathers had said and went on from there to propose my own definition: "Humility is a grace in the soul and with a name known only to those who have had experience of it. It is indescribable wealth, a name and a gift from God. 'Learn from Me,' He said; that is, not from an angel, not from a man, not from a book, but 'from Me,' that is, from My dwelling within you, from My illumination and action within you, for 'I am gentle and meek of heart' (Matt. 11:29) in thought and in spirit, and your souls will find rest from conflicts and relief from evil thoughts."

The appearance of this sacred vine is one thing during the winter of passions, another in the springtime of flowering, and still another in the harvesttime of all the virtues. Yet all these appearances have one thing in common, namely, joy and the bearing of fruit, and they all give sure signs and evidence of the harvest to come. As soon as the cluster of holy humility begins to flower within us, we come, after hard work, to hate all earthly praise and glory. We rid ourselves of rage and fury; and the more this queen of virtues spreads within our souls through spiritual growth, the more we begin to regard all our good deeds as of no consequence, in fact as loathsome. For every day we somehow imagine that we are adding to our burden by an ignorant scattering, that the very abundance of God's gifts to us is so much in excess of what we deserve that the punishment due to us becomes thereby all the greater. Hence our minds remain secure, locked up in the purse of modesty, aware of the knocks and the jeers of thieves and yet untroubled by them, because modesty is an unassailable strongroom.

We have so far risked a few words of a philosophical kind regarding the blossoming and the growth of this everblooming fruit. But those of you who are close to the Lord Himself must find out from Him what the perfect reward is of this holy virtue, since there is no way of measuring the sheer abundance of such blessed wealth, nor could words convey its quality. Nevertheless, we must try to express the thoughts that occur to us about its distinguishing characteristics.

Real repentance, mourning scrubbed of all impurity, and holy humility among beginners are as different and distinct from one another as yeast and flour from bread. The soul is ground and refined by visible repentance. The waters of true mourning bring it to a certain unity. I would even go so far as to speak of a mingling with God. Then, kindled by the fire of the Lord, blessed humility is made into bread and made firm without the leaven of pride. The outcome of all this is a three-stranded cord (cf. Eccles. 4:12), a heavenly rainbow coming together as a single power and energy, with its own effects and characteristics. Speak of one and we imply the other two. And I will now briefly try to prove the truth of what I am saying.

The first and principal token of this excellent and admirable triad is the delighted readiness of the soul to accept indignity, to receive it with open arms, to welcome it as something that relieves and cauterizes diseases of the soul and grevious sins. The second token is the wiping out of anger—and modesty over the fact that it has subsided. Third and preeminent is the honest distrust of one's own virtues, together with an unending desire to learn more.

"The end of the law and the prophets is Christ, for the justification of every believer" (Rom. 10:4). And the end of impure passions is vainglory and pride for every man who fails to deal with the problem. But their destroyer is a spiritual stag[86] which keeps the man who lives with it safe from every poison. The deadly bane of hypocrisy and of calumny can surely never appear where there is humility. Where will this snake nestle and hide? Will it not be pulled out from the heart's earth to be killed and done away with? Where there is hu-

86. The stag was thought to be able to kill snakes after first drawing them out of their holes with the breath of its nostrils (cf. Origen, *Hom. 2, 11 in Cant.* : *PG* 13, 56C).

mility there will be no sign of hatred, no species of quarrelsomeness, no whiff of disobedience—unless of course some question of faith arises. The man with humility for his bride will be gentle, kind, inclined to compunction, sympathetic, calm in every situation, radiant, easy to get along with, inoffensive, alert and active. In a word, free from passion. "The Lord remembered us in our humility and delivered us from our enemies" (Ps. 135:23–24), that is, from our passions and from our impurities.

A humble monk will not preoccupy himself with mysteries. A proud monk busies himself with the hidden judgments of God.

Demons once heaped praise on one of the most discerning of the brothers. They even appeared to him in visible form. But this very wise man spoke to them as follows: "If you cease to praise me by way of the thoughts of my heart, I shall consider myself to be great and outstanding because of the fact that you have left me. But if you continue to praise me, I must deduce from such praise that I am very impure indeed, since every proudhearted man is unclean before the Lord (cf. Prov. 16:5). So leave me, and I shall become great, or else praise me, and with your help I shall earn more humility." Struck by this dilemma, they vanished.

Let not your soul be a hollow in the stream of life, a hollow sometimes full and sometimes dried up by the heat of vainglory and pride. Instead, may your soul be a spring-head of dispassion that wells up into a river of poverty. Friend, remember that corn and the fruit of the spirit will stand high in the valleys (cf. Ps. 64:14). The valley is a soul made humble among the mountains of labors and virtues. It always remains unproud and steadfast. In Scripture are the words, "I humbled myself, and the Lord hastened to rescue me" (Ps. 114:6); and these words are there instead of "I have fasted," "I have kept vigil," "I lay down on the bare earth."

Repentance lifts a man up. Mourning knocks at heaven's gate. Holy humility opens it. This I say, and I worship a Trinity in Unity and a Unity in Trinity.

The sun lights up everything visible. Humility reaches across everything done according to reason. Where there is no light, all is in darkness. Where there is no humility, all is rotten.

In the entire universe there is a unique place that saw the sun just once. And there is a unique thought that has given rise to humility. There was a unique day on which the whole world rejoiced. And there is a unique virtue the demons cannot imitate.[87]

To exalt oneself is one thing, not to do so another, and to humble oneself is something else entirely. A man may always be passing judgment on others, while another man passes judgment neither on others nor on himself. A third, however, though actually guiltless, may always be passing judgment on himself.

There is a difference between being humble, striving for humility, and praising the humble. The first is a mark of the perfect, the second of the obedient, and the third of all the faithful.

A man truly humble within himself will never find his tongue betraying him. What is not in the treasury cannot be brought out through the door.

A solitary horse can often imagine itself to be at full gallop, but when it finds itself in a herd it then discovers how slow it actually is.

A first sign of emerging health is when our thoughts are no longer filled with a proud sense of our aptitudes. As long as the stench of pride lingers in the nose, the fragrance of myrrh will go unnoticed.

Holy humility had this to say: "The one who loves me will not condemn someone, or pass judgment on anyone, or lord it over someone else, or show off his wisdom until he has been united with me. A man truly joined to me is no longer in bondage to the Law."

The unholy demons once began to murmur praise in the heart of an ascetic who was struggling to achieve blessed humility. However, God inspired him to use a holy trick to defeat the cleverness of these spirits. The monk got up and on the wall of his cell he wrote in sequence the names of the major virtues: perfect love, angelic humility, pure prayer, unassailable chastity, and others of a similar kind. The result was that whenever vainglorious thoughts began to puff him up, he would say: "Come! Let us go to be judged." Going to the wall he would read the names there and would cry out to himself: "When you

87. The scholiast explains two of these allusions as follows: "The unique place is the floor of the Red Sea during the crossing of Israel. The day of universal joy is none other than the day of the resurrection of our Lord and Savior, on which our race was freed from the eternal bonds of Hades. Others say that it is the day of the nativity, on which the glory to God in the highest of the angels was heard. Others say that it is the day on which Noah and his companions came out of the ark" (scholion 10 [1005B]). According to another scholion, attributed to John of Raithu, the unique thought is "the constant thought of death, and meditation on eternal judgment and on the Cross and death of Christ" (*PG* 88, 1236C). The unique virtue is humility.

have every one of these virtues within you, then you will have an accurate sense of how far from God you still are."

No one of us can describe the power and nature of the sun. We can merely deduce its intrinsic nature from its characteristics and effects. So too with humility, which is a God-given protection against seeing our own achievements. It is an abyss of self-abasement to which no thief can gain entry. It is a tower of strength against the enemy. "Against him the enemy will not prevail and the son (or, rather, the thought) of iniquity will do him no harm and he will cut off his enemies before him" (Ps. 88:23–24) and will put to flight those who hate him.

The great possessor of this treasure has other properties in his soul besides those referred to above. These properties, with one exception, are manifest tokens of this wealth. You will know that you have this holy gift within you and not be led astray when you experience an abundance of unspeakable light together with an indescribable love of prayer. Even before reaching this stage, you may have it, if in your heart you pass no judgment on the faults of others. And a precursor of what we have described is hatred of all vainglory.

The man who has come to know himself with the full awareness of his soul has sown in good ground. However, anyone who has not sown in this way cannot expect humility to flower within him. And anyone who has acquired knowledge of self has come to understand the fear of the Lord, and walking with the help of this fear, he has arrived at the doorway of love. For humility is the door to the kingdom, opening up to those who come near. It was of that door, I believe, that the Lord spoke when He said: "He shall go in and come out of life" and not be afraid "and he shall find pasture" (John 10:8–9) and the green grass of Paradise. And whoever has entered monastic life by some other door is a thief and a robber of his own life.

Those of us who wish to gain understanding must never stop examining ourselves and if in the perception of your soul you realize that your neighbor is superior to you in all respects, then the mercy of God is surely near at hand.

Snow cannot burst into flames. It is even less possible for humility to abide in a heretic. This achievement belongs only to the pious and the faithful, and then only when they have been purified.

Most of us would describe ourselves as sinners. And perhaps we really think so. But it is indignity that shows up the true state of the heart.

Whoever is eager for the peaceful haven of humility will never cease to do all he possibly can to get there, and with words and thoughts, with considerations and explanations, with questionings and probings, with every device, with prayer and supplication, with meditation and reflection, he will push onward, helped by God, humiliated and despised and toiling mightily, and he will sail the ship of his soul out from the ever-stormy ocean of vainglory. For the man delivered from this sin wins ready pardon for all his other sins, like the publican in Scripture.

Some drive out empty pride by thinking to the end of their lives of their past misdeeds, for which they were forgiven and which now serve as a spur to humility. Others, remembering the passion of Christ, think of themselves as eternally in debt. Others hold themselves in contempt when they think of their daily lapses. Others come to possess this mother of graces by way of their continuous temptations, weaknesses, and sins.[88] There are some—and I cannot say if they are to be found nowadays—who humble themselves in proportion to the gifts they receive from God and live with a sense of their unworthiness to have such wealth bestowed on them, so that each day they think of themselves as sinking further into debt. That is real humility, real beatitude, a real reward! And you may be sure that it is by this particularly blessed route that anyone has traveled who in a few short years has arrived at the summit of dispassion.

Love and humility make a holy team. The one exalts. The other supports those who have been exalted and never falls.

There is a difference between contrition, self-knowledge, and humility.

Contrition is the outcome of a lapse. A man who has lapsed breaks down and prays without arrogance, though with laudable persistence, disarrayed and yet clinging to the staff of hope, indeed using it to drive off the dog of despair.

Self-knowledge is a clear-eyed notion of one's own spiritual advance. It is also an unwavering remembrance of one's lightest sins.

Humility is a spiritual teaching of Christ led spiritually like a bride into the inner chamber of the soul of those deemed worthy of it, and it somehow eludes all description.

88. HTM has a fuller version of this sentence: "Others, as a result of their besetting temptations, infirmities and sins, have mortified their pride. Others for want of graces have appropriated the mother of graces (i.e. humility)."

A man says that he is experiencing the full fragrance of this myrrh within him. Someone happens to praise him, and if he feels the slightest stir of the heart or if he grasps the full import of what is being said, then he is certainly mistaken, and let him have no illusion about that fact.

"Not to us, not to us, but to Your name, O Lord, give glory" (Ps. 113:9). I once heard a man say this with total sincerity. He was a man who well understood that human nature is such that it cannot remain unharmed by praise. "My praise shall be from You in the great assembly, Lord" (Ps. 21:26), that is, in the life to come, and I cannot accept it before that without risk to myself.

If the outer limit, the rule, and the characteristic of extreme pride is for a man to make a show of having virtues he does not actually possess for the sake of glory, then surely the token of extreme humility will be to lower ourselves by claiming weaknesses we do not really have. This was what one man did when he took the bread and cheese in his hands.[89] This too was the way of the man who was free of all fleshly lust but who used to take his clothes off and parade naked through the whole city.[90] Men like these do not worry about giving scandal, for through prayer they have received the power to reassure all men invisibly. Indeed, to be afraid of censure is to show lack of ability in prayer. And when God is ready to hear our prayers we can achieve anything.

Better to offend man than God. For God is delighted when He sees us courting dishonor for the purpose of crushing, striking, and destroying our empty self-esteem. And virtue of this sort comes only from a complete abandonment of the world and only the really great can endure the derision of their own folk. This should not surprise you. The fact is that no one can climb a ladder in a single stride. And in this matter it is not on account of the devils subjected to us that men will recognize us as disciples of God, but because our names are written in the heaven of humility (cf. Luke 10:20).

A lemon tree naturally lifts its branches upwards when it has no fruit. The more its branches bend, the more fruit you will find there. The meaning of this will be clear to the man disposed to understand it.

Holy humility receives from God the power to yield fruit thirty-

89. Abba Simon: *The Sayings of the Desert Fathers,* Simon.

90. Sarapion the Sindonite: Palladius, *The Lausiac History,* ch. 37.

fold, sixtyfold and a hundredfold. The dispassionate attain that last degree, the courageous the middle, and everyone can rise to the first.

The man who has come to know himself is never fooled into reaching for what is beyond him. He keeps his feet henceforth on the blessed path of humility.

Just as birds fear the sight of a hawk, those who practice humility fear the sound of an argument.

Many have attained salvation without the aid of prophecies, illumination, signs and wonders. But without humility no one will enter the marriage chamber, for humility is the guardian of such gifts. Without it, they will bring disaster on the frivolous.

Because of our unwillingness to humble ourselves, God has arranged that no one can see his own faults as clearly as his neighbor does. Hence our obligation to be grateful not to ourselves but to our neighbor and to God for our healing.

A humble man will always hate his own will as a cause of error. In his petitions to the Lord which he makes with unwavering faith he learns what he should do and obeys. He does not spend his time scrutinizing the lifestyle of his superiors. He lays all his burden on the God Who used an ass to teach Balaam what had to be done. All the acts, thoughts, and words of such a man are directed to the will of God and he never trusts himself. Indeed, to a humble man, self-confidence is as much a thorn and a burden as the orders of someone else are to a proud man.

In my opinion, an angel is characterized by the fact that he is not tricked into sinning. And I hear those words of an earthly angel:[91] "I am aware of nothing against myself and yet I am not thereby justified. It is the Lord Who is my Judge" (1 Cor. 4:4). So we must always condemn and criticize ourselves in order that by means of deliberately chosen humiliations we may protect ourselves from unwitting sin. And if we do not do this, our punishment at death will be heavy indeed.

The man who asks God for less than he deserves will certainly receive more, as is shown by the publican who begged forgiveness but obtained salvation (cf. Luke 18:10–14). And the robber asked only to be remembered in the kingdom, yet he inherited all of Paradise (cf. Luke 23:43).

In the created world fire cannot naturally be both small and

91. In Greek "angel" means "messenger."

great at one and the same time. Humility cannot be genuine and at one and the same time have a worldly strain.[92] Genuine humility is not in us if we fall into voluntary sin, and this is the sign that there is something material still within us.

The Lord understood that the virtue of the soul is shaped by our outward behavior. He therefore took a towel and showed us how to walk the road of humility (cf. John 13:4). The soul indeed is molded by the doings of the body, conforming to and taking shape from what it does. To one of the angels it was the fact of being a ruler that led to pride, though it was not for this reason that the prerogative was originally granted to him.

A man who sits on a throne acts in one way, and the man who sits on a dunghill acts in another. That, perhaps, is the reason why that great and just man[93] sat on the dunghill outside the city. Totally humbled, he said in all sincerity, "I despise myself, waste away" (Job 42:6), and have regarded myself as dust and ashes.

I note that Manasseh sinned like no other man. He defiled the temple of God with idols and he contaminated the sacred Liturgy (cf. 4 [2] Kings 21:4). A fast by all the world could not have made reparation for his sin, and yet humility could heal his incurable wound. "If You wanted sacrifice I would have given it," David says to God, "but You will not be satisfied with holocausts," that is, with bodies worn out by fasting. "The sacrifice for God is a contrite spirit. God will not despise a humble and contrite heart" (Ps. 50:17). Following on adultery and murder, blessed humility once cried out to God, "I have sinned against the Lord," and the reply was heard: "The Lord has put away your sin" (2 Kings [2 Sam.] 12:13).

The wonderful Fathers proclaimed physical labor to be the way to and the foundation of humility. To this I would add obedience and honesty of heart, since these are by nature opposed to self-aggrandizement.

If pride turned some of the angels into demons, then humility can doubtless make angels out of demons. So take heart, all you sinners.

---

92. This passage is obscure. It may be translated alternatively: "It is impossible to see a fire, whether small or great, existing by nature in any creature. Similarly, it is impossible to see any trace of the form of matter (i.e., sin) existing in genuine humility."

93. I.e., Job.

Let us strive with all our might to reach that summit of humility, or let us at least climb onto her shoulders. And if this is too much for us, let us at least not tumble out of her arms, since after such a tumble a man will scarcely receive any kind of everlasting gift.

Humility has its signs. It also has its sinews and its ways, and these are as follows—poverty, withdrawal from the world, the concealment of one's wisdom, simplicity of speech, the seeking of alms, the disguising of one's nobility, the exclusion of free and easy relationships, the banishment of idle talk.

Nothing can ever so humble the soul as destitution and the subsistence of a beggar. We will show ourselves true lovers of wisdom and of God if we stubbornly run away from all possibility of aggrandizement.

If you wish to fight against some passion, take humility as your ally, for she will tread on the asp and the basilisk of sin and despair, and she will trample under foot the lion and the serpent of physical devilishness and cunning (cf Ps. 90:13).

Humility is a heavenly waterspout which can lift the soul from the abyss up to heaven's height.

Someone discovered in his heart how beautiful humility is, and in his amazement he asked her to reveal her parent's name. Humility smiled, joyous and serene: "Why are you in such a rush to learn the name of my begetter? He has no name, nor will I reveal him to you until you have God for your possession. To Whom be glory forever." Amen.

The sea is the source of the fountain, and humility is the source of discernment.

Step 26

ON DISCERNMENT

Among beginners, discernment is real self-knowledge; among those midway along the road to perfection, it is a spiritual capacity to distinguish unfailingly between what is truly good and what in nature is opposed to the good; among the perfect, it is a knowledge resulting from divine illumination, which with its lamp can light up what is dark in others. To put the matter generally, discernment is—and is recognized to be—a solid understanding of the will of God in all times, in all places, in all things; and it is found only among those who are pure in heart, in body, and in speech.

The man who has devoutly destroyed within himself the three has also destroyed the five.[94] If he has neglected any of the former, then he will not be able to overcome even a single passion.

Discernment is an uncorrupted conscience. It is pure perception.

No one seeing or hearing something in monastic life that has a force over and beyond nature should, out of ignorance, become unbelieving. For much that is supernatural happens where the supernatural God abides.

Every demonic upheaval within us arises from the following three related causes, namely, carelessness, pride, or the envy of de-

94. According to Evagrius (*Phil.*, p.38), the three principal evil thoughts are gluttony, vainglory and avarice; these give rise to the other five, lust, despondency, pride, dejection and anger. Cf. Climacus, 26 (1021C), p. 235; also the Preface, p. 64.

mons. The first is pitiable, the second deplorable, but the third is blessed.

Let our God-directed[95] conscience be our aim and rule in everything so that, knowing how the wind is blowing, we may set our sails accordingly.[96]

Amid all our efforts to please God, three pitfalls lie, prepared for us by demons. First is their attempt to impede any sort of worthwhile achievement; and if this fails, they strive secondly to ensure that what we do should not be in accordance with the will of God. And if the scoundrels fail in this too, then they stand quietly before our soul and praise us for the fact that in every respect we are living as God would wish. We should fight these risks, the first by zeal and fear of death, the second by obedience and self-abasement, the third by unceasing self-condemnation. "This work is ahead of us until the fire of God shall enter our sanctuary" (cf. Ps. 72:16–17), and then indeed the power of our predispositions will no longer constrain us. For our God is a fire consuming all lusts, all stirrings of passion, all predispositions, and all hardness of heart, both within and without, both visible and spiritual.

Demons, on the other hand, bring about the very opposite to all this. Grabbing a soul, they put out the light of the mind until in our wretchedness we find ourselves lacking sobriety or discernment, self-knowledge or shame; and we are burdened instead with indifference, insensitivity, want of discernment, and blindness.

All of this is well known to those who have abandoned fornication and become chaste, who have reined in their tongues and switched from shamelessness to modesty. They know that when the mind was cleansed, its callousness ended, or rather its mutilation healed, shame filled them for what they said and did previously in the season of their blindness.

---

95. HTM reads *meta theon* instead of *kata theon:* "After God, let us have our conscience," etc.

96. The scholiast comments: "A ship is sometimes overwhelmed by storms from without, and sometimes sinks through springing a leak within. We too sometimes perish through sins committed externally, and sometimes are destroyed by evil thoughts within. We must therefore both keep watch for the external attacks of spirits, and bail out the impurity of evil thoughts within. Only more effort must be made with the understanding against evil thoughts" (scholion 4 [1037AB]).

If the day of our soul does not turn to evening and become dark, no thieves will come then to rob or slay or ruin our soul.[97]

Robbery is a hidden bondage of the soul. The slaying of the soul is the death of a rational mind that has fallen into evil ways. Ruin is despair of oneself following on a breach of God's law.

No one should plead inability to do what is asked of us in the gospels, since there are souls who have accomplished far more than is commanded. Of this truth you will be entirely persuaded, given what is said about the man who loved his neighbor more than himself and who laid down his life for him, in spite of the fact that the Lord had not ordered him to do so.[98]

Those who have been humbled by their passions should take heart. Even if they tumble into every pit, even if they are trapped by every snare, even if they suffer every disease, still after their return to health they become a light to all, they prove to be doctors, beacons, pilots. They teach us the characteristics of every malady and out of their own experience they can rescue those about to lapse.

Anyone in the grip of previous bad habits and yet still able to give teaching, although only by their words, should do so. (Of course, they should not hold positions of authority.) Shamed by their own words, they may finally begin to practice what they preach. And there may even happen in their case what I have seen happen with people stuck in the mud. Mired themselves, they warned passersby, telling how they had sunk, explaining this for their salvation so that they too might not fall in the same manner, and the omnipotent God rescued them from the mud so that the others might be saved.

But anyone who is dominated by passions and who quite willingly embraces pleasure should be a lesson by his very silence. Jesus began both "to do and to teach" (Acts 1:1).

We humble monks have to travel a truly dangerous sea, a sea full of winds, rocks, and whirlpools, of pirates, waterspouts, and shallows, of monsters and waves. A rock in the soul is wild and sudden anger. A whirlpool is the hopelessness that lays hold of the mind on every side and struggles to drag it into the depths of despair. A shallow is

97. HTM adds two sentences: "Theft is loss of property. Theft is doing what is not good as if it were good."

98. Abba Leo of Cappadocia, who gave his life to redeem three captive monks; see John Moschus, *Pratum Spirituale*, ch. 112.

the ignorance that makes a good of what is evil. A monster is this gross and savage body. Pirates are those deadly servants of vainglory who snatch our cargo, the hard-won earnings of our virtues. A wave is the swollen and packed stomach that by its gluttony hands us over to the beast. A waterspout is pride, the pride that flings us down from heaven, bears us up to the sky, and then dashes us into the lowest depths.

Educators can distinguish between the programs of study suitable for beginners, for the intermediate, and for teachers. And we ought to ensure that we do not spend an unduly long time at the beginner's stage, for it would be a disgrace to have an old man going to kindergarten.

Here for everyone is an excellent alphabet: A—obedience, B—fasting, Γ—sackcloth, Δ—ashes, E—tears, Z—confession, H—silence, Θ—humility, I—vigil, K—bravery, Λ—cold, M—struggle, N—hard work, Ξ—humiliation, O—contrition, Π—forgetfulness of wrongs, P—brotherly love, Σ—meekness, T—simple and unquestioning faith, Y—freedom from worldly concern, Φ—unhating rejection of parents, X—detachment, Ψ—innocent simplicity, Ω—voluntary abasement.

For the advanced, the following is a good plan and indeed a sign of progress: lack of vainglory, freedom from anger, good hope, stillness, discernment, continuous remembrance of the judgment, compassion, hospitality, gentleness in criticism, passionless prayer, lack of avarice.

And a measure, rule, and law for those in the flesh aiming at perfection in spirit and body is the following: A—an unfettered heart, B—perfect love, Γ—a well of humility, Δ —a detached mind, E—an indwelling of Christ, Z—an assurance of light and of prayer, H—an outpouring of divine illumination, Θ—a wish for death, I—hatred of life, K—flight from the body, Λ—an ambassador for the world, M—an importuner of God, N—fellow worshiper with the angels, Ξ—a depth of knowledge, O—a dwelling place of mysteries, Π—a custodian of holy secrets, P—a savior of men, Σ—lord over the demons, T—master of the passions, Y—lord of the body, Φ—controller of nature, X—a stranger to sin, Ψ—home of dispassion, Ω—with God's help an imitator of the Lord.

We have to be particularly vigilant whenever the body is sick, for at such a time the demons, observing our weakness and our inability to fight against them as usual, rush in to attack us. In times of illness the demon of anger and even of blasphemy may be discovered around those who live in the world. Those leading a religious life but having all they need of a material kind may suffer the onslaught of the demon of gluttony and fornication. But ascetics who live without comforts may find themselves plagued by the tyrant of despondency and ingratitude.

And I have noticed how the wolf of fornication increased the sufferings of the sick and, while they were laid low, caused stirrings of the flesh and even emissions. It was amazing to see how the body, for all its agonies, could still rage and lust. And when I looked once more I saw sick men comforted by the power of God or by the workings of compunction, and because they were comforted they kept the pain at bay and even arrived at a disposition where they had no wish to recover from their illness. At other times I saw men freed from their souls' passion by grave sickness, as though it were some kind of penance, and I could only praise the God who cleans clay with clay.

A mind disposed to the things of the spirit is certainly endowed with spiritual perception and this is something that, whether we possess it or not, we should always seek to have. And when it comes, our senses desist from their natural activities. This is why a wise man once said, "You shall obtain a sense of what is divine."[99]

In the matter of actions, words, thoughts, and movements, the monastic life has to be lived with a perceptive heart.[100] Otherwise it will not be monastic or indeed angelic.

One has to distinguish between divine providence, divine assistance, divine protection, divine mercy, and divine consolation. Providence is shown in all of nature, assistance among the faithful alone, protection among those believers whose faith is most alive, mercy among those who serve God, and consolation among those who love Him.

One man's medicine can be another man's poison, and something can be a medicine to the same man at one time and a poison at another. So I have seen an incompetent physician who by inflicting dishonor on a sick but contrite man produced despair in him, and I have seen a skillful physician who cut through an arrogant heart with the knife of dishonor and thereby drained it of all its foul-smelling pus. I

99. HTM says that a Russian note attributes this saying to St. Nilus of Sinai (i.e., presumably Nilus of Ancyra).

100. The scholiast adds: "Because the monk must carefully investigate all his movements, even those of his thoughts" (scholion 18 [1040D]).

have seen a sick man striving to cleanse his impurity by drinking the medicine of obedience, by moving, walking, and staying awake. That same man when the eye of his soul was sick did not move, made no noise, and was silent. Therefore, "he who has ears to hear, let him hear" (Luke 14:35).

Since I am not so proud as to pry into the gifts of God, I cannot say why it is that some people appear to be naturally inclined to temperance or silence or purity or modesty or meekness or contrition. Others have to fight hard against their own natures to acquire these, they have to force themselves on to the best of their ability, suffering occasional defeat on the way; and it seems to me that the very fact of having to struggle against their own natures somehow puts them into a higher category than the first kind.

Never boast, man, about the wealth you acquired without having to work for it. The heavenly Giver anticipates how you may be injured, weakened, or ruined and therefore gives you some help by way of those gifts, which you certainly did not deserve.

What we learned as children, our education and our studies, may be a help or a hindrance to us in virtue in monastic life, when we come of age.

Angels are a light for monks and the monastic life is a light for all men. Hence monks should spare no effort to become a shining example in all things, and they should give no scandal in anything they say or do. For if the light becomes dark, then all the deeper will be the darkness of those living in the world.

And if you will lend a willing ear to what I have to say, you will agree that it would be bad for us to spread ourselves too thinly, to have our wretched souls pulled in all directions, to take on, alone, a fight against thousands upon thousands and ten thousands upon ten thousands of enemies, since the understanding of their evil workings, indeed even the listing of them, is far beyond our capacities. Instead, let us summon the Holy Trinity to help us as we marshal three against three.[101] If we fail to do this we will make very hard work for ourselves. For if God really dwells in us, the God Who made dry land of the sea, then the Israel within us, the mind that looks to God, will surely make a safe crossing of this sea and it will look on the Egyp-

101. Self-control, love and humility, says the scholiast, against sensuality, avarice and ambition (scholion 29 [1044AB]): the three latter are the principal evil thoughts according to Evagrius (see note 94, p. 229).

tians sunk in the waters of tears. But if God has not yet arrived in us, who will understand the roaring waves of the sea, that is, of our bodies? Whereas if, because of our works, God rises within us, His enemies will be scattered; and if we draw near to Him through contemplation, "those who hate Him will run from before His face" (Ps. 67:2) and from ours.

Let us seek to discover the things of heaven through the sweat of our efforts, rather than by mere talk, for at the hour of death it is deeds, not words, that must be displayed.

Those who learn of treasure hidden away somewhere look for it, and when they find it, they make sure to hold on to what they have found. But those who get rich without any effort are quick to squander what they have.

It is hard to shake off old habits, especially bad ones; and when others are added to these, despair can result and obedience proves to be without value. Still, I know that God can do anything, that for Him nothing is impossible.

Certain people put a particular question to me, a question very difficult to solve and certainly beyond my capacities. Nor is it dealt with in any of the books that have come my way. The question took this form: "What are the special offspring of the eight deadly sins, and which of the three chief sins produce the other five?" To my credit, I pleaded ignorance and was therefore put in the position of being able to learn the following from those men of great holiness: "Gluttony is the mother of lust and vainglory is the mother of despondency. Dejection and anger are the offspring of those three,[102] and the mother of pride is vainglory."

The statement of these ever-memorable fathers inspired me to put more questions regarding the lineage of the eight sins, which produced which. And these men, free as they were from passion, kindly instructed me, saying that no order or reason can be found among the irrational passions, that indeed every brand of disorder and chaos may be discovered in them. The blessed Fathers confirmed all this with persuasive examples and numerous proofs, some of which I include in this section. They will be a light by which to analyze the others.

---

102. I.e. (in the Evagrian scheme) of gluttony, vainglory and avarice. But Climacus does not in fact mention avarice in the present passage, although he treats it as one of the three chief vices in Step 17.

For instance, jokes at the wrong time can be the product of lust, or of vainglory when a man impiously pretends to be pious, or high living. Excessive sleep can arise from luxury, from fasting when those who fast become proud of it, from despondency, or sometimes from nature. Garrulity sometimes comes from gluttony, and sometimes from vainglory. Despondency can derive now from high living, now from lack of fear of God. Blasphemy is properly the child of pride, but can often arise out of the readiness to condemn one's neighbor for the same offense, or it can be due to the untimely envy of demons. Hardheartedness is sometimes the consequence of gluttony, frequently of insensitivity, and also of being grasping. And to be grasping can be due to lust, avarice, gluttony, vainglory, and indeed to many other causes. Malice comes from conceit and from anger, while hypocrisy comes from independence and self-direction.

The virtues opposed to these are born of opposing parents. And since I have not the time to examine them in detail, I will merely observe that the remedy for all the passions listed above is humility. Those who possess that virtue have won the whole battle.

The mother of all wickedness is pleasure and malice. If these are in a man, he will not see the Lord; and to abstain from the first without also giving up the second will not be of much use.

The fear we have in the presence of rulers and of wild beasts could serve as an example of fear of the Lord, and physical love can be a paradigm of the longing for God. (There is nothing wrong with using opposites for the purposes of finding examples of the virtues.)

This present generation is wretchedly corrupt. It is full of pride and hypocrisy. It works as hard as the Fathers of old, but it has none of their graces. And yet there has been no era so much in need of spiritual gifts as today. Still, we got what we deserved, since God is made manifest not in labors but in simplicity and in humility. If the power of the Lord is brought to perfection in weakness, the Lord will definitely not reject a humble worker.

If we happen to observe that one of our spiritual athletes is seriously ill, we must not maliciously try to discover the reason for his illness. Simply and lovingly we should do what we can to heal him as though he were a part of our own body and because he is a fellow campaigner hurt in battle.

Illness can occur sometimes to cleanse us from our sins and sometimes to humble our thinking. When our ever-gracious Master and Lord discovers people getting lazy in their religious lives, He may humble their bodies by illness, as if by a lighter form of asceticism. Illness too can sometimes purify the soul from evil thoughts and passions.

Whatever happens to us, whether seen or unseen, can be accepted by us well, or passionately, or in some intermediate fashion. I once saw three brothers punished. One was angry, one did not feel any grief, but the third profited greatly from the fact that he rejoiced in his punishment.

I have watched farmers sowing the same type of seed, and yet each one had different ideas of what he was doing. One was planning to pay off his debts. Another was hoping to get rich. Another wanted to be able to bring gifts to honor the Lord. Another was hoping to earn praise for his work from the passers-by in life. Someone else wanted to irritate a jealous neighbor, while there was yet another who did not want to be reproached by men for laziness. And as for the seeds thrown into the earth, their names are fasting, keeping vigil, almsgiving, service, and suchlike. So let our brethren in the Lord keep a careful eye on their motives.

When we draw water from a well, it can happen that we inadvertently also bring up a frog. When we acquire virtues we can sometimes find ourselves involved with the vices which are imperceptibly interwoven with them. What I mean is this. Gluttony can be caught up with hospitality; lust with love; cunning with discernment; malice with prudence; duplicity, procrastination, slovenliness, stubbornness, wilfulness, and disobedience with meekness; refusal to learn with silence; conceit with joy; laziness with hope; nasty condemnation with love again; despondency and indolence with tranquillity; sarcasm with chastity; familiarity with lowliness. And behind all the virtues follows vainglory as a salve, or rather a poison, for everything.

We must not become upset if for a while the Lord seems to allow our requests to go unheard. Naturally the Lord would be delighted if in one moment all men became disspasionate. But He knows, in His providence, that this would not be to their advantage.

When requests are made to God and are not immediately answered, the reason may be one of the following: either that the petition is premature, or because it has been made unworthily or vaingloriously, or because, if granted, it would lead to conceit, or because negligence and carelessness would result.

Demons and passions quit the soul entirely or for some length of time. No one can deny that. However, the reasons for such a departure are known to very few.

Some of the faithful and even of the unfaithful have found themselves in the position of being bereft of all passions except one, and that one proved so overwhelming an evil that it took the place of all the others and was so devastating that it could lead to damnation.

The material of the passions is done away with when consumed by divine fire. It is uprooted, and all evil urges retire from the soul unless the man attracts them back again by his worldly habits and by his laziness.

Demons leave us alone so as to make us careless, then pounce on our miserable souls. And those beasts have another trick, of which I am aware; namely, to depart when the soul has become thoroughly imbued with the habits of evil, when it has turned into its own betrayer and enemy. It is rather like what happens to infants weaned from the mother's breast, who suck their fingers because the habit has taken hold of them.

There is a fifth kind of dispassion. It comes from great simplicity and from admirable innocence. "To such is help rightly given by the God Who saves the upright of heart" (Ps. 7:11) and Who rids them of all evil without their perceiving it. They are like infants who when undressed have no realization of the fact that they are naked.

Evil or passion is not something naturally implanted in things. God is not the creator of passions. On the other hand, there are many natural virtues that have come to us from Him. These clearly include the following: mercy, something even the pagans have; love, for even dumb animals bewail the loss of one of their own; faith, which all of us can generate of ourselves; hope, since we all lend, and take to the sea, and sow seed, expecting to do well out of it. Hence if love comes naturally to us—and it has been shown to be so—if it is the bond and the fulfilment of the law, virtues cannot be too far from nature. For which reason, those who claim to be unable to practice the virtues should be very ashamed of themselves.

At a level above nature are chastity, freedom from anger, humility, prayer, keeping vigil, fasting, uninterrupted compunction, and we learn about these from men, from angels, and from the Teacher and Giver, God the Word.

When confronted by evils, we should choose the least. For instance, we are standing at prayer and some brothers approach us. We have to do one of two things, either to cease praying or to upset a brother by ignoring him. Now love is greater than prayer, since the latter is a particular virtue while the former embraces all virtues.

Long ago, in my young days, I came to a city or to a village, and while sitting at table I was afflicted at the same time by thoughts of gluttony and of vainglory. Knowing and fearing the outcome of gluttony, I decided to give in to vainglory. I also knew that in the young, the demon of gluttony often overcomes the demon of vainglory. This is not to be wondered at, for among people of the world love of money is the root of all evil, whereas in monks it is gluttony.

God in His providence often leaves some vestiges of passion in people of a very spiritual disposition. He does so in order that, by their endless condemnation of what are very minor defects, they may obtain a wealth of humility that no one can plunder.

Humility can come only when you have learned to practice obedience. When a man has a self-taught skill, he may start having high notions about himself.

The Fathers say that two virtues dominate the active life, namely, fasting and obedience. They are quite right about this, since fasting destroys sensuality and obedience completes the destruction by bringing in humility. Mourning too has a double effect by destroying sin and producing humility.

A pious man tends to give to anyone who asks. Someone more than usually pious gives even to those who do not ask. But to omit the opportunity to demand the return of something from the person who took it is characteristic, I think, only of the dispassionate.

Regarding every vice and every virtue, we must unceasingly scrutinize ourselves to see what point we have reached, a beginning, a middle, or the end.

Attacks by demons afflict us for three reasons: because we are sensual, because we are proud, or because the demons envy us. The last is a ground for rejoicing, the middle for pity, and where the first is concerned, the prospect is lifelong failure.

Endurance of hardship is a kind of perception or habit. The man who has it will never be afraid of pain, or toil or hardship, nor will he run from them. It was this marvelous grace that enabled the souls of the martyrs to rise superior to their torments.

Keeping guard over one's thoughts is one thing; watching over one's mind another. Distant from each other as the east from the west, the latter is more significant and more laborious than the former.

It is one thing to pray for rescue from bad thoughts, another to stand up against them, and another still to despise and ignore them. The first situation is exemplified by the one who said: "O God, come and help me" (Ps. 69:2); the second by, "I will speak a word of contradiction to those who reproach me" (Ps. 118:42), and "You have made us a contradiction to our neighbors" (Ps. 79:7). And of the third the witness is the psalmist: "I was silent and did not open my mouth, I put a guard on my mouth when the sinner was before me" (Ps. 38:10); "The proud have gone too far in breaking the law, but I have not turned aside from my contemplation of You" (Ps. 118:51). So the man who stands in the middle position will often make use of the first of these, since he is insufficiently prepared, whereas the man who is still at the first stage cannot use the second method as a way of overcoming his enemies. However, the man who has come as far as the third step will completely ignore the demons.

The incorporeal cannot be hemmed in by what is corporeal; but the man who has God for his possession can do anything at all.

Everyone with a healthy sense of smell can detect hidden perfumes, and a pure soul can quickly recognize in others the sheer fragrance of goodness that he himself has received from God. And indeed he can also recognize—as others cannot—the foul odor from which he himself has been liberated.

Not everyone can achieve dispassion. But all can be saved and can be reconciled to God.

Have a care that alien thoughts may not secure a hold over you. I mean those that push you into being anxious to probe either the unspeakable decisions of God's providence or those visions that by coming to others give rise to the notion that the Lord shows favoritism. Such thoughts are the manifest outcome of pride.

There is a demon of avarice that often takes on the guise of humility. There are demons of vainglory and of sensuality and these encourage the giving of alms. If we can keep ourselves clear of these, we ought to do the works of mercy without cease.

Some hold that demons work against each other. But I do know that all of them work to destroy us.

Our own determination and intention together with the help of God come into play in every spiritual act of ours, visible or not, and the latter is unlikely to operate without the former.

Ecclesiastes declares that there is a time for everything under heaven (cf. Eccles. 3:1), and "everything" may be taken to refer to our spiritual life. If this is so, then we ought to examine the matter; and we should do everything in proper season. For those entering the struggle—I mean novices—there is a time for dispassion and a time for passion. There is a time for tears and a time for hardness of heart, a time for obedience and a time for command, a time for fasting and a time for eating, a time for the battle against the body our enemy and a time for quiet in our flesh. There is a time for the soul's upheaval and a time for calm in the mind, a time for heart's sorrow and a time for joy of spirit, a time for teaching and a time for listening, a time for pollutions, perhaps on account of conceit, and a time for cleansing by humility, a time for effort and a time for secure rest, a time for stillness and a time for undistracted distraction, a time for unceasing prayer and a time for honest service. Proud zeal must therefore never be allowed to deceive us and we should never strain for what will come in its own good time, since winter is not the time for summer's goods nor seedtime the proper season for the harvest. There is a time for the sowing of labors and a time to reap the astounding fruits of grace; and if it were otherwise we would not receive in due time whatever was proper to the season.

God in His unspeakable providence has arranged that some received the holy reward of their toils even before they set to work, others while actually working, others again when the work was done, and still others at the time of their death. Let the reader ask himself which one of them was made more humble.

There is a despair that results from the great number of one's sins. It comes from a burdened conscience and intolerable grief, when the soul, engulfed by the mass and the burden of its wounds, slips into the deep waters of hopelessness. But there is also another kind of sorrow. It comes from pride and conceit and arises when a man thinks it unfair that he lapsed in some way. Now there is a distinctive aspect to each of these conditions which the observant will discover. The one man gives himself over to indifference, the other continues to practice his ascetic disciplines even though his despair persists in him, which is a contradiction. Temperance and good hope can heal the first man; the other will be cured by humility and by the practice of judging no one.

We should be neither amazed nor shocked when we find ourselves watching someone do evil behind a cloak of fine words. After all, it was overweening pride that destroyed the serpent in Paradise.

Whatever you do, however you live, whether you live under obedience or whether you are independent, in what you do openly or in your spiritual life, let it be your rule and practice to ask if what you do is in accordance with the will of God. When we novices, for instance, do something and the humility deriving from that action is not added to the possessions of our souls, then the action, great or small, has not been undertaken in deference to the divine will. For those of us who are untried recruits in the life of the spirit, growth in humility comes out of doing what the Lord wants; for those who have reached midway along that route, the test is an end to inner conflict; and for the perfect there is increase and, indeed, a wealth of divine light.

The tiniest thing may not seem so to the great. But to those who are small, even great things are not quite perfect.

The sun is bright when clouds have left the air; and a soul, freed of its old habits and also forgiven, has surely seen the divine light.

Distinctions have to be made between sin, idleness, indifference, passion, and a lapse. The man who can analyze such matters, with God's help, should do so.

Some people are full of praise for the gift of miracle working and for those other spiritual gifts that can be seen. What they do not know is that there are many more important gifts and that these are hidden and are therefore secure.

A perfectly purified man can look into the soul of his neighbor—not of course into its actual substance—and can discern its present state. He who progresses further can even tell the state of the soul from the body.

A small fire can wipe out an entire forest and a small fault can ruin all our work.

There comes a breathing space from hostility when the powers of the mind are awakened without stirring the fire of passion. There is too an exhaustion of the body that can actually evoke the flesh's lust. So "we shall put no trust in ourselves" (2 Cor. 1:9). We ought, rather, to depend on God, Who in His own secret way can mortify our living lusts.

If it comes to our attention that there are some who love us in the Lord, we must be very careful to keep our distance from them, since nothing can so damage love and produce hatred as familiarity.

The eye of the soul is spiritual and very beautiful and next to incorporeal beings it surpasses everything. And so it happens that people who are still subject to the effects of the passions can frequently tell what the thoughts are of others because of their great love for them. This is particularly true of those who have not been overwhelmed by the defilements of the flesh. For there is nothing so directly opposed to immaterial nature as material nature. Let him who reads understand.

For laymen, superstitious observances are contrary to God's providence. But for monks they are contrary to spiritual knowledge.

Faltering souls should recognize the visitation of the Lord from their bodily circumstances and dangers and outward temptations. The perfect should recognize it from the coming of the Holy Spirit and the acquisition of graces.

There is a demon who attacks us when we are lying in bed. He fires evil and dirty thoughts at us, so that, too lazy to get up and arm ourselves against him with prayer, we might fall asleep with all these dirty thoughts in us and have dirty dreams.

There is a demon called the forerunner. He lays hold of us as soon as we awaken and defiles our very first thought.

Give the first fruits of your day to the Lord, for it will determine the rest of the day. An excellent servant of the Lord once said to me something well worth hearing. "I can tell from my morning how the rest of the day will go."

There are many roads to holiness—and to hell. A path wrong for one will suit another, yet what each is doing is pleasing to God.

Demons, using the temptations that occur to us, fight to make us say or do something improper. If they cannot get at us in this way, they turn quiet and whisper to us that we should offer up arrogant thanks to God.

Those with minds centered on the things of heaven, after the separation of soul and body rise up on high in two parts.[103] Those with minds directed to what is below will travel that downward route, for there is no intermediate halting place for souls separated from their bodies. Only one of God's creations has its being in something else and not in itself.[104] Yet it is amazing how it can come to exist outside that in which it received being.

103. I.e., first the soul and then, after the resurrection, the body.

104. I.e., the soul has its being in the body.

Pious mothers bear pious daughters, and the mothers themselves are born of the Lord. And it makes good sense to apply this norm in reverse.

The coward should not go out to battle. This was the injunction of Moses, or rather of God Himself (cf. Deut. 20:8), and the reason, a good one, was in case the last spiritual lapse should be worse than the first fall of the body.

Our eyes are a light to all the body. Discernment of the virtues is a light to all the mind.

On Expert Discernment

As the hart parched with thirst pants for running water (cf. Ps. 41:2), the monk longs for a knowledge or grasp of the good and divine will. And indeed he longs also for knowledge of what is not totally of God, even of what is opposed to God. There is here a vitally important theme, and one not easily explained. What I mean is this. What should we do at once, with no delay and as soon as possible, as is recommended in the saying, "Woe to him who delays from day to day" (Ecclus. 5:7–8) and from period to period? On the other hand, what should be done moderately and with discretion, in accordance with the saying, "War is made by leadership" (Prov. 20:18) and "Let all things be done decently and in due order" (1 Cor. 14:40)? Not everyone can make quick and precise decisions in such delicate matters and even that man who had God within him and the Holy Spirit speaking for him, even he prays for this gift and says: "Teach me to do Your will, since You are my God" (Ps. 142:10), and "Direct me to your truth" (Ps. 24:5), and "Show me, Lord, the road I must travel, for I have lifted up my soul to You" (Ps. 142:8) from all the cares and passions of this life.

Those who wish to discover the will of God must begin by mortifying their own will. Then having prayed in faith and simplicity, all malice spent, they should turn humbly and in confidence to the fathers or even the brothers and they should accept their counsel, as though from God Himself, even when that counsel goes against the grain, even when the advice comes from those who do not seem very spiritual. God, after all, is not unjust. He will not lead astray the souls who, trusting and guileless, yield in lowliness to the advice and decision of their neighbor. Even if those consulted are stupid, God immaterially and invisibly speaks through them and anyone who faithfully submits to this norm will be filled with humility. If a man can express on a harp whatever ails him, surely a rational mind and a reasonable soul can provide better teaching than something inanimate.

Yet this perfect and easy rule is rejected by many for reasons of pride. Instead they have sought to discover the will of God by their own resources and within themselves and have then proceeded to offer us numerous and different opinions on this whole issue.

Some of those trying to discover the will of God abandoned every attachment. They asked God to be the arbiter of any thoughts they might have concerning the stirrings of their souls, whether to do something or to resist it. They prayed hard for a fixed number of days and they laid aside any inclination of their own. In this way they found out what God willed, either through some direct manner of intelligible communication from Him or by the complete evaporation from their souls of whatever it was they had proposed to do.

Others found so much trouble and distraction in whatever they were doing that they were led to think that bother of this sort could only have come from God, in accordance with the saying, "We wanted to come to you once and once again, but Satan prevented us" (1 Thess. 2:18).

But there were others who found that a venture of theirs had proved unexpectedly successful, and so they inferred that it had pleased God, and they went on to declare that God helps everyone who chooses to do the right thing (cf. Rom. 8:28).

The man who through illumination has come to possess God within himself both in things requiring immediate action and in those that take time will find immediate divine reassurance by the second way.

Wavering judgment and lingering doubt are the signs of an unenlightened and vainglorious soul.

God is not unjust. He will not slam the door against the man who humbly knocks.

In everything we do, in what has to be done now or later, the objective must be sought from God Himself; and every act that is not the product of personal inclination or of impurity will be imputed to us for good, especially if done for the sake of God and not for someone else. This is so, even if the actions themselves are not completely good.

There is always a danger in seeking for what is beyond our immediate reach, and what God has decided for us is hard to penetrate. In His providence, He often conceals His will from us, for He knows that even if we knew about it, we would disobey it, thereby rendering ourselves liable to greater punishment.

An honest heart is unshaken by the various sorts of distraction. It sails along safely in the ship of innocence.

There are brave souls who lovingly and humbly undertake tasks that are well beyond them. There are proud hearts that do the same. Now it often happens that our enemies deliberately inspire us to do things beyond our capacities, and their objective is to make us falter so that we abandon even what lies within our power, and make ourselves ridiculous to our enemies.

I have observed men who were sick in soul and body and who, out of a sense of the great number of their sins, tried to do what was beyond their power, and therefore failed. To these I say that God judges our repentance not by our exertions but by our humility.

Sometimes one's upbringing may be responsible for the greatest evils. Sometimes it may be the company we keep. And often it may be the sheer perversity of the soul that produces disaster. The monk who is free of the first two may escape the third as well. But the man afflicted by the third is discredited everywhere, for there is no place safer than heaven.[105]

In any conflict with unbelievers or heretics, we should stop after we have twice reproved them (cf. Titus 3:10). But where we are dealing with those who are eager to learn the truth, we should never grow tired of doing the right thing (cf. Gal. 6:9). And we should use both situations to test our own steadfastness.

A man who despairs of himself after hearing about the supernatural achievements of the saints is very unreasonable. In fact they should teach you one of two things, either to be courageous like them in the striving for excellence, or else to be deeply humble and conscious of your inherent weakness by way of thrice-holy humility.

Some of the impure demons are worse than others. They tell us not to sin alone but to bring company with us, and they tell us this in order that our punishment may be all the more severe. I have witnessed the case of someone who learned a sinful habit from another. The latter came to his senses, repented, and desisted from evil, but his change of heart was of no use because of what his disciple was doing.

The wickedness of the evil spirits is truly astounding and it is something not witnessed by many, and indeed even those few who

105. Yet Satan fell from heaven.

appreciate it see it only in part. How is it, for instance, that when we are living in luxury and abundance we can keep vigil and remain awake, whereas while fasting and wearing ourselves down with toil, we are wretchedly overcome by sleep? Why is it that our hearts grow calloused when we are dwelling alone in silence, and yet compunction may be stirred in us when we are involved with others? How is it that dreams tempt us when we are hungry and omit to do so when we are full? Amid want we become gloomy and incapable of compunction, while after some wine we grow happy and are quite able to be contrite. (Anyone who, with God's help, can shed light on this ought to do so, for the sake of the unenlightened. For we really are unilluminated where all this is concerned.) But switches of this sort, of course, do not always come from demons. In my own case—and for reasons I do not understand—I too experience this kind of change as a result of the temperament which I have been given and my burden of grubby and greedy flesh.

Regarding these changes mentioned above, changes that are so hard to explain, let us sincerely and humbly pray to the Lord. But if after time and prayer we still experience the same force at work in us, we should accept that this is due to nature and not to demons. And divine providence often likes to help us by means of adversity and to restrain our pride in every way.

It is a hardy enterprise to inquire into the depths of God's judgment, for the inquisitive sail in the ship of conceit.[106]

Someone asked this question of a discerning man: "Why is it that God confers gifts and wonder-working powers on some, even though He knows in advance that they will lapse?" His answer was that God does this so that other spiritual men may grow cautious, and to show that the human will is free, and to demonstrate that on the day of judgment there will be no excuse for these who lapsed.

The Law, in its imperfection, says: "Attend to yourself" (Deut. 4:9). The Lord, in His perfection, tells us to correct our brother, saying, "If your brother sins against you, etc." (Matt. 18:15). If your reproof, or rather your reminder, can be pure and humble, then do as the Lord commanded, particularly in the case of those who will accept it. But if your progress has not reached this far, at least do what the Law says.

106. HTM adds: "Yet because of the weakness of many, something should be said."

You should not be surprised if those you love turn against you after you have rebuked them. The frivolous are instruments of the demons, and are used, especially against the demons' enemies.

There is one thing about us that never ceases to amaze me. Why is it that when we have Almighty God, the angels, and the saints to help us toward virtue, and when only the devil is against us, we still incline so readily to the passions? I do not want to go into detail on this. In fact I cannot. And if everything that has come into being continues to hold onto its nature, how is it, as the great Gregory puts it, that I am the image of God, yet mingled with clay?[107] Is it not a fact that a creature of God that has strayed from its created nature will continuously try to return to its original condition? Indeed everyone should struggle to raise his clay, so to speak, to a place on the throne of God. And no one should refuse to make the ascent, since the way and the door lie open. To hear about the achievements of the spiritual Fathers stirs mind and soul to imitation.[108]

Doctrine listened to is a light in darkness, a road home to the lost traveler, an illumination for the blind. A discerning man is a discoverer of health, a destroyer of sickness.

Those who look with admiration on trifles do so for two reasons: either through profound ignorance or else because they make much of what their neighbors achieve so that they themselves may reach humility.

We should not spar with demons. We should make outright war on them. In the first case a fall is sometimes given or taken, but in the latter case the enemy is always under fierce attack.

The man who has conquered the passions has injured the demons, and by pretending to be still subject to them he deceives his enemies and remains invulnerable to them. A brother once suffered a disgrace but in his heart he was untroubled by it and in his mind he was prayerful. However, he lamented aloud and by feigned passion hid his dispassion. Another pretended to be eager for the job of father superior when in fact he had no wish at all for it. And how am I to speak of the chastity of the brother who entered a brothel for what

107. Not Pope Gregory the Great of Rome but Gregory of Nazianzus: *Or.* 14, 6 (*PG* 35, 865A).

108. HTM has a longer version of this sentence: "It excites the mind and soul to emulation to hear the spiritual feats of the Fathers, and their zealous admirers are led to imitate them through listening to their teaching."

appeared as a determination to commit sin, and who actually enticed the harlot to take up the ascetic life?[109] Or, again, it once happened that a bunch of grapes was brought early one morning to an ascetic. When the person who brought the grapes had left, the hermit ate them, seeming to stuff them in, but in fact taking no pleasure in them, and in this way he fooled the demons into imagining that he was a glutton. Another one of the brethren once lost a few palm leaves[110] and he pretended all day to be very upset about this.

However, people like this should be wary. In their efforts to fool the demons they may fool themselves. It was to these that the reference was made: "As deceivers and yet true" (2 Cor. 6:8).

If anyone wishes to present to the Lord a pure body and a clean heart, he must persevere in freedom from anger and in chastity. All our work is useless if we lack these.

Eyes show different colors and the sun of the spirit may shine in different ways in the soul. There is the way of bodily tears and there is the way of the tears of the soul. There is the way of the contemplation of what is before us and the way of the contemplation of what remains unseen. There is the way of things heard at second hand and the way of spontaneous joy within the soul. There is the way of stillness and the way of obedience. And in addition to these there is the way of rapture, the way of the mind mysteriously and marvelously carried into the light of Christ.

There are virtues, and there are begetters of virtues, and it is with these latter that a wise man would have his dealings. The teacher of these parent virtues is God Himself in His proper activity, and there are plenty of teachers for the derivative virtues.

We should be careful not to make up for lack of food by sleeping too much, and vice versa. This is a practice of foolish men. I have seen ascetics who, having yielded a little to their appetites, afterwards punished their poor stomachs by standing all night, thus teaching them to be content if they were not filled up.

The demon of avarice fights hard against those who have nothing. When it fails to overcome them, it begins to tell them about the wretched conditions of the poor, thereby inducing those in the religious life to become concerned once more with material things.

---

109. Sarapion the Sindonite; see F. Nau, "Histoire de Thais", *Annales du Musée Guimet* xxx, p. 51.

110. See note 28, p. 105.

When you are depressed, bear in mind the Lord's command to Peter to forgive a sinner seventy times seven (cf. Matt. 18:22). And you may be sure that He Who gave this command to another will Himself do very much more. But if, on the other hand, we become too self-assured, let us remember what has been said about the person who keeps the whole spiritual law and yet, having slipped into one passion, that of pride, is guilty of all (cf. James 2:10).

Some evil and jealous spirits of their own accord leave holy men so as to deprive these of the opportunity to win the prize of victory over them.

Blessed are the peacemakers (Matt. 5:9). No one will deny this. But I have seen foemakers who are also blessed. Two monks once developed an unhealthy fondness for one another. But a discerning and very experienced father brought them to the stage of detesting each other. He made them enemies by telling each man he was being slandered by the other, and by this piece of chicanery he warded off the demon's malice, and by causing hatred he brought an end to what was an unclean affection.

Again, there are some who infringe a commandment for the sake of a commandment. I have known young men who were bound by ties of honorable affection but who, to avoid any scandal, agreed to avoid each other's company for a time.

Like a wedding and a funeral, pride and despair are opposites. But sufficient confusion can be caused by demons to make them seem of a kind.

When we begin religious life, some unclean demons give us lessons in the interpretation of scripture. This happens particularly in the case of people who are either vainglorious or who have had a secular education, and these are gradually led into heresy and blasphemy. One may detect this diabolical teaching about God, or rather war against God, by the upheaval, confusion, and unholy joy in the soul during lessons.

The things that have come into being have received from the Creator their proper place, their beginning and, in some cases, their end. But there is no boundary to virtue. The psalmist says, "I have seen the end of all perfection, but Your commandment is very broad and is without limit" (Ps. 118:96). Now if it is true that some good ascetics pass from the strength of action to the strength of contemplation (cf. Ps. 83:7), and if it is true that love never fails (1 Cor. 13:8), and that the Lord will guard the coming in of your fear and the going out of your love (cf. Ps. 120:8), then love has no boundary, and both in the present and in the future age we will never cease to progress in it, as we add light to light. Perhaps this may seem strange to many. Nevertheless it has to be said, and the evidence we have, blessed Father, would lead me to say that even the angels make progress and indeed that they add glory to glory and knowledge to knowledge.

Do not be surprised if demons often inspire good thoughts in us, together with the reasoned arguments against them. What these enemies of ours are trying to do is to get us to believe that they know even our innermost thoughts.

Do not be a harsh critic of those who resort to eloquence to teach many important things, but who have few actions to match their words. For edifying words have often compensated for a lack of deeds. All of us do not get an equal share of every good, and for some the word is mightier than the deed (cf. Ps. 102:20–21; 1 Pet. 5:8) and *vice versa* for others.

God neither caused nor created evil and, therefore, those who assert that certain passions come naturally to the soul are quite wrong. What they fail to realize is that we have taken natural attributes of our own and turned them into passions. For instance, the seed which we have for the sake of procreating children is abused by us for the sake of fornication. Nature has provided us with anger as something to be turned against the serpent, but we have used it against our neighbor. We have a natural urge to excel in virtue, but instead we compete in evil. Nature stirs within us the desire for glory, but that glory is of a heavenly kind. It is natural for us to be arrogant—against the demons. Joy is ours by nature, but it should be joy on account of the Lord and for the sake of doing good to our neighbor. Nature has given us resentment, but that ought to be against the enemies of our souls. We have a natural desire for food,[111] but not surely for profligacy.

An active soul is a provocation to demons, yet the greater our conflicts the greater our rewards. There will be no crown for the man who has never been under attack, and the man who perseveres in spite of any failures will be glorified as a champion by the angels.

111. HTM reads "pleasure" (*tryphis*) for "food" (*trophis*).

He Who was three nights in the earth came back and lived forever. He who has conquered three hours will never die.[112]

If, after rising in us, the sun "knows his going down" (Ps. 103:19) for our providential chastening, "he made darkness the place of his concealment" (Ps. 17:12). The night came on, the night in which the fierce young lions go prowling once more after they had left us alone, the lions and all the beasts of the woods of thorny passions, roaring to seize the hope that is in us, and seeking from God their food of the passions either in thought or in deed. Through the darkness of our humility, the sun rises over us, and the wild beasts gather where they belong, in sensual hearts and not in ours (cf. Ps. 103:22). Then the demons speak to one another: "The Lord delighted in doing great things for them." And we speak: " 'He has done great things for us and we are glad' (cf. Ps. 135:4) but you are banished." "See, the Lord rides on a swift cloud," on the soul raised above earthly longings, "and He shall come into Egypt," into the darkened heart, "and He shall shatter the man-made idols" (Isa. 19:1), the empty fashionings of the mind.

Christ, although all-powerful, fled bodily from Herod. So let the foolish learn not to fling themselves into temptation. It is said: "Let not your foot be moved and let not your guardian angel slumber" (cf. Ps. 120:3).

Like bindweed round a cypress, vanity twines itself around courage. And we must be ever on guard against yielding to the mere thought that we have achieved any sort of good. We have to be really careful about this, in case it should be a trait within us, for if it is, then we have certainly failed.

If we watch out continually for signs of the passions, we will discover that there are many within us which, in our sickness, we never noticed. We were too weak, or they were too deeply rooted.

God judges us by our intentions, but because of His love for us

112. What is meant by "three hours" is obscure. Scholion 21a (1081A), quoting a saying of Abba Elias, suggests that they are death, the coming into the presence of God, and judgment. Scholion 21b (1081A) offers other interpretations: youth, maturity and old age, or pleasure, vainglory and avarice, or the three temptations of the demon (presumably the three temptations of Christ in the wilderness). As the conqueror of the three hours is Christ Himself, the expression could well refer to the three hours on the cross.

He only demands from us such actions as lie within our power. Great is the man who does all that lies within his power, but greater still is the man who, in all humility, tries to do more.

Demons often prevent us from doing what would be easy and valuable for us. Instead they like to push us into trying what is harder.

I find that Joseph is deemed blessed because he avoided an occasion of sin and not because he showed evidence of dispassion (cf. Gen. 39:12). Hence the question of the type and number of sins, the avoidance of which is rewarded by a crown. There is a difference between running from a shadow and the greater act of hastening toward the sun of righteousness. For to be in darkness is to stumble and to stumble is to fall, and to fall is to die.

Those brought down by wine often wash with water, but those brought down by passion wash with their tears.

There is a distinction between clouding, darkness, and blindness. Temperance will cure the first, solitude the second. The third will be cured by obedience and by the God Who for our sakes became obedient (cf. Phil. 2:8).

Two examples, drawn from the world, will provide useful analogies for those with minds intent on the things of heaven. A monastic community living according to the Lord is like a laundry where the dirt, grossness, and deformity of the soul are scrubbed away; and the solitary life for those who are moving from the monastery to total seclusion is like the dye-works where lust, the harboring of wrongs, and anger are erased.

Some would claim that our repeated lapses in some matter are caused by our failure to do adequate penance for earlier falls. But the problem then arises as to whether those who have not fallen into the same type of sin over and over again have actually repented as they should. People commit the same sin again and again either because they have thoroughly forgotten their previous sins, or because in their own pleasure-loving way they keep thinking that God is merciful, or because they have given up all hope of salvation. Now—and I may be severely criticized for this—it seems to me that their real difficulty is that they have not had the strength to grip firmly what in fact is a dominating habit.

Here is a question. Why does the incorporeal soul fail to perceive the real character of the evil spirits that come to dwell with it? The answer, perhaps, lies in the union of the soul with the body; but it is known only to the One Who bound them together in the first place.

An experienced man once asked me earnestly to tell him which spirits were accustomed to depress the mind when we sin and which to exalt it. The question left me at a loss, and I had to swear my ignorance. So this man, himself so eager for knowledge, taught me, saying: "I shall give you the leaven of discernment briefly and I shall leave you to find out the rest by your own efforts. The spirits of lust, of anger, of gluttony, of despondency, and of sleepiness do not usually raise up the horn of the mind. But the spirits of money-grubbing, of ambition, of talkativeness, and many others pile evil onto evil. This also is the reason why the spirit of criticism is so near the latter."

A monk who has spent an hour or a day visiting people out in the world or entertaining them as guests should rejoice at the time of parting, like someone released from a trap. If however what he feels is a pang of regret, then this shows that he has become the plaything either of vainglory or of lust.

We must always find out which way the wind blows, lest we set our sails against it.

Show kindness and give a little respite to old men leading the active life whose bodies are worn out by ascetical practice. But insist that young men who have exhausted their souls with sin must be restrained and must think of the eternal torments.

I have already said that at the beginning of one's life as a monk one cannot suddenly become free of gluttony and vainglory. But we must not counter vainglory with high living simply because among novices, to defeat gluttony is to run into vainglory. So let us fight it by way of frugality. The time will come—and indeed is already here for those really wishing it—when the Lord will enable us to trample on this vice.

At the start of religious life, the young and those of advanced years are not troubled by the same passions, since very often they have quite opposite failings. Hence the fact that humility is so truly blessed, for it makes repentance safe and effective for both young and old.

Do not make a fuss about what I am going to say now. There are souls, true, upright, and rare, who know nothing of malice, hypocrisy and deceit, and who are quite unable to live in religious communities. Helped by a spiritual director, they can leave the harbor of solitude and rise heavenward without ever wishing for and experiencing the ups and downs, the stumbling blocks of community life.

Men can heal the lustful. Angels can heal the malicious. Only God can heal the proud.

It may be that an aspect of love is to allow a neighbor who comes on frequent visits to do what he pleases. Certainly we must show him every kindness.

Here is another problem. Is there a kind of repentance that can destroy good in the same way as evil? If so, how, to what extent, and in what circumstances?

We must be very shrewd in the matter of knowing when to stand up against sin, when and to what extent to fight against whatever nourishes the passions, and when to withdraw from the struggle. Because of our weakness there are times when we must choose flight if we are to avoid death. We must watch and see (for perhaps there are times when we can neutralize gall with bitterness) which of the demons uplift us, which depress us, which make us hard, which bring us consolation, which darken us, which pretend to enlighten us, which make us lazy, which shifty, which make us sad and which cheerful.

At the start of our religious lives, we may find that our passions are stronger than they were when we were in the world. This should not upset us, and if we remove the causes of our sickness, then health will come to us. Those beasts were formerly concealed in us, but they did not reveal themselves.

It may happen that those who are otherwise attaining perfection are tripped up by the demons on some minor matter. They should at once use every means to wrench this out of themselves a hundred times over.

Like the winds, which sometimes in calm weather ruffle only the surface of the sea and at other times stir up the depths, so there are the dark blasts of evil. Think about them. They reach down to disturb the very hearts of those dominated by the passions, whereas among those who have made progress, they merely ruffle the surface of the mind. That is why the latter soon recover their usual calm for their hearts were left undefiled.

It is characteristic of the perfect that they always know whether a thought comes from within themselves, or from God, or from the demons. Remember that demons do not automatically propose evil at the outset. Here we have a problem truly hard to penetrate.

Two corporeal eyes give light to the body, and the eyes of the heart are enlightened by discernment in things seen and unseen.

A BRIEF SUMMARY OF ALL THE PRECEDING STEPS

A strong faith is the mother of renunciation. The opposite of this is quite evident.

Unswerving hope is the gateway to detachment. The opposite of this is perfectly obvious.

Love of God is the foundation of exile. The opposite of this is quite evident.

Self-criticism begets obedience and the longing for health.

Self-control is the mother of health. The mother of self-control is the thought of death and the memory of the gall and vinegar of God our Lord.

The solitary life is the helper and the foundation of chastity. Fasting quenches the fires of the flesh. And contrition of heart is the foe of dirty thoughts.

Faith and withdrawal from the world are the death of avarice.

Compassion and love are betrayers of the body.

Unremitting prayer is the death of despondency.

Remembrance of the judgment is an encouragement to zeal.

Love of being dishonored is a cure for anger. And the singing of hymns, the display of compassion, and poverty are quenchers of sorrow.

Detachment from the things perceived by the senses means the vision of things spiritual.

Silence and solitude are the foes of vainglory. If you are in a crowd, seek out dishonor.

A gloomy environment will cure open pride, but only He who is invisible from all eternity can cure the pride hidden within us.

The deer destroys all visible serpents and humility destroys those of the spirit.[113]

We can learn to perceive intelligible things clearly by means of every thing that exists in the natural world.

A snake can shed its old skin only if it crawls into a tight hole, and we can shed our old tendencies, our worn-out soul, and the garment of the old man only if we take the straight and narrow path of fasting and dishonor.

Just as a large-bodied bird cannot fly heavenward, neither can anyone who feeds his flesh and gives in to it.

Dried-up mud draws no pigs. Dried-up flesh harbors no demons.

Too many sticks can choke a fire and put it out, causing a lot of smoke. An excess of sorrow can often make a soul turn smoky and dark and dries up the stream of tears.

A blind archer is useless. An argumentative disciple is a lost one.

Tempered iron can sharpen what is untempered. A zealous brother can frequently save a lazy one.

Eggs warmed in dung[114] hatch out. Unconfessed evil thoughts hatch evil actions.

Galloping horses vie with each other. A zealous community encourages individual zeal.

Clouds hide the sun. Evil thoughts bring shadows to the mind and ruin it.

A condemned man on his way to execution does not discuss the theater. A man genuinely lamenting his sins will never pander to his stomach.

Poor men are all the more conscious of their own deprivation when they look at regal treasures. A soul reading of the great virtues of the Fathers adopts a much more humble outlook.

Iron is drawn willy-nilly by a magnet. A man in the grip of bad habits is mastered by them.

Oil tames the reluctant sea. Fasting puts down the involuntary fires of the body.

---

113. See note 86, p. 220.

114. Rader reads "the bosom" *(kolpo)* for "dung" *(kopro)*.

Dammed waters run back upstream. The soul constricted by dangers often returns to God and is saved by repentance.

A wearer of perfume is detected, whether he wishes it or not, by the aromas around him. A carrier of God's Spirit is detected in his speech and in his lowliness.[115]

Winds stir the deep and temper stirs the mind more than anything else.

What the eye has not seen and what has only been heard of does not greatly stir desire. So ignorance is therefore a great help to the chaste.

Thieves do not pounce where royal armor is stored. Spiritual thieves do not readily pounce on the man who has united his heart with prayer.

Fire does not give birth to snow, and those seeking honor here will not come to enjoy it in heaven.

One spark has often set fire to a great forest, and it has been found that one good deed can wipe away a multitude of sins (cf. James 3:5, 5:20).

It is impossible to destroy wild beasts without arms. It is impossible to achieve freedom from anger without humility.

Just as by nature we cannot exist without food, we cannot afford to slip into carelessness even for an instant at any time up to the moment of death.

Like the sun's ray passing through a crack and lighting up the house, showing up even the finest dust, the fear of the Lord on entering the heart of a man shows up all his sins.

Crabs are easy to catch, for sometimes they walk forward and sometimes backward. In the same way, the soul that tries laughter now, grief then, high living some other time, cannot make progress.

The sleepy are easily robbed and those living close to the world are easily despoiled of their virtue.

When a man fights a lion, it is fatal to glance away for even a moment. So too with the man fighting against his body, who yields for the merest instant.

It is dangerous to climb a rotten ladder, and in the same way all honor, glory, and power pose a danger to humility.

A man eager for salvation thinks of death and the judgment in

---

115. HTM adds a sentence: "As the sun makes gold glitter, so virtue makes manifest the man who possesses it."

the same way that a starving man thinks of bread.

Tears can wash away sins as water washes away something written. And as some, lacking water, use other means to wipe off what is written, souls lacking tears beat and scour away their sins with grief, groans, and deep sorrow.

A dung heap breeds worms in abundance. Piles of food breed an abundance of lapses, evil thoughts, and dreams.

A man whose legs are bound cannot walk freely. Those who hoard treasures cannot climb to heaven.

A new wound can easily be cured, but the very opposite is true of souls with long-standing wounds. If they are healed at all, it is only with the greatest difficulty.

A dead man cannot walk. A man in despair cannot be saved.

A man who asserts that he has the true faith and yet continues to sin is like a man without eyes. And the man who has no faith but who does good is like someone who draws water and then pours it into a barrel with holes.

A ship with a good navigator comes safely to port, God willing. A soul with a good shepherd climbs easily heavenward, even if it has earlier done much wrong.

A man, no matter how prudent, may easily go astray on a road if he has no guide. The man who takes the road of monastic life under his own direction may easily be lost, even if he has all the wisdom of the world.

If anyone is weak in body and if he has suffered grievous falls, let him turn onto the path of humility, taking on himself what is typical of that way, for there is no other road to salvation.

Just as someone in the grip of a long illness cannot return to instant health, it is not possible to overcome passions—not even one of them—in a quick moment.

Keep track of the exact condition of each passion and of each virtue, and you will know exactly how you are making progress.

Those who take mud in exchange for gold are suffering a loss. So too with those who hold forth on things spiritual for the sake of material advantage.

Many have been speedily forgiven their sins. But no one has rapidly acquired dispassion, for this requires much time and longing,[116] and God.

---

116. Rader gives "labor" (*ponou*) as an alternative to "longing" (*pothou*).

We should find out which animals and which birds seek to harm us at the time of sowing, at the time when the shoots are green, and at the time of harvest, and we should arrange our traps accordingly.

A man in a fever ought not to commit suicide. And right up to the moment of death we should never despair.

It would be quite wrong for a man to go straight from burying his father to his own wedding, and it would be quite wrong for those in mourning for their sins to look for honor, rest, or glory in this life from men.

Citizens live in one sort of place, convicts in another. So too there ought to be a difference in status between those who mourn their sins and those who are innocent.

A king ordains that a soldier badly wounded in his presence in battle should not be dismissed but, in fact, promoted. In the same way, the King of heaven gives a crown to the monk who has endured many perils from demons.

Perception is a property of the soul. Sin is a battering of this property. Perception brings about the end or the lessening of evil, and it is a product of conscience. Conscience is the word and censure that come from our guardian angel, and we have it from the time of baptism. And it is for this reason that the unbaptized do not feel very much bitterness of soul for their evil deeds.

The lessening of evil yields abstinence from evil, and such abstinence is the starting point of repentance. The beginning of repentance is the beginning of salvation, and the beginning of salvation is a good intention, which, in turn, is the begetter of labors. The beginning of labors is virtue and the beginning of virtue is a flowering, and the flowering of virtue is the beginning of activity.

The offspring of virtue is perseverance. The fruit and offspring of perseverance is habit, and the child of habit is character.

Good character begets fear, and fear begets observance of the commandments, by which I mean those of heaven and earth. To keep the commandments is to show love, and the starting point of love is an abundance of humility, which in turn is the daughter of dispassion. To have dispassion is to have the fullness of love, by which I mean the complete indwelling of God in those who, through dispassion, are pure of heart for they shall see God (Matt. 5:8). To Him be glory forever and ever. Amen.

Step 27

ON STILLNESS

We are like purchased slaves, like servants under contract to the unholy passions. And because this is so, we know a little of their deceits, ways, impositions and wiles. We know of their evil despotism in our wretched souls. But there are others who fully understand the tricks of these spirits, and they do so because of the working of the Holy Spirit and because of the freedom they themselves have managed to achieve. We in our sickness can only imagine the sort of relief that would come with good health; but they, being healthy, can understand and talk about the weakness that goes hand in hand with sickness.

Now this is why, being weak and infirm, I hesitate to hold forth to you in this discourse on the haven of solitude. I know only too well that at the table of good fellowship there is always some dog waiting to grab a piece of bread, a soul in other words, to run off with it in its mouth and to devour it at leisure. Therefore I want nothing said by me to give room to that dog, to give a chance to those on the lookout for such an opportunity. I do not think it right to talk about peace to those brave followers of our King, those warriors who are in the midst of battle. I will merely say that crowns of peace and calm are ready for those who do not weaken in the fight.

Still, the subject should be mentioned so as not to offend anyone. I shall therefore, with your permission, speak briefly about stillness.

Stillness of the body is the accurate knowledge and management of one's feelings and perceptions. Stillness of soul is the accurate knowledge of one's thoughts and is an unassailable mind.

Brave and determined thinking is a friend of stillness. It is always on the watch at the doors of the heart, killing or driving off invading notions. What I mean by this will be well understood by the man who practices stillness in the deep places of the heart, while the novice will have no experience or knowledge of it.

A shrewd hesychast requires no words. He is enlightened by deeds rather than by words.

The start of stillness is the rejection of all noisiness as something that will trouble the depths of the soul. The final point is when one has no longer a fear of noisy disturbance, when one is immune to it. He who when he goes out does not go out in his intellect[117] is gentle and wholly a house of love, rarely moved to speech and never to anger. The opposite to all this is manifest.

Strange as it may seem, the hesychast is a man who fights to keep his incorporeal self shut up in the house of the body.

The cat keeps hold of the mouse. The thought of the hesychast keeps hold of his spiritual mouse. Do not mock the analogy. Indeed, if you do, it shows you still do not understand the meaning of stillness.

A solitary is not the same as a monk living with another monk. A solitary has to be very much on guard, and his mind has to be alert. The second kind of monk often helps his brother, but an angel helps the solitary.

The powers of heaven join in living and worship with the man who practices stillness in his soul. I shall not say anything to you about the opposite situation.

The profundities of dogma are great and the mind of the solitary leaps over them not without danger.[118]

It is risky to swim in one's clothes. A slave of passion should not dabble in theology.

The cell of a hesychast is the body that surrounds him, and within him is the dwelling place of knowledge.

When a man sick with a passion in his soul attempts the solitary life, he resembles a man jumping from a ship into the sea and imagining that he will reach shore safely on a plank.

---

117. I.e., who maintains inner solitude when he goes out of his hermitage.

118. Or: "capers among them not without danger." HTM translates: "leaps over them safely."

A solitary life is suitable for someone who is fighting his clay, provided the time is right and provided he has a spiritual director. The fact is that you need the strength of an angel if you are to live a solitary life. Here, of course, I am talking of those who live a real life of solitude in soul and body.

When a hesychast gets lazy, he starts telling lies. He hints at others to get him out of his solitude, and when he leaves his cell he puts the blame on devils. What he does not know is that he has turned into his own devil.

I have known hesychasts whose flaming urge for God was limitless. They generated fire by fire, love by love, desire by desire.

A hesychast is like an angel on earth. With the paper of love and the letters of zeal, he has freed his prayer from sloth and carelessness. Openly he cries out: "O God, my heart is ready" (Ps. 56:8). He says, "I sleep, but my heart is awake" (Song of Songs 5:2).

Close the door of your cell to your body, the door of your tongue to talk, and the gate within to evil spirits. The endurance of the sailor is tried by the noonday sun or when he is becalmed, and the endurance of the solitary is tested by his lack of necessary supplies. The one jumps into the water and swims when he is impatient, the other goes in search of a crowd when he is discouraged.

Do not be afraid of loud nonsense. The spirit of mourning is neither afraid of it nor upset by it.

Those with a mind accustomed to true prayer talk directly to the Lord, as if to the ear of the emperor. Those praying aloud fall down in front of the Lord as if before the entire senate. Those who live in the world make their pleas to the emperor in the midst of bustling crowds. Now if you have learned the technique of prayer systematically, you will certainly grasp what I am saying.

Sit in a high place and keep watch if you can, and you will see the thieves come, and you will discover how they come, when and from where, how many and what kind they are as they steal your clusters of grapes.

When the watchman gets tired, he stands up and he prays. And then, sitting down once more, he bravely carries on with his task.

A man knew about all these things from experience and wanted to describe them in close detail. But he was afraid. He did not wish to discourage those already engaged in this or by his words to scare off those on the point of embarking on this way.

A man who begins to talk subtly and with knowledge about stillness stirs up the demons against himself, for there is no one else who can so hold up their evil work to contempt.

He who has achieved stillness has arrived at the very center of the mysteries, but he would never have reached these depths if he had not first seen and heard the sound of the waves and of the evil spirits, if he had not even been splashed by those waters. Paul confirms this. If he had not been caught up into Paradise as into stillness, he would never have heard the unspeakable words (cf. 2 Cor. 12:4). The ear of the solitary will hear wonders from God. Hence the words of the all-wise Job: "Will not my ear receive amazing things from Him?" (Job 4:12).

The solitary runs away from everyone, but does so without hatred, just as another runs toward the crowd, even if without enthusiasm. The solitary does not wish to be cut off from the divine sweetness.

Go now. At once. Give away everything you have. ("Sell what you own." That needs time.) Give to the poor monks so that their prayers may be with you in your solitude. Take up your cross, carrying it in obedience, and endure strongly the burden of your thwarted will. And then, "Come, follow me" (Matt. 19:21). Come to union with most blessed stillness and I will teach you the workings and the behavior of the spiritual powers. They never grow tired of their everlasting praise of their Maker, nor does he who has entered into the heaven of stillness cease to praise his Creator. Spirits have no thought for what is material, and those who have become immaterial in a material body will pay no attention to food, for the former know nothing of it and the latter need no promise of it; the former are unconcerned about money and chattels and the latter are heedless of the malice of evil spirits. In those dwelling above, there is no yearning for the visible creation, while those on earth below have no longing for what can be sensed, because the former never cease to make progress in love and the latter will never cease to imitate them. The former know well the value of their progress; the latter understand their own love and longing for the ascent to heaven. The former will desist only when they rise to the realm of the Seraphim; the latter will grow tired only when they come at last to be angels. Blessed is he who hopes; thrice blessed is he who lives to see the promise of being an angel.

The Differences between the Various Kinds of Stillness

As everyone knows, there are differences of concept and aim in each of the sciences. There are defects in all, because of some failure of zeal or strength. Hence some enter this harbor, this sea, or indeed the abyss of solitary life because they cannot control their tongues or because of some previous habit of the flesh. Others do so because they have a bad temper, which they cannot restrain in company, or because they arrogantly think it better to sail on their own rather than under the guidance of someone else. Others do so because if they live amid material things they cannot do without them. Some think that a life of solitude will enhance their zeal, and some wish to punish themselves in secret for their faults. Some think of the glory a solitary life will earn them. And there are some—may the Son of Man find them on earth when He comes back—who undertake this holy way of life because of a delight in, a thirst for the love and sweetness of God, and they achieve a union of this kind only after they have shed all despondency. For to link despondency to the loving of God is rather like committing adultery.

I have put together a ladder of ascent, though my meager knowledge makes me something of a second-rate architect. Still, let each one take note of the step on which he is standing. Is it on the step of self-will, of fame, of a loose tongue, of hot temper? Or of possessiveness? Is it on the step of atonement for sin, of greater zeal, of loving fire added to fire? "The last shall be first and the first last" (Matt. 19:30). The first seven are the work of the world's week, and some are good while others are not. But the eighth clearly bears the mark of the age to come.

O solitary monk, watch out for the hour of the wild beasts, because if you do not, then you will be unable to get ready the appropriate traps. If you have managed to shake off despondency, this task will be superfluous, but if it still plagues you, I do not know how you can endure the life alone.

Why is it that there were not as many lights among the holy fathers at Tabennisi as at Scetis?[119] Cope with that question if you can. I cannot say why. Or rather, I do not wish to.

119. Tabennisi in Upper Egypt was the site of St Pachomius' first monastery. Its characteristic features were a strict community life under an abbot with meals and

Some work to reduce the passions. Others sing psalms and spend most of their time in prayer. Some turn to the depths of contemplation. But whatever the situation is, let it be investigated in accordance with the ladder and accepted in the Lord.

There are some idle souls in the monasteries. Giving way to whatever feeds that idleness, they come to an utterly bad end. Others by living in community strip themselves of idleness. This often occurs not only with the careless but with the zealous too.

The same may be said regarding the solitary life, for it has received many experienced monks but has rejected them because of their self-direction and proved them to be lovers of pleasure. It has accepted others and made them zealous and fervent by fear and concern for the burden of their judgment.

The man who is foul-tempered and conceited, hypocritical and a nurse of grievances, ought never to enter the life of solitude, for fear he should gain nothing but the loss of his sanity. Someone free of these faults will know what is best. Or perhaps, I think, not even he.

The following are the signs, the stages, and the proofs of practicing stillness in the right way—a calm mind, a purified disposition, rapture in the Lord, the remembrance of everlasting torments, the imminence of death, an insatiable urge for prayer, constant watchfulness, the death of lust, no sense of attachment, death of worldliness, an end to gluttony, a foundation for theology,[120] a well of discernment, a truce accompanied by tears, an end to talkativeness, and many other such things alien to most men.

The following are signs of stillness practiced wrongly—poverty of spiritual treasures, anger on the increase, a growth of resentment, love diminished, a surge of vanity. And I will say nothing about all that follows from these.

Our chapter has now reached the point at which we must deal with those living in obedience, especially as this step is directed for the most part towards them.

With regard to those who lawfully, chastely, and in pure fashion

---

worship in common. Scetis (the Wadi Natrun) in Lower Egypt was a center for hermitages, where stillness could be practiced by solitaries or small groups of monks. Scetis was sometimes used as a general name to include Nitria as well, some forty miles to the north. Many of the famous Fathers whose sayings are recorded in the great collections of the Apophthegmata came from Scetis or Nitria.

120. Theology here means the direct experience of God.

are wedded to this orderly and admirable way of obedience, there are manifestations—validated by the divinely inspired Fathers and brought to perfection in their own time—manifestations accompanied by daily increase and progress. There is an advance in basic humility. There is lessening of bad temper, which must after all diminish as the gall is depleted. Darkness is scattered and love approached. There is an estrangement from passions, an escape from hatred. Lust, under ceaseless criticism, diminishes; despondency is unknown; and zeal grows. There is compassionate love and a banishment of pride. This is what everyone must seek, though few will be completely successful. A well without water does not deserve its name, and hence the obvious conclusion for those with understanding.

A young wife who strays from her marriage defiles her body. A soul unfaithful to his vow defiles his spirit. The former is denounced, hated, beaten, and, most pitiable of all, thrown out.[121] For the latter there is pollution, forgetfulness of death, an insatiable belly, eyes out of control, vainglory at work, a longing for sleep, a calloused heart, insensitivity, a storing up of bad thoughts, an increase of consent, captivity of heart, spiritual upheaval, disobedience, argumentativeness, attachment to things, unbelief, doubt, talkativeness, and—most serious this—free and easy relationships. Most wretched of all is a heart without compunction, which, in the careless, is succeeded by insensitivity, the mother of devils and of lapses.

Of the eight evil spirits, five attack the solitary and three assail those living in obedience.[122]

A monk practicing stillness and struggling against despondency is often harmed, for the time to be given to prayer and contemplation is wasted in the tricks and wrestlings needed to fight his problem.

I was once sitting in my cell having become slack. Indeed I was thinking of leaving it. But some visitors came, and when they began to praise me for leading the life of a hesychast, my slackness gave way

121. The ancient discipline of the Church allowed separation from an unfaithful spouse. Indeed a priest was required to divorce his wife if she committed adultery. There was no question, however, of remarriage.

122. Scholion 14 (1120C) identifies the five as despondency, vainglory, pride, dejection and anger, and the three as gluttony, lust, and avarice. For a slightly different subdivision, cf. note 94, p. 229.

to vainglorious thoughts and I was amazed by the manner in which this three-horned demon stood up against all the others.

The spirit of despondency is your companion. Watch him every hour. Note his stirrings and his movements, his inclinations and his changes of face. Note their character and the direction they take. Someone with the gift of calm from the Holy Spirit well understands what I have in view.

The first task of stillness is disengagement from every affair good and bad, since concern with the former leads on to the latter. Second is urgent prayer. Third is inviolable activity of the heart. And just as you have to know the alphabet if you are to read books, so if you have missed out on the first task, you cannot enter upon the other two.

I myself was occupied with the second of these tasks and entered the intermediate stage. A light came to me as I was thirsting and I asked there what the Lord was before He took visible form. The angel could not tell me because he was not permitted to do so. So I asked him: "In what state is He now?" and the answer was that He was in the state appropriate to Him, though not to us. "What is the nature of the standing or sitting at the right hand of the Father?" I asked. "Such mysteries cannot be taken in by the human ear," he replied. Then I pleaded with him right then to bring me where my heart was longing to go, but he said that the time was not yet ripe, since the fire of incorruption was not yet mighty enough within me. And whether, during all this, I was in the body or out of it, I cannot rightly say (cf. 2 Cor. 12:2).

It is very hard to shake off the sleep of midday, particularly in summer time. Then—and perhaps only then—is manual work to be permitted.

The demon of despondency, as I have discovered, opens the way for the demon of lust. It greatly weakens the body and causes that sleep which brings about pollutions in those practicing stillness. Fight hard against these demons and they in turn will furiously attack you. They will try to force you to desist from your labors, which, they will tell you, are of no value. But there is no better proof of the failure of the demons than the violence with which they attack us.

When you come out in public, be sure to protect what you have accumulated. When the cage doors are opened, the birds fly out. And if that happens, then there is no point in continuing with stillness.

A small hair disturbs the eye. A minor concern interferes with stillness, for, after all, stillness means the expulsion of thoughts and the rejection of even reasonable cares.

He who has truly attained stillness ignores the flesh. God does not make false promises.

The man who wishes to offer a pure mind to God but who is troubled by cares is like a man who expects to walk quickly even though his legs are tied together.

There are not many outstanding experts in worldly philosophy. But I would claim that rarer still are those who are truly expert in the philosophy of stillness.

A man without experience of God ought not to undertake the solitary life. He leaves himself open to many hazards. Stillness chokes the inexperienced. Never having tasted the sweetness of God, such people waste time in being set upon, robbed, made despondent, distracted.

A man who has experienced the value of prayer avoids crowds like a wild donkey. After all, it is prayer that makes him resemble the donkey and makes him shun everybody.

A man who is gripped by passions and lives in the desert listens to their prattle. I was taught this by that blessed elder, George Arsilaites,[123] whom your reverence[124] knows. He was once the director of my useless soul and the guide who brought me to stillness. "I have observed," he said, "that the demons of vainglory and concupiscence usually attack us in the morning. In the middle of the day, the attack comes from the demons of despondency, gloom, and anger; and it comes in the evening from the dung-loving demons of the miserable stomach."

It is better to live poor and obedient than to be a solitary who has no control over his thoughts.

The man who has entered on stillness for a good reason but who fails to see how it benefits him daily is either practicing it in the wrong way or is being robbed of it by self-esteem.

Stillness is worshipping God unceasingly and waiting on Him.

123. A spiritual master whose name occurs in the narratives of Anastasius, *Narratives*, §§ 9 and 12.

124. I.e., John, Abbot of Raithu, at whose request *The Ladder* was written.

Let the remembrance of Jesus[125] be present with your every breath. Then indeed you will appreciate the value of stillness.

Self-will is the ruin of the monk living in obedience. But ruin for the solitary is the interruption of prayer.

If you rejoice because visitors have come to your cell, you should realize that you are taking a holiday not just from despondency but from God. So the model for your prayer should be the widow wronged by her adversary (cf. Luke 18:1–8), and for your stillness that great and angelic hermit Arsenius.[126] In your solitude think of this marvelous hesychast and remember how he used to send away those who came to visit him, lest he be deprived of the better part.

I am aware of the fact that demons often persuade foolish footloose people to go around visiting right-living hermits.[127] The demons do this to create some hindrance, if they can, even through these. So watch out for such people and do not worry about offending them by your devout behavior. Indeed, offensiveness of this kind may stop their footloose career. But be careful. Do not make the mistake of offending a soul who in his thirst has come to draw water from you. Discretion is necessary in everything.

The life of stillness, especially when practiced by solitaries, must be guided by conscience and common sense. If you run the race as it should be run, if every enterprise, utterance, thought, step, move-

---

125. The remembrance of Jesus is usually the context in which the Jesus Prayer is practiced. Here it seems to be equivalent to the Prayer itself (cf. note 51 and the Preface, p. 48).

126. Arsenius was a Roman of senatorial rank who had held office in the imperial palace. He was mistakenly thought by hagiographic sources to have been the tutor of the Emperor Theodosius' sons Arcadius and Honorius. Toward the end of the fourth century he left Rome and retired to a hermitage in Scetis, where he lived until its devastation by barbarian nomads in 434. He was at Canopus near Alexandria for a time, where he was frequently consulted by Archbishop Theophilus (d. 412). After the devastation of Scetis he lived at Troë, between Cairo and Helouan. He was famous for his austerity and avoidance of visitors. The alphabetical collection of *The Sayings of the Desert Fathers* assigns forty-four sayings or maxims to him, with a further two under R attributed to a monk of Rome. For a full list of references see *DHGE* iv, cols. 745–7.

127. From the late fourth century onward visitors came to the Egyptian desert in large numbers to see for themselves how the monks lived. Some were serious inquirers like Basil, Rufinus, Jerome and Palladius. Others were mere tourists. On the irritation caused by some visitors see, for example, *The Sayings of the Desert Fathers*, Arsenius 28, and *The Lives of the Desert Fathers* I, 19–24.

ment, is done according to the Lord, then the Lord's work is done with spiritual perception as if He were there Himself. But if a person is somehow robbed, then he is not yet living in accordance with virtue.

"With the harp I will expound what I have to say" (Ps. 48:5) and what I wish. And it will be in accordance with my imperfect judgment. And in my prayer I will offer up my will, and from God I will draw assurance.

Faith is the wing of prayer, and without it my prayer will return to my bosom. Faith is the unshaken stance of the soul and is unmoved by any adversity. The believing man is not one who thinks that God can do all things, but one who trusts that he will obtain everything. Faith is the agent of things unhoped for, as the thief proved (cf. Luke 23:42–3). The mother of faith is hard work and an upright heart; the one builds up belief, the other makes it endure. Faith is the mother of the hesychast, for after all, how can he practice stillness if he does not believe?

A man chained in prison is fearful of his judge, and the monk in his cell is fearful of God. But the court holds less terror for the one than the judgment seat of God for the other. My good friend, you have to be very much afraid if you are to practice stillness, and nothing else is quite so effective in scattering despondency. The prisoner is always on the watch for the judge to come to the jail, and the true worker is ever on the watch for the coming of death. A weight of sorrow bears down on the one, while for the other there is a fountain of tears.

Take hold of the walking stick of patience, and the dogs will soon stop their impudent harassment. Patience is a labor that does not crush the soul. It never wavers under interruptions, good or bad. The patient monk is a faultless worker who has turned his faults into victories. Patience sets a boundary to the daily onslaught of suffering. It makes no excuses and ignores the self. The worker needs patience more than food, since the one brings him a crown while the other brings destruction. The patient man has died before his death, his cell being his tomb. Patience comes from hope and mourning, and indeed to lack those is to be a slave to despondency.

The warrior of Christ knows how to attack some enemies at a distance and some at close quarters. Sometimes the fight earns a crown and sometimes the unwillingness to fight has produced disaster. Hard and fast rules cannot be laid down for such matters, since we all have differences of character and disposition.

Keep a special watch for the one spirit that unfailingly attacks you whether you stand, walk, sit, stir, get up, pray, or sleep.

Some who preside over the race of stillness always keep before them the words: "I see the Lord before me continually" (Ps. 15:8). But all the loaves of heavenly bread do not have the same appearance. Others therefore keep to the words: "In your patience possess your souls" (Luke 21:19). Others: "Watch and pray" (Matt. 26:41). Others: "Prepare your works for your death" (Prov. 24:27). Others: "I was humbled and He saved me" (Ps. 114:6). Others: "The sufferings of the present time are not to be compared with the glories of the future" (Rom. 8:18). Others constantly ponder the words: "Lest he snatch you away and there be no one to deliver you" (Ps. 49:22). All race, but only one receives the prize without effort.

Someone who has made progress is at work not only when awake but also when he is asleep. Some, therefore, even in sleep show their contempt for the demons who approach them, and urge chastity on the wanton women of their imaginings. On the other hand, do not be on the lookout for these visitations, preparing for them in advance, because the condition of stillness is essentially simple and free.

Anyone planning to construct a tower and cell of stillness will first begin the job by sitting down to count the cost. He will feel his way by prayer. He will ponder whether he has within himself what it takes to complete the task, and he will be careful not to lay the foundations and then prove a joke to his enemies and a hindrance to others who labor (cf. Luke 14:28–30).

Pay careful attention to whatever sweetness there may be in your soul, in case it has been concocted by cruel and crafty physicians.

You should spend most of the night in prayer and only what is left of it in psalmody. And during the day prepare yourself as best you can.

Light and recollection come to the mind by way of reading the Scriptures. The words are those of the Holy Spirit, and they provide guidance to the readers. Let your reading be a preliminary to action, since you are a doer (cf. James 1:22). Put the words into practice, and then further reading will be unnecessary. Try to be enlightened by the words of salvation through your labors and not from books. And until you have acquired spiritual power, do not read works that have various levels of meaing[128] since, being obscure, they may bring darkness over the weak.

A single cup is sufficient to reveal the flavor of a wine, and a single word from a hesychast can reveal to those with taste his whole inner condition and activity.

Let the soul's eye be ever on the watch for conceit, since nothing else can produce such havoc.

Once outside your cell, watch your tongue, for the fruits of many labors can be scattered in a moment.

Stay away from what does not concern you, for curiosity can defile stillness as nothing else can.

When people visit you, offer them what they need for body and spirit. If they happen to be wiser than we are, then let our own silence reveal our wisdom. If they are brothers who share with us the same type of life, we should open the door of speech to them in proper measure. Best of all, however, is to deem everyone our superior.

I would have liked to forbid novices to engage in any toil during times of vigil in common. But I demurred because of the monk who all night carried sand in his cloak.[129]

Doctrine tells of the holy, uncreated, and adorable Trinity. And there is a contrast here with what is said about the providential incarnation of One of the Persons of the hymned Trinity. What is plural in the Trinity is single in Him. What there is single is plural here.[130] Similarly, some practices are appropriate for the way of stillness, and others for those living in obedience.

The divine Apostle said: "Who has known the mind of the Lord?" (Rom. 11:34). I will say:"Who has known the mind of the man who is a hesychast in body and spirit?"

Wealth and numerous subjects constitute the power of a king. Abundance of prayer constitutes the power of the hesychast.

---

128. I.e., works of an allegorical nature, for which spiritual discernment is necessary in order to penetrate to the true meaning.

129. The young Pachomius was thus trained by his abba, Palamon, to stay awake during vigils (though in fact they carried the sand in baskets): Pachomius, *Vita Prima,* § 6; Rosweyde, *Vitae Patrum,* p. 115.

130. In the Trinity there are three Persons but one nature; in Christ there is one Person but two natures.

Step 28

ON PRAYER

Prayer is by nature a dialog and a union of man with God. Its effect is to hold the world together. It achieves a reconciliation with God.

Prayer is the mother and daughter of tears. It is an expiation of sin, a bridge across temptation, a bulwark against affliction. It wipes out conflict, is the work of angels, and is the nourishment of all bodiless beings. Prayer is future gladness, action without end, wellspring of virtues, source of grace, hidden progress, food of the soul, enlightenment of the mind, an axe against despair, hope demonstrated, sorrow done away with. It is wealth for monks, treasure of hermits, anger diminished. It is a mirror of progress, a demonstration of success, evidence of one's condition, the future revealed, a sign of glory. For the man who really prays it is the court, the judgment hall, the tribunal of the Lord—and this prior to the judgment that is to come.

Let us arise and pay heed to what that holy queen of the virtues cries out to us in a loud voice, saying: " 'Come to me, all of you who labor and are weighed down, and I will give you rest. Take upon yourselves my yoke, and you will find rest for your souls' (Matt: 11:28–29), and a balm for the blows that fall on you. 'For my yoke is easy' (ibid. 30) and is a remedy for great sins."

Those of us wishing to stand before our King and God and to speak with Him should not rush into this without some preparation, lest it should happen that—seeing us from afar without arms and without the dress appropriate to those who appear before the King—He should command His servants and His slaves to lay hold of us, to drive us out of His sight, to tear up our petitions and to throw them in our faces.

When you set out to appear before the Lord, let the garment of your soul be woven throughout with the thread of wrongs no longer remembered. Otherwise, prayer will be useless to you.

Pray in all simplicity. The publican and the prodigal son were reconciled to God by a single utterance.

The attitude of prayer is the same for all, but there are many kinds of prayer and many different prayers. Some talk and deal with God as with a friend and master, lifting their praises and their requests to Him not for themselves but for others. Some look for greater spiritual treasures and glory and for greater assurance in their prayers. Some beg to be freed entirely from their adversary. Some look for rank and others for relief from all their debts. Some seek freedom from gaol or for charges against them to be dropped.

But heartfelt thanksgiving should have first place in our book of prayer. Next should be confession and genuine contrition of soul. After that should come our request to the universal King. This method of prayer is best, as one of the brothers was told by an angel of the Lord.

If you ever found yourself having to appear before a human judge, you may use that as an example of how to conduct yourself in prayer. Perhaps you have never stood before a judge nor witnessed a cross-examination. In that case, take your cue from the way patients appeal to surgeons prior to an operation or a cautery.

In your prayers there is no need for high-flown words, for it is the simple and unsophisticated babblings of children that have more often won the heart of the Father in heaven.

Try not to talk excessively in your prayer, in case your mind is distracted by the search for words. One word from the publican sufficed to placate God, and a single utterance saved the thief. Talkative prayer frequently distracts the mind and deludes it, whereas brevity[131] makes for concentration.

If it happens that, as you pray, some word evokes delight or re-

131. Gk *monologia*, i.e. short prayers of varied content. See the Preface, p. 44; *DS* viii (1972), col. 1131.

morse within you, linger over it; for at that moment our guardian angel is praying with us.

However pure you may be, do not be forward in your dealings with God. Approach Him rather in all humility, and you will be given still more boldness. And even if you have climbed the whole ladder of the virtues, pray still for the forgiveness of sins. Heed Paul's cry regarding sinners "of whom I am the first" (1 Tim. 1:15).

Oil and salt are the condiments of food; chastity and tears give flight to prayer.

If you are clothed in gentleness and in freedom from anger, you will find it no trouble to free your mind from captivity.

Until we have acquired true prayer, we are like those who introduce children to walking.

Make the effort to raise up, or rather, to enclose your mind within the words of your prayer; and if, like a child, it gets tired and falters, raise it up again. The mind, after all, is naturally unstable, but the God Who can do everything can also give it firm endurance. Persevere in this, therefore, and do not grow weary; and He Who sets a boundary to the sea of the mind will come to you too during your prayer and will say, "Thus far you shall come, and no farther" (Job 38:11). Spirit cannot be bound, but where He is found everything yields to the Creator of spirit.

If you have ever seen the Sun, you will be able to converse with Him in an appropriate way. But if you have not, then how can you truly talk to Him?

The beginning of prayer is the expulsion of distractions from the very start by a single thought;[132] the middle stage is the concentration on what is being said or thought; its conclusion is rapture in the Lord.

Prayer brings one sort of joy to those living in community, and another to those praying in stillness. Elation is sometimes characteristic of the former, but humility is always to be found in the latter.

If you are careful to train your mind never to wander, it will stay by you even at mealtimes. But if you allow it to stray freely, then you will never have it beside you. "I would prefer to speak five words with my understanding" (1 Cor. 14:19) and so on, says the mighty practitioner of great and high prayer. But prayer of this sort is foreign to infant souls, and so because of our imperfection we need

132. Gk *monologistōs*, which may mean "by a repeated short prayer."

quantity as well as quality in the words of our prayer, the former making a way for the latter, in accordance with the saying about giving prayer to him who prays resolutely, albeit impurely and laboriously (cf. 1 Kings [1 Sam.] 2:9).

There is a difference between the tarnish of prayer, it disappearance, the robbery of it, and its defilement. Prayer is tarnished when we stand before God, our minds seething with irrelevancies. It disappears when we are led off into useless cares. It is robbed when our thoughts stray without our realization of the fact. And it is defiled when we are in any way under attack.

If we happen not to be alone at the time of prayer, let us form within ourselves the demeanor of someone who prays. But if the servants of praise are not sharing our company, we may openly put on the appearance of those at prayer. For among the weak, the mind often conforms to the body.

Total contrition is necessary for everyone, but particularly for those who have come to the King to obtain forgiveness of their sins. While we are still in prison, let us listen to him who told Peter to put on the garment of obedience, to shed his own wishes, and, having been stripped of them, to come close to the Lord in prayer, seeking only His will (cf. Acts 12:8). Then you will receive the God Who takes the helm of your soul and pilots you safely.

Rise from love of the world and love of pleasure. Put care aside, strip your mind, refuse your body. Prayer, after all, is a turning away from the world, visible and invisible. What have I in heaven? Nothing. What have I longed for on earth besides You? Nothing except simply to cling always to You in undistracted prayer. Wealth pleases some, glory others, possessions others, but what I want is to cling to God and to put the hopes of my dispassion in Him (cf. Ps. 72:25, 28).

Faith gives wings to prayer, and without it no one can fly upward to heaven.

Those of us who are swept by passion must ceaselessly pray to the Lord, for all the passionate have advanced from passion to dispassion.

Even if the judge has no fear of God, yet because a soul widowed from God by sin and by a fall disturbs Him, He will take revenge on the body, the soul's adversary, and on the spirits who declare war on her (cf. Luke 18:1–7).

Our good Redeemer, by speedily granting what is asked, draws to His love those who are grateful. But He keeps ungrateful souls praying a long time before Him, hungering and thirsting for what they want, since a badly trained dog rushes off as soon as it is given bread and leaves the giver behind.

After a long spell of prayer, do not say that nothing has been gained, for you have already achieved something. For, after all, what higher good is there than to cling to the Lord and to persevere in unceasing union with Him?

A convicted man does not fear his sentence as much as a zealous man the time of prayer. So if he is shrewd and sensible, he will remember this and will therefore be able to avoid reproach, anger, anxiety, concerns, affliction, satiety, temptation, and distractions.

Get ready for your set time of prayer by unceasing prayer in your soul. In this way, you will soon make progress. I have observed that those who were outstanding in obedience and who tried as far as possible to keep in mind the thought of God were in full control of their minds and wept copiously as soon as they stood in prayer, for holy obedience had prepared them for this.

One can be held back and distracted by the singing of psalms in a congregation. This does not happen when one is a solitary. However, despondency can assail the latter, while in the former situation the brethren can give help by their zeal.

War reveals the love of a soldier for his king, and the time and practice of prayer show up a monk's love for God. So your prayer shows where you stand. Indeed, theologians say that prayer is a monk's mirror.

Someone who is occupied with some task and continues with it at the hour of prayer is being fooled by the demons, for these thieves aim to steal one hour after another from us.

Do not refuse a request to pray for the soul of another, even when you yourself lack the gift of prayer. For often the very faith of the person making the request will evoke the saving contrition of the one who is to offer the prayer.

Do not become conceited when you have prayed for others and have been heard, for it is their faith which has been active and efficacious.

A child is examined each day without fail regarding what he has learned from his teacher. And it is reasonable to ask that there be a reckoning of each prayer we have undertaken, in order that we may have an idea of the power we have received from God. You should see to this. And when you have prayed soberly, you will soon have to cope with bouts of ill temper, something our enemies aim for.

Every virtuous act we do—and this is particularly true of prayer—should be done with great sensitivity. A soul prays with sensitivity when it has overcome anger.

Whatever is obtained as a result of long and persistent prayer will remain.

When a man has found the Lord, he no longer has to use words when he is praying, for the Spirit Himself will intercede for him with groans that cannot be uttered (cf. Rom. 8:26).

Do not form sensory images during prayer, for distraction will certainly follow.

The confident expectation of gaining that for which one is begging will show up during prayer. Confidence is doubt absent. Confidence is proof of the uncertain.

If prayer is a matter of concern to you, then show yourself to be merciful. Monks will receive a hundredfold if they are merciful, and they will receive everything else in the life to come.

When fire comes to dwell in the heart it resurrects prayer; and after prayer has been revived and taken up into heaven, a descent of fire takes place into the upper chamber of the soul.

Some claim that prayer is better than the remembrance of death. But for my part, my praise goes out to the two natures in one person.[133]

When a good horse is mounted, it warms up and quickens its pace. The singing of psalms is the pace and a determined mind is the horse. It scents the battle from afar, is ready for it, and dominates the scene.

It would be very wrong to snatch water from the mouth of a thirsty person. Worse, however, is the case of a soul that is praying with compunction and is snatched away from its task before it has completed its longed-for prayer.

Do not stop praying as long as, by God's grace, the fire and the water have not been exhausted,[134] for it may happen that never again in your whole life will you have such a chance to ask for the forgiveness for your sins.

A man with a taste for prayer may defile his mind with one care-

---

133. Prayer and the remembrance of death (love and fear) form a unity analogous to that between the divine and human natures in Christ.

134. I.e., as long as fervor and tears remain.

less word, and then at prayer he will not get what he wants in the way he used to.

To keep a regular watch over the heart is one thing; to guard the heart by means of the mind is another for the mind is the ruler and high priest offering spiritual sacrifices to Christ. When heaven's holy fire lays hold of the former, it burns them because they still lack purification. This is what one of those endowed with the title of Theologian tells us.[135] But as for the latter, it enlightens them in proportion to the perfection they have achieved. It is one and the same fire that is called that which consumes (cf. Heb. 12:29) and that which illuminates (cf. John 1:9). Hence the reason why some emerge from prayer as from a blazing furnace and as though having been relieved of all material defilements. Others come forth as if they were resplendent with light and clothed in a garment of joy and of humility. But as for those who emerge without having experienced either of these effects, I would say that they have prayed in a bodily, not to say a Jewish, manner, and not spiritually.

A body changes in its activity as a result of contact with another body. How therefore could there be no change in someone who with innocent hands has touched the Body of God?[136]

We may note that our all-good King, like some earthly monarch, sometimes distributes His gifts to His soldiers Himself, sometimes through a friend or a slave, and sometimes in a hidden way. But certainly it will be in accordance with the garment of humility worn by each of us.

A man stands before an earthly monarch. But he turns his face away and talks to the enemies of the king, and the king will be offended. In the same way, the Lord will be offended by someone who at prayer time turns away toward unclean thoughts. So if the dog keeps coming, drive him off with a stick and never give in to him, however much he may persist.

Ask with tears, seek with obedience, knock with patience. For so it goes that he "who asks receives, and he who seeks finds, and to him who knocks it will be opened" (Matt. 7:8).

In your prayers be careful not to beg too much on behalf of the

135. St. Gregory of Nazianzus: cf. *Or.* 21, 2 (*PG* 35, 1084D).

136. I.e., how are we not transformed by receiving the Body of Christ in Holy Communion?

opposite sex, for the enemy may come at you from the unprotected side.[137]

Do not insist on confessing your carnal acts in detail, since you might become a traitor to yourself.

The hour of prayer is no time for thinking over necessities, nor even spiritual tasks, because you may lose the better part (cf. Luke 10:42).

Hold on to the staff of prayer and you will not fall. And even a fall will not be fatal, since prayer is a devout coercion of God (cf. Luke 18:5).

The value of prayer can be guessed from the way the demons attack us during services in church, and its fruit may be inferred from the victory over the enemy. "By this I know You are on my side because the enemy will not come to gloat over me" (Ps. 40:12) in the hour of battle. "I cried out with all my heart," said the psalmist (Ps. 118:145). He is referring to body, soul, and spirit, and where the last two are gathered, God is in the midst of them (cf. Matt. 18:20).

We are not all the same, either in body or soul. Some profit from singing the psalms quickly, others from doing so slowly, the one fighting distraction, the others coping with ignorance.

If you are always in dialog with the King in regard to your enemies, take heart whenever they attack you. A long struggle will not be necessary for you, for they will soon give up of their own accord. These unholy beings are afraid that you may earn a crown as a result of your battle against them through prayer, and besides, when scourged by prayer they will run away as though from a fire.

Always be brave, and God will teach you your prayer.

You cannot learn to see just because someone tells you to do so. For that, you require your own natural power of sight. In the same way, you cannot discover from the teaching of others the beauty of prayer. Prayer has its own special teacher in God, who "teaches man knowledge" (Ps. 93:10). He grants the prayer of him who prays. And He blesses the years of the just.

137. I.e., from the side of the weapon (prayer) rather than from the side of the shield (ascesis).

Step 29

ON DISPASSION

So here we are, stuck in the deepest pit of ignorance, in the dark passions of the body, in death's shadow, and still we have the temerity to hold forth on the subject of heaven on earth!

Stars adorn the skies and dispassion has the virtues to make it beautiful. By dispassion I mean a heaven of the mind within the heart, which regards the artifice of demons as a contemptible joke. A man is truly dispassionate—and is known to be such—when he has cleansed his flesh of all corruption; when he has lifted his mind above everything created, and has made it master of all the senses; when he keeps his soul continually in the presence of the Lord and reaches out beyond the borderline of strength to Him. And there are some who would claim that dispassion is resurrection of the soul prior to that of the body, while others would insist that it is a perfect knowledge of God, a knowledge second only to that of the angels.

Dispassion is an uncompleted perfection of the perfect. I have been told this by someone who has tasted it. Its effect is to sanctify the mind and to detach it from material things, and it does so in such a way that, after entering this heavenly harbor, a man, for most of his earthly life, is enraptured, like someone already in heaven, and he is lifted up to the contemplation of God. Someone with an experience of this says, finely, somewhere that "God's mighty ones of the earth have become greatly exalted" (Ps. 46:10); and such a man, as we happen to know, was that Egyptian[138] who joined others in lengthy prayer and held out his hands without ever resting them.

One man is dispassionate, another is more dispassionate than the dispassionate.[139] The one will loathe evil while the other will have the blessing of an inexhaustible store of virtues. Purity is also said to be dispassion, and this is right, for it is a foretaste of the general resurrection and of the incorruption of the corruptible. A dispassionate man was he who said that he had the mind of the Lord (cf. 1 Cor. 2:16), and the same is true of the Egyptian[140] who asserted that he was no longer afraid of the Lord. Similar too was the man who prayed that his passions might return to him.[141] Has anyone been granted so much dispassion prior to the coming glory as that Syrian?[142] David, the most glorious of the prophets, says to the Lord: "Spare me so that I may recover my strength" (Ps. 38:14); but the athlete of God[143] cries: "Spare me from the waves of Your grace."

A dispassionate soul is immersed in virtues as a passionate being is in pleasure.

If the height of gluttony is that you force yourself to eat even when you are not hungry, then the height of temperance in a hungry man is that he restrains even the justifiable urges of nature. If the height of lechery is that one raves even over animals and over inanimate things, then the height of purity is to look on everyone in the same way that one would regard inanimate objects. If the ultimate stage of cupidity is to gather without ever being satisfied, the ultimate stage of poverty is the willingness to dispense with one's own body. If the final point of despondency is to have no patience even when living in total peace, the final point of patience is to consider oneself to be at rest even in the midst of affliction. If to be furious even in solitude is talked of as a sea of wrath, then calmness, whether your slanderer be present or not, will be a sea of long-suffering. If the high

138. Abba Tithoes: *The Sayings of the Desert Fathers*, Tithoes 1.

139. The man who is dispassionate, says scholion 3 (1153B), is unattached to things; the man who is more than dispassionate is unattached even to the remembrance of things.

140. St. Antony the Great: *The Sayings of the Desert Fathers*, Antony the Great 32.

141. St. John Kolovos (the Dwarf): *The Sayings of the Desert Fathers*, John the Dwarf 13.

142. St. Ephraim the Syrian.

143. St. Ephraim the Syrian.

point of vainglory is for a person to put on airs even when no one is present to praise him, the sure proof of its absence is that you keep your thoughts under control when someone is praising you to your face. If it is a sign of perdition, that is pride, to be arrogant even when poorly dressed, then surely amid high doings and great success lowly thoughts betoken saving humility. If complete enslavement to passion is indicated by the fact that one quickly submits to whatever the demons have sown in us, I take it then that a mark of holy dispassion is to be able to say unambiguously: "I did not recognize the evil one as he slipped away from me" (Ps. 100:4), nor did I know the time of his coming, the reasons for it, nor how he went. I am completely unaware of such matters because I am and will ever be wholly united with God.

The man deemed worthy to be of this sort during his lifetime has God always within him, to guide him in all he has to say or do or think. The will of the Lord becomes for him a sort of inner voice through illumination. All human teaching is beneath him. " 'When shall I come to appear before the face of God?' " he says (Ps. 41:3). "I can no longer endure the force of love. I long for the undying beauty that You gave me before this clay."

What more has to be said? The dispassionate man no longer lives himself, but it is Christ Who lives in him (cf. Gal. 2:20). This is what we are told by the man who fought the good fight, completed the course, and stayed with the faith (cf. 2 Tim. 4:7).

Just as a royal crown is not made up of one stone, so dispassion is incomplete if we neglect even one of the most ordinary virtues.

Think of dispassion as a kind of celestial palace, a palace of the King of heaven. Think of the numerous mansions (cf. John 14:2) as so many dwelling places within this city. Think of the forgiveness of sins as being the fortifying wall of this Jerusalem. O my brothers, we should run to enter the bridal chamber of this palace, and if some burden of past habits or the passage of time should impede us, what a disaster for us! Let us at least take up residence in one of the mansions near the bridal chamber. But if we begin to falter or weaken, we ought to ensure that at least we are inside the walls, since the man who does not get there before the end, who does not climb that wall, must camp out in the desert.[144] This is the reason for the prayer of the man who said: "By my God I will climb a wall" (Ps. 17:30). An-

144. HTM adds: "of fiends and passions."

other, as if in the person of God Himself, says: "Is it not your sins that separate you and Me?" (Isa. 59:2).

Friends, let us break through this wall of separation (cf. Eph. 2:14), this wall that in our disobedience we built to our own harm. Let us look there for the forgiveness of our sins, since there is no one in hell who can pardon us. Brothers, let us commit ourselves to this, for our names are on the lists of the devout. There must be no talk of "a lapse," "there is no time," or "a burden." To everyone who has received the Lord in baptism,[145] "He has given the power to become children of God" (John 1:12). " 'Be still and know that I am God' (Ps. 45:11) and am Dispassion," He says. To Him be glory forever and ever. Amen.

Blessed dispassion raises the poor mind from earth to heaven, raises the beggar from the dunghill of passion. And love, all praise to it, makes him sit with princes, that is with holy angels, and with the princes of God's people (cf. Ps. 112:7–8).

145. Literally: "in the bath of regeneration," a standard patristic synonym for baptism.

Step 30

ON FAITH, HOPE, AND LOVE

And now at last, after all that has been said, there remains that triad, faith, hope, and love, binding and securing the union of all. "But the greatest of these is love" (1 Cor. 13:13), since that is the very name of God Himself (cf. 1 John 4:8). To me they appear, one as a ray, one as light, and one as a disk,[146] and all as a single radiance and a single splendor. The first can make and create all things, the mercy of God encircles the second and keeps it from confusion, while the third never falls, never halts on its way, never gives respite to the man wounded by its blessed rapture.

The man who wants to talk about love is undertaking to speak about God. But it is risky to talk about God and could even be dangerous for the unwary. Angels know how to speak about love, but even they do so only in proportion to the light within them.

"God is love" (1 John 4:16). But someone eager to define this is blindly striving to measure the sand in the ocean.

Love, by its nature, is a resemblance to God, insofar as this is humanly possible. In its activity it is inebriation of the soul. Its distinctive character is to be a fountain of faith, an abyss of patience, a sea of humility.

Love is the banishment of every sort of contrariness, for love thinks no evil.

146. A common image among the Fathers to express the unity of the Trinity.

Love, dispassion, and adoption are distinguished by name, and name only. Light, fire, and flame join to fashion one activity. So too with love, dispassion, and adoption.

Fear shows up if ever love departs, for the man with no fear is either filled with love or is dead in spirit.

There is nothing wrong about offering human analogies for longing, fear, concern, zeal, service, and love of God. Lucky the man who loves and longs for God as a smitten lover does for his beloved. Lucky the man whose fear of God is in no way less than the fear of the accused in front of a judge. Lucky the man who is caught up with the zeal of loyal slaves toward their owner. Lucky the man who is as passionately concerned with the virtues as a jealous husband watching over his wife. Lucky the man who prays before God like a courtier before the king. Lucky the man who strives without end to please the Lord as others try to please men.

Not even a mother clings to her nursing child as a son of love clings to the Lord at all times.

Someone truly in love keeps before his mind's eye the face of the beloved and embraces it there tenderly. Even during sleep the longing continues unappeased, and he murmurs to his beloved. That is how it is for the body. And that is how it is for the spirit. A man wounded by love had this to say about himself—and it really amazes me—"I sleep (because nature commands this) but my heart is awake (because of the abundance of my love)" (Song of Songs 5:2). You should take note, my brother, that the stag,[147] which is the soul, destroys reptiles and then, inflamed by love, as if struck by an arrow,[148] it longs and grows faint for the love of God (cf. Ps. 41:1).

The impact of hunger is not always obvious, but thirst has a definite and clear effect. It reveals to all the presence of a fever. Hence someone who yearns for God has this to say: "My soul is thirsty for God, for the mighty and living God" (cf. Ps. 41:3).

If the sight of the one we love clearly makes us change completely, so that we turn cheerful, glad, and carefree, what will the face of the Lord Himself not do as He comes to dwell, invisibly, in a pure soul?

When fear arises from the deeper reaches of the soul, it destroys

147. See note 86, p. 220.

148. Or: "venom" (i.e. of the reptiles).

and devours impurity. "Nail down my flesh with fear of You" (Ps. 118:120). So it is said.

Holy love has a way of consuming some. This is what is meant by the one who said, "You have ravished our hearts, ravished them" (Song of Songs 4:9). And it makes others bright and overjoyed. In this regard it has been said: "My heart was full of trust and I was helped, and my flesh has revived" (Ps. 27:7). For when the heart is cheerful, the face beams (cf. Prov. 15:13), and a man flooded[149] with the love of God reveals in his body, as if in a mirror, the splendor of his soul, a glory like that of Moses when he came face to face with God (cf. Exod. 34:29–35).

Men who have attained this angelic state often forget to eat, and I really think they do not even miss their food. No wonder, since an opposite desire drives out the very wish to eat, and indeed I suspect that the bodies of these incorruptible men are immune to sickness, for their bodies have been sanctified and rendered incorruptible by the flame of chastity which has put out the flame.[150] My belief is that they accept without any pleasure the food set out in front of them, for just as subterranean waters nourish the roots of a plant, the fires of heaven are there to sustain their souls.

The growth of fear is the starting point of love, and total purity is the foundation for theology.[151]

When a man's senses are perfectly united to God, then what God has said is somehow mysteriously clarified. But where there is no union of this kind, then it is extremely difficult to speak about God.

The consubstantial[152] Word brings purity to completion, and His presence destroys death, and when death is done away with, the disciple of sacred knowledge is illuminated. The Word of the Lord, being from the Lord, remains eternally pure.

The man who does not know God speaks about Him only in probabilities.

Purity makes of a disciple someone who can speak of God, and he can move on to a knowledge of the Trinity.

He who loves the Lord has first loved his brother, for the latter is proof of the former. Someone who loves his neighbor will never tol-

---

149. Literally: "somewhat commingled."
150. I.e., of the passions.
151. The knowledge of God from experience rather than from study.
152. Or: "the indwelling Word" (*enousios*).

erate slanderers and will run from them as though from a fire. And the man who claims to love the Lord but is angry with his neighbor is like someone who dreams he is running.

Hope is the power behind love. Hope is what causes us to look forward to the reward of love. Hope is an abundance of hidden treasure. It is the abundant assurance of the riches in store for us. It is a rest from labor, a doorway of love. It lifts despair and is the image of what is not yet present. When hope fails, so does love. Struggles are bound by it, labors depend on it, and mercy lies all around it. The hopeful monk slays despondency, kills it with his sword. Hope comes from the experience of the Lord's gifts, and someone with no such experience must be ever in doubt. Hope is destroyed by anger, for hope does not disappoint and the angry man has no grace.

Love grants prophecy, miracles. It is an abyss of illumination, a fountain of fire, bubbling up to inflame the thirsty soul. It is the condition of angels, and the progress of eternity.

Most beautiful of all the virtues, tell us where you feed your flock, where you take your noonday rest (cf. Song of Songs 1:7). Enlighten us, end our thirst, lead us, show us the way, since we long to soar up to you. You rule everything, and now you have enraptured my soul. I am unable to hold in your flame, and therefore I will go forward praising you. "You rule the power of the sea, you make gentle (and deaden) the surge of its waves. You make humble the proud thought as a wounded man. With your powerful arm you have scattered your enemies" (cf. Ps. 88:9–10), and you have made your lovers invincible.

I long to know how Jacob saw you fixed above the ladder (cf. Gen. 28:12). That climb, how was it? Tell me, for I long to know. What is the mode, what is the law joining together those steps that the lover has set as an ascent in his heart? (cf. Ps. 83:6). I thirst to know the number of those steps, and the time required to climb them. He who discovered Your struggle and Your vision has spoken to us of the guides. But he would not—perhaps he could not—tell us any more.

This empress,[153] as if coming from heaven, spoke thus in my soul's hearing: "My love, you will never be able to know how beauti-

153. I.e., love. HTM adds: "or I think I might properly say King" (i.e. God).

ful I am unless you get away from the grossness of the flesh. So let this ladder teach you the spiritual union of the virtues. And I am there on the summit, for as the great man said, a man who knew me well: 'Remaining now are faith, hope, and love, these three. But love is the greatest of them all' (1 Cor. 13:13)."

A BRIEF SUMMARY AND EXHORTATION

Ascend, my brothers, ascend eagerly. Let your hearts' resolve be to climb. Listen to the voice of the one who says: "Come, let us go up to the mountain of the Lord, to the house of our God" (Isa. 2:3), Who makes our feet to be like the feet of the deer, "Who sets us on the high places, that we may be triumphant on His road" (Hab. 3:19).[154]

Run, I beg you, run with him who said, "Let us hurry until we all arrive at the unity of faith and of the knowledge of God, at mature manhood, at the measure of the stature of Christ's fullness" (Eph. 4:13). Baptized in the thirtieth year of His earthly age, Christ attained the thirtieth step on the spiritual ladder, for God indeed is love, and to Him be praise, dominion, power. In Him is the cause, past, present, and future, of all that is good forever and ever. Amen.

154. Gk *odo*. HTM reads "with His song" (*odi*). The textus receptus of Hab. 3:19 is *odi* but Sinaiticus, lectio prima, has *odo*.

INDEX TO THE PREFACE AND INTRODUCTION

INDEX

INDEX

INDEX TO THE TEXT

INDEX

INDEX

INDEX

INDEX

INDEX

Other Volumes in this Series

Julian of Norwich • SHOWINGS

Jacob Boehme • THE WAY TO CHRIST

Nahman of Bratslav • THE TALES

Gregory of Nyssa • THE LIFE OF MOSES

Bonaventure • THE SOUL'S JOURNEY INTO GOD, THE TREE OF LIFE, and THE LIFE OF ST. FRANCIS

William Law • A SERIOUS CALL TO DEVOUT AND HOLY LIFE, and THE SPIRIT OF LOVE

Abraham Isaac Kook • THE LIGHTS OF PENITENCE, LIGHTS OF HOLINESS, THE MORAL PRINCIPLES, ESSAYS, and POEMS

Ibn 'Ata' Illah • THE BOOK OF WISDOM and **Kwaja Abdullah Ansari** • INTIMATE CONVERSATIONS

Johann Arndt • TRUE CHRISTIANITY

Richard of St. Victor • THE TWELVE PATRIARCHS, THE MYSTICAL ARK, and BOOK THREE OF THE TRINITY

Origen • AN EXHORTATION TO MARTYRDOM, PRAYER AND SELECTED WORKS

Catherine of Genoa • PURGATION AND PURGATORY, THE SPIRITUAL DIALOGUE

Native North American Spirituality of the Eastern Woodlands • SACRED MYTHS, DREAMS, VISIONS, SPEECHES, HEALING FORMULAS, RITUALS AND CEREMONIALS

Teresa of Avila • THE INTERIOR CASTLE

Apocalyptic Spirituality • TREATISES AND LETTERS OF LACTANTIUS, ADSO OF MONTIER-EN-DER, JOACHIM OF FIORE, THE FRANCISCAN SPIRITUALS, SAVONAROLA

Athanasius • THE LIFE OF ANTONY, A LETTER TO MARCELLINUS

Catherine of Siena • THE DIALOGUE

Sharafuddin Maneri • THE HUNDRED LETTERS

Martin Luther • THEOLOGIA GERMANICA

Native Mesoamerican Spirituality • ANCIENT MYTHS, DISCOURSES, STORIES, DOCTRINES, HYMNS, POEMS FROM THE AZTEC, YUCATEC, QUICHE-MAYA AND OTHER SACRED TRADITIONS

Symeon the New Theologian • THE DISCOURSES

Ibn Al'-Arabī • THE BEZELS OF WISDOM

Hadewijch • THE COMPLETE WORKS

Philo of Alexandria • THE CONTEMPLATIVE LIFE, THE GIANTS, AND SELECTIONS

George Herbert • THE COUNTRY PARSON, THE TEMPLE

Unknown • THE CLOUD OF UNKNOWING

John and Charles Wesley • SELECTED WRITINGS AND HYMNS

Meister Eckhart • THE ESSENTIAL SERMONS, COMMENTARIES, TREATISES AND DEFENSE

Francisco de Osuna • THE THIRD SPIRITUAL ALPHABET

Jacopone da Todi • THE LAUDS

Fakhruddin 'Iraqi • DIVINE FLASHES

Menahem Nahum of Chernobyl • THE LIGHT OF THE EYES

Early Dominicans • SELECTED WRITINGS